AF327225

MANOLO
VALDÉS

MANOLO VALDÉS

SCULPTURES IN NEW YORK

PHOTOGRAPHS
ANDREA SANTOLAYA

TEXTS
ANTONIO LUCAS

.TF. EDITORES

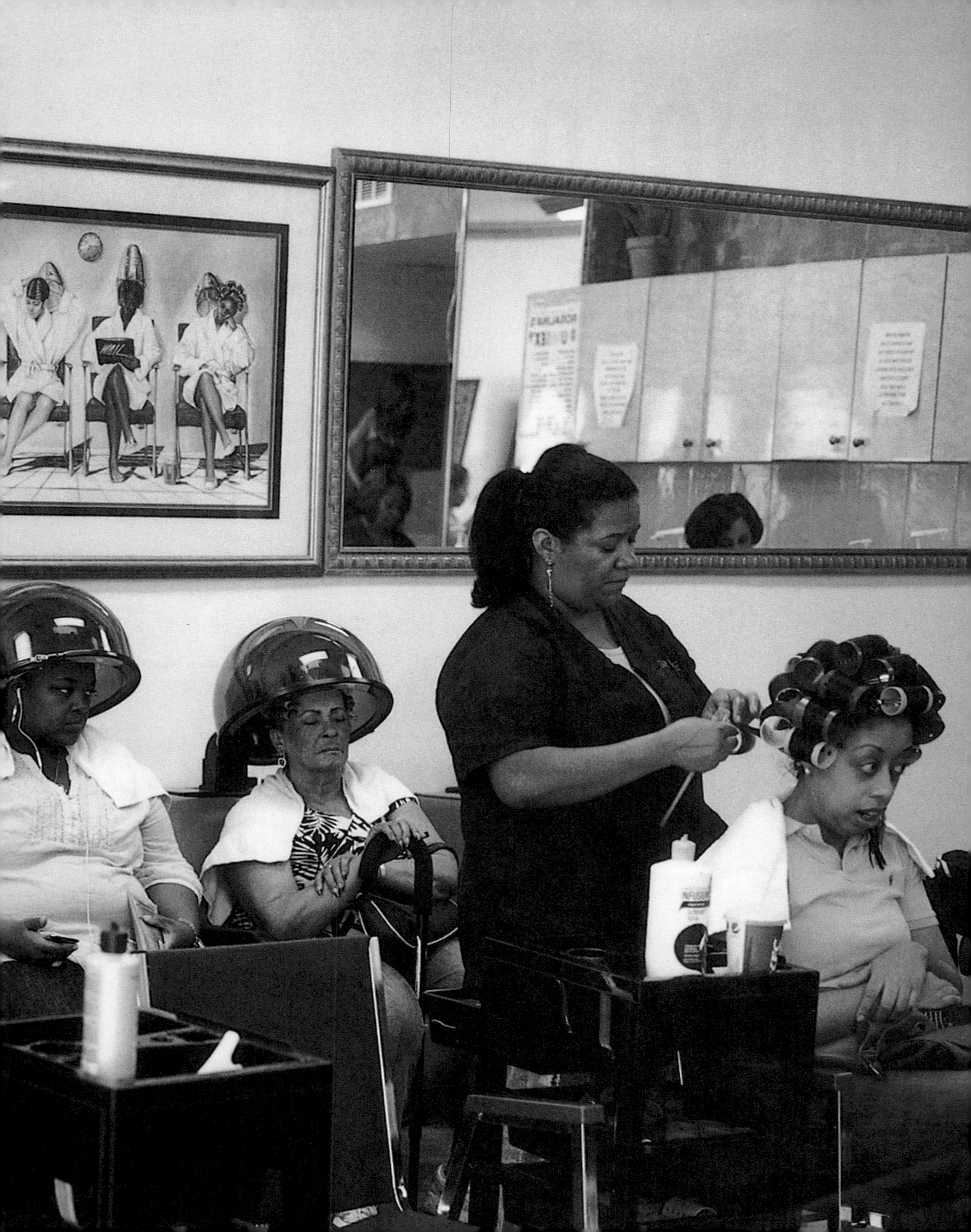

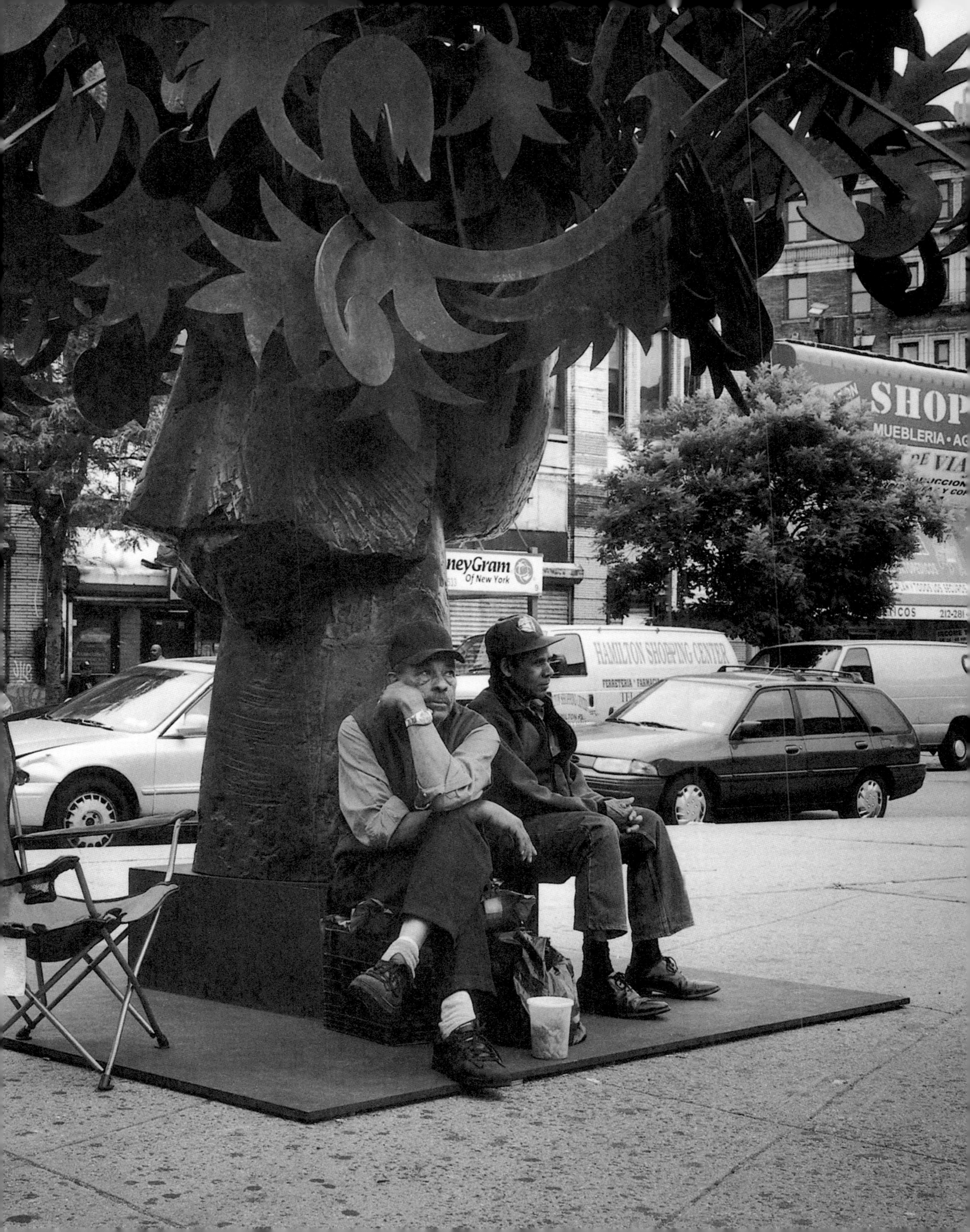
SHOP
MUEBLERIA · AG
DE VIA
MoneyGram
Of New York
HAMILTON SHOPPING CENTER
FERRETERIA · FARMACIA
TEL

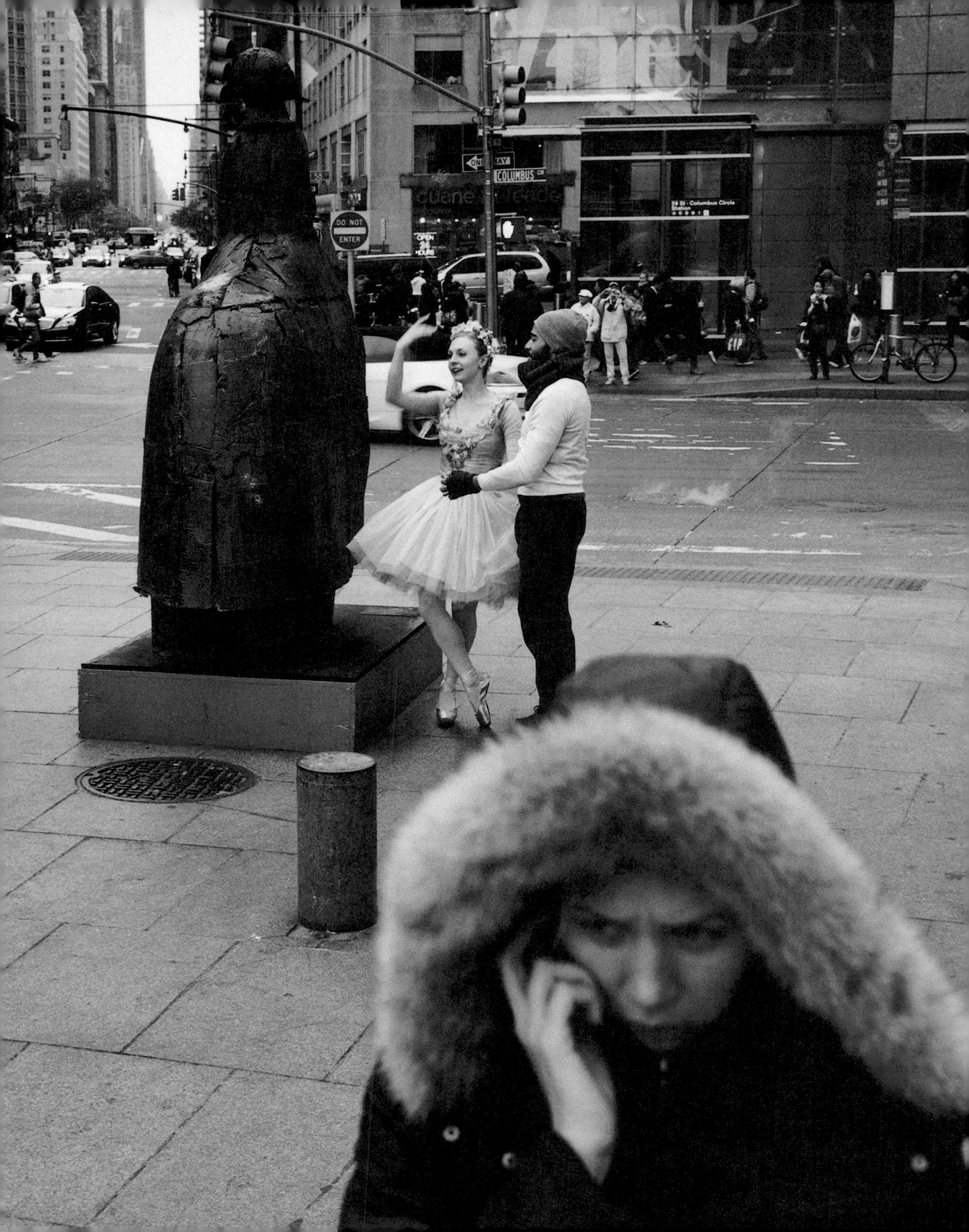

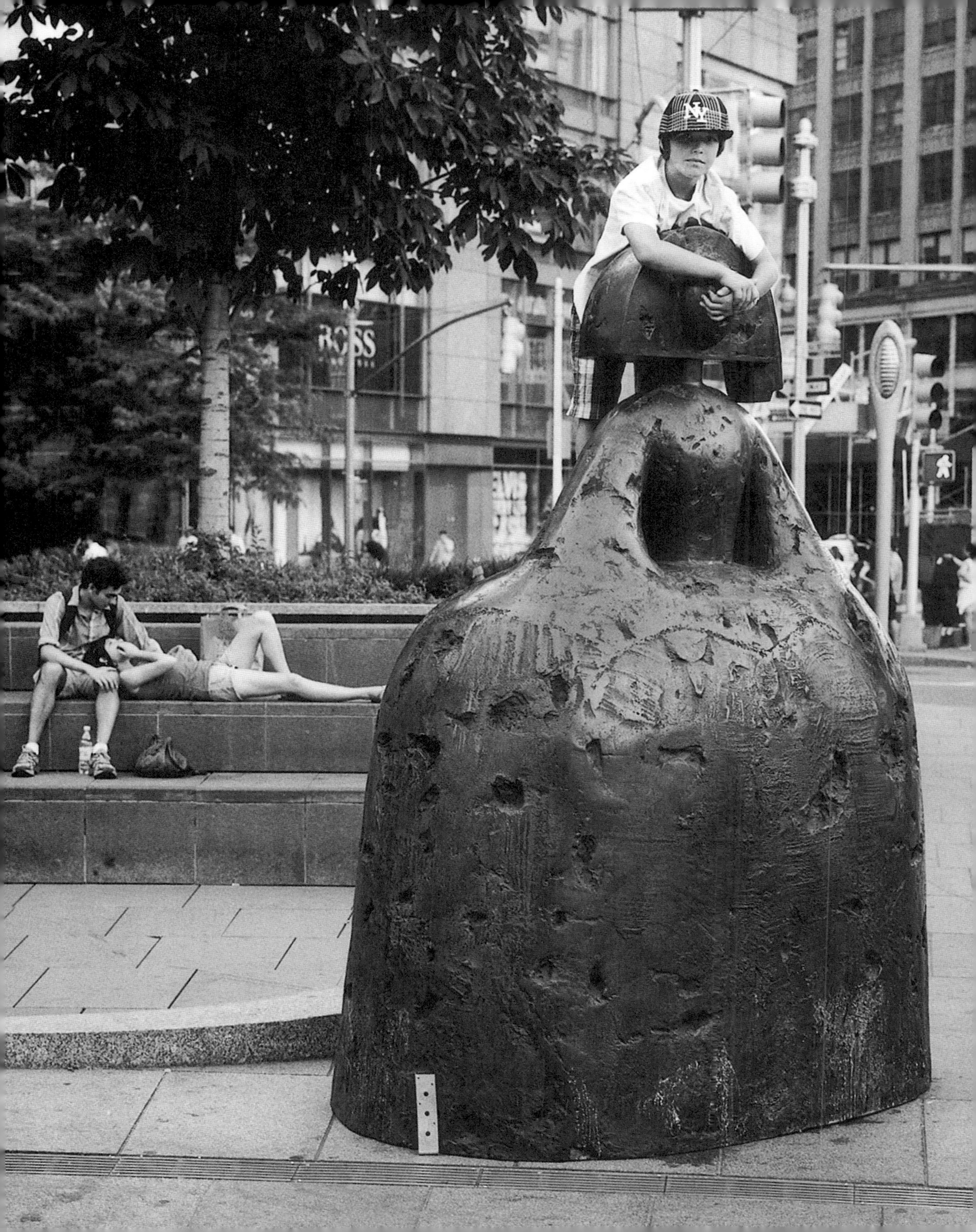

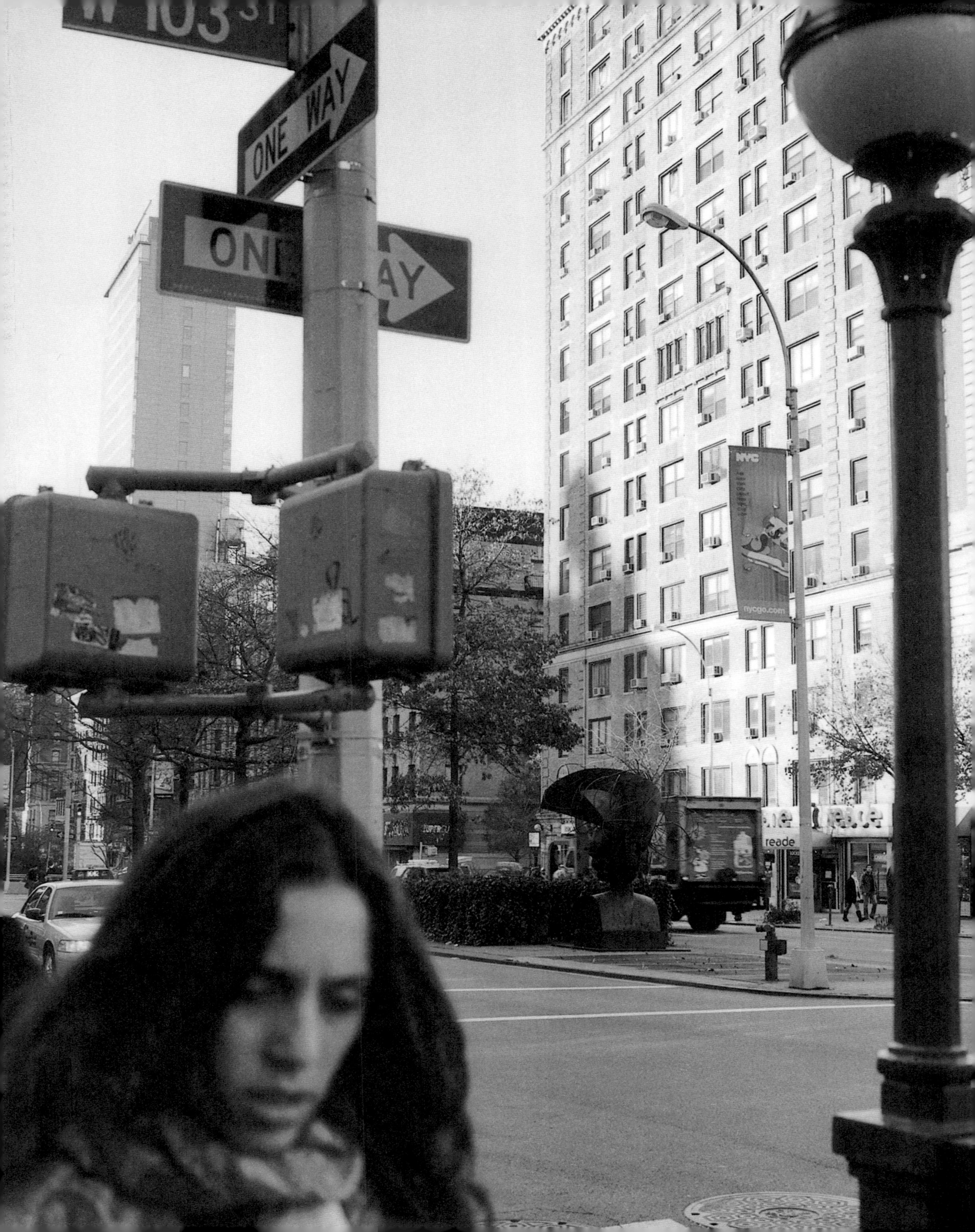

W 103 ST
ONE WAY
ONE WAY
NYC
nycgo.com
reade

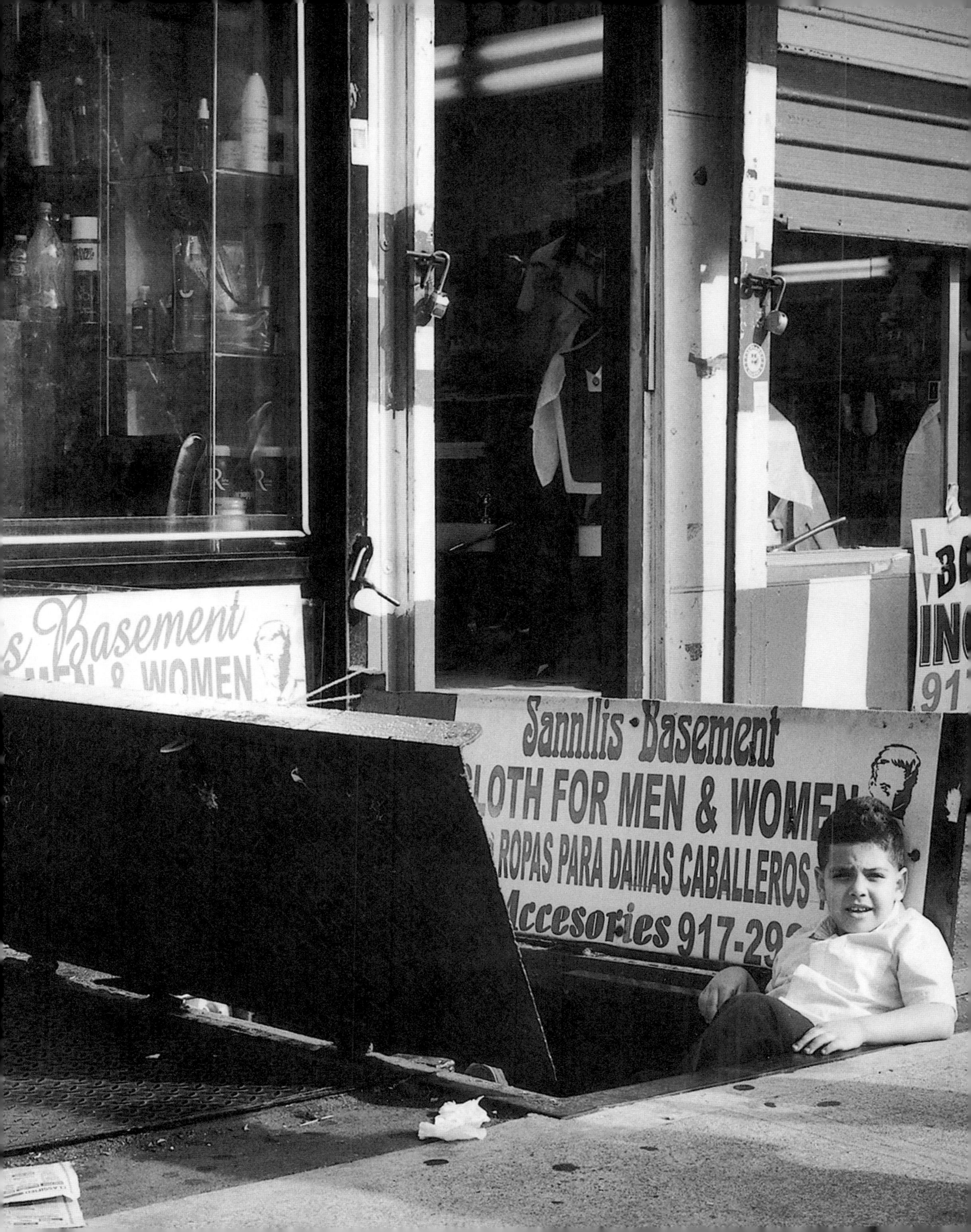

s..Basement
WOMEN
Sannllis • Basement
LOTH FOR MEN & WOMEN
ROPAS PARA DAMAS CABALLEROS
Accesories 917-29
B
IN
91

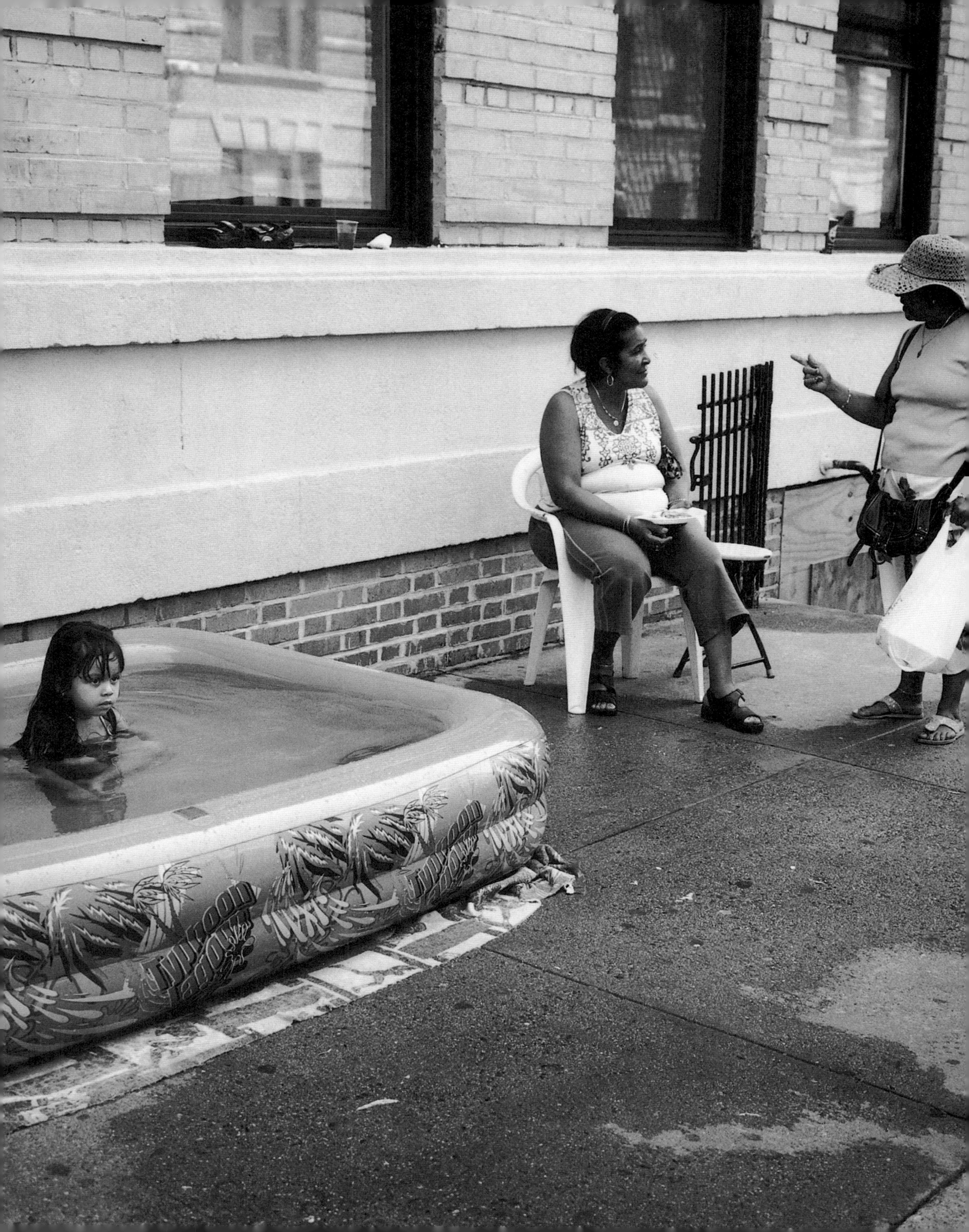

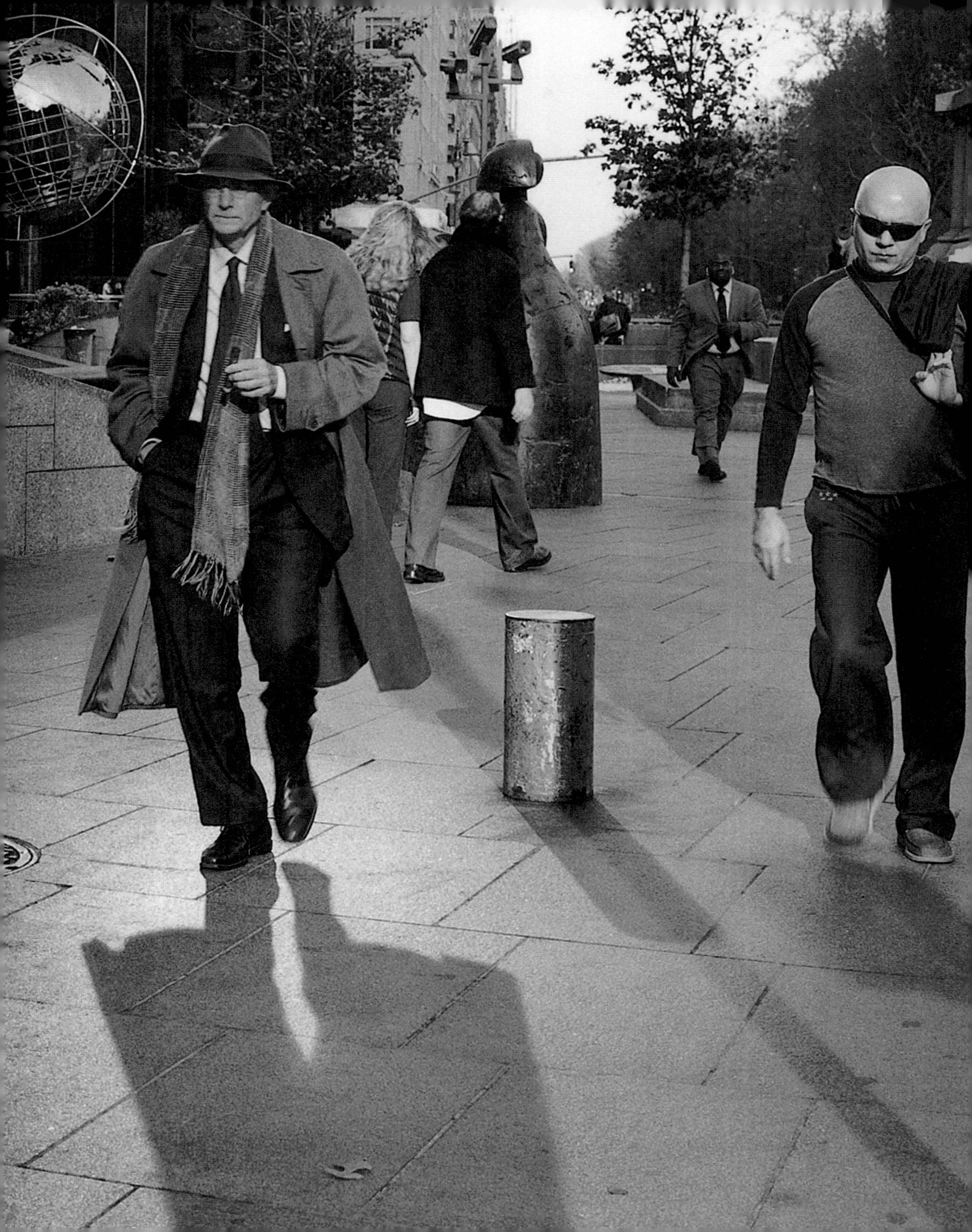

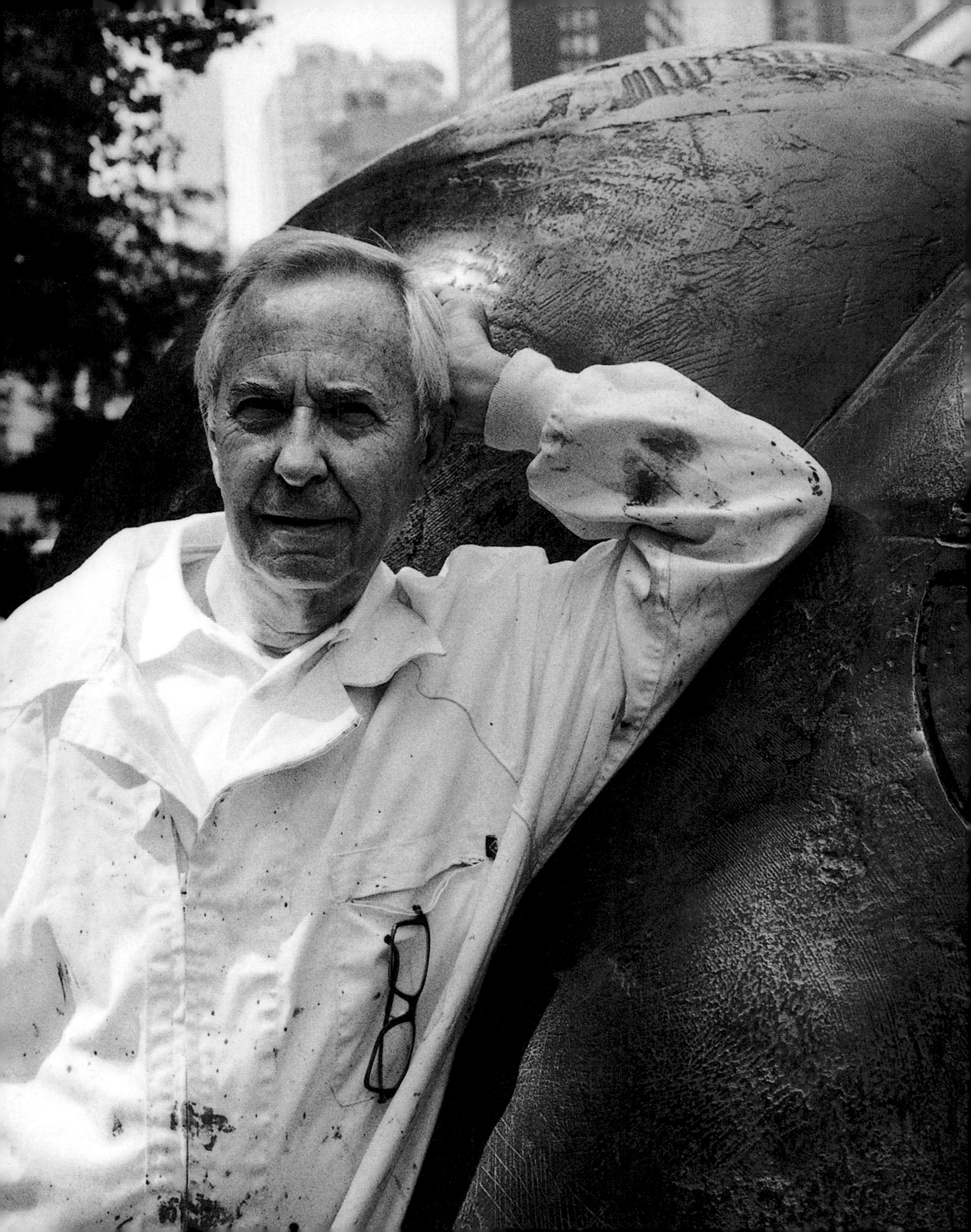

KEYS TO THE ITINERARY

From May 2010 to January 2011 the Marlborough Gallery displayed a set of sixteen monumental sculptures by Manolo Valdés on the stretch of Broadway that goes from 166th Street to Columbus Circle. These sculptures acted as beacons of the singular iconography of the Valencian artist. They were all made in New York, the city in which he has lived for more than twenty years. This is the first time that a Spanish creative artist has occupied such a vast space in the complex urban area of Manhattan. During the nine months that the works were installed, they became referents integrated into the changing landscape where each one of them was carefully exhibited: on sidewalks and boulevards, in parks and at subway entrances...Around them the routine of the neighborhoods followed its course, from the unhurried pace of the Dominican Harlem to the acceleration of the Lincoln Center. And the result was an experience which confirms that art can become an inseparable part of the pulse of life, as photographer Andrea Santolaya was able to show in her unique exploit of capturing the living traces of this initiative in which man and sculpture merged together in a daily adventure for nearly a year.

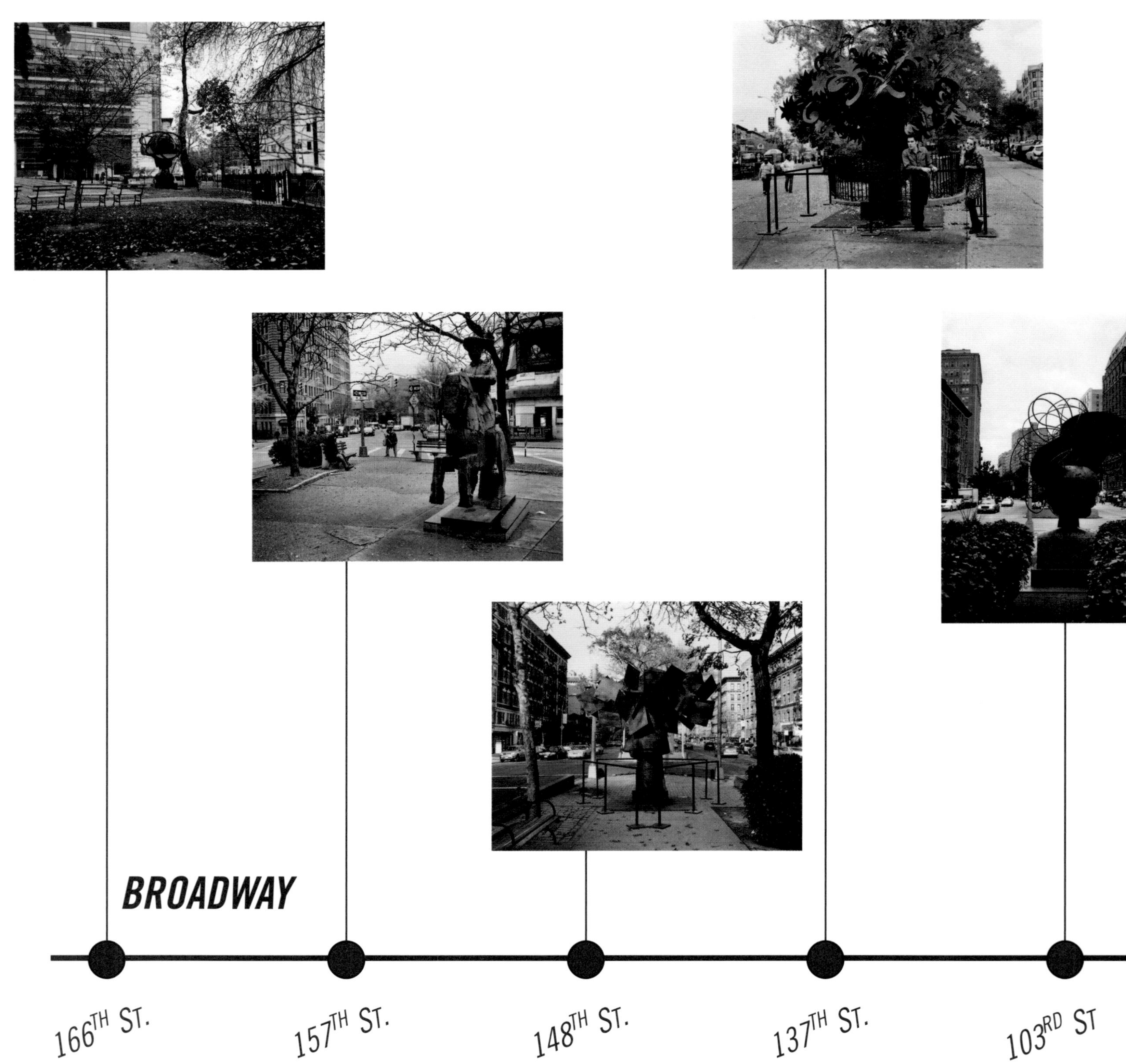

BROADWAY
166TH ST.
157TH ST.
148TH ST.
137TH ST.
103RD ST

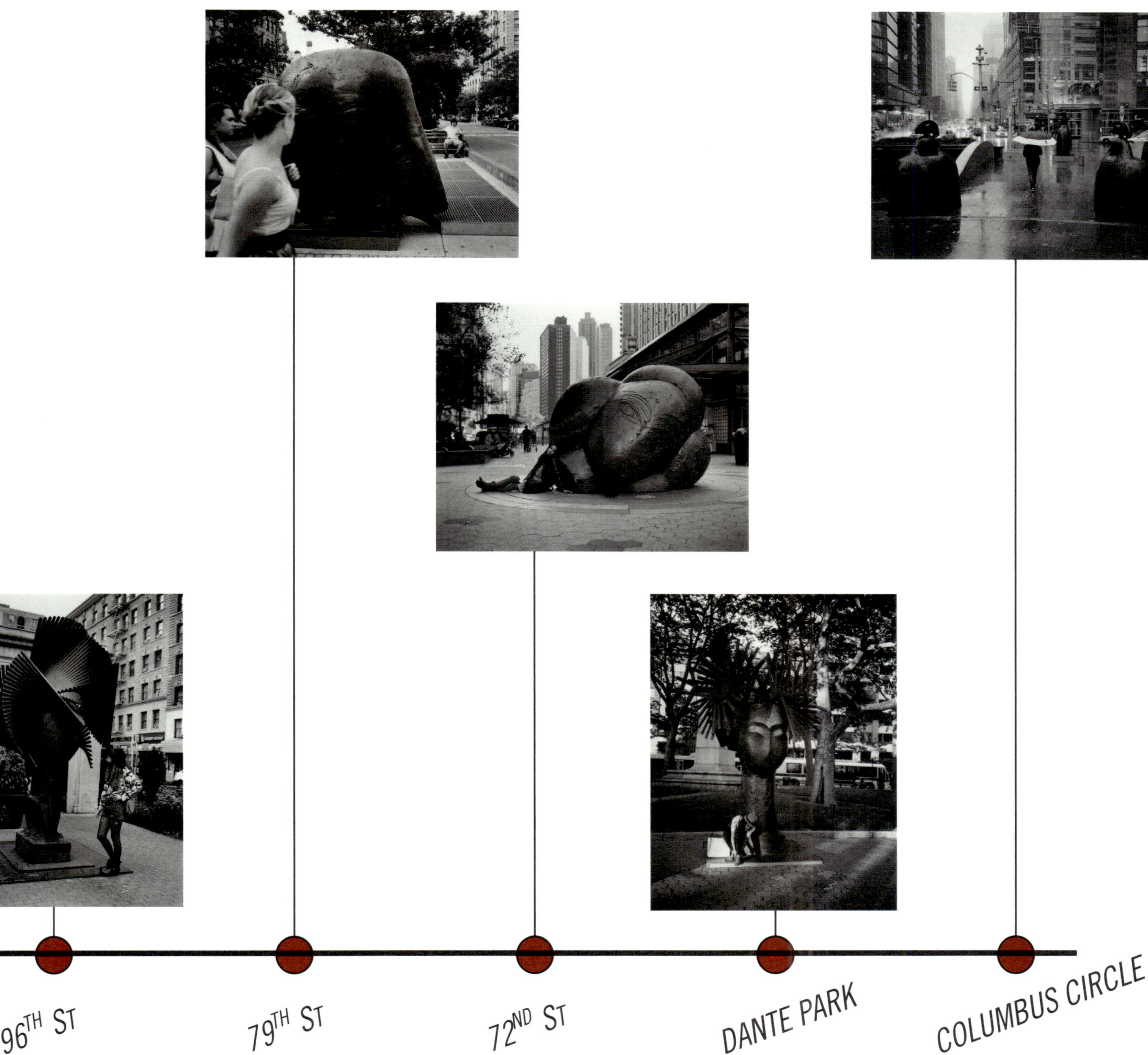

96TH ST
79TH ST
72ND ST
DANTE PARK
COLUMBUS CIRCLE

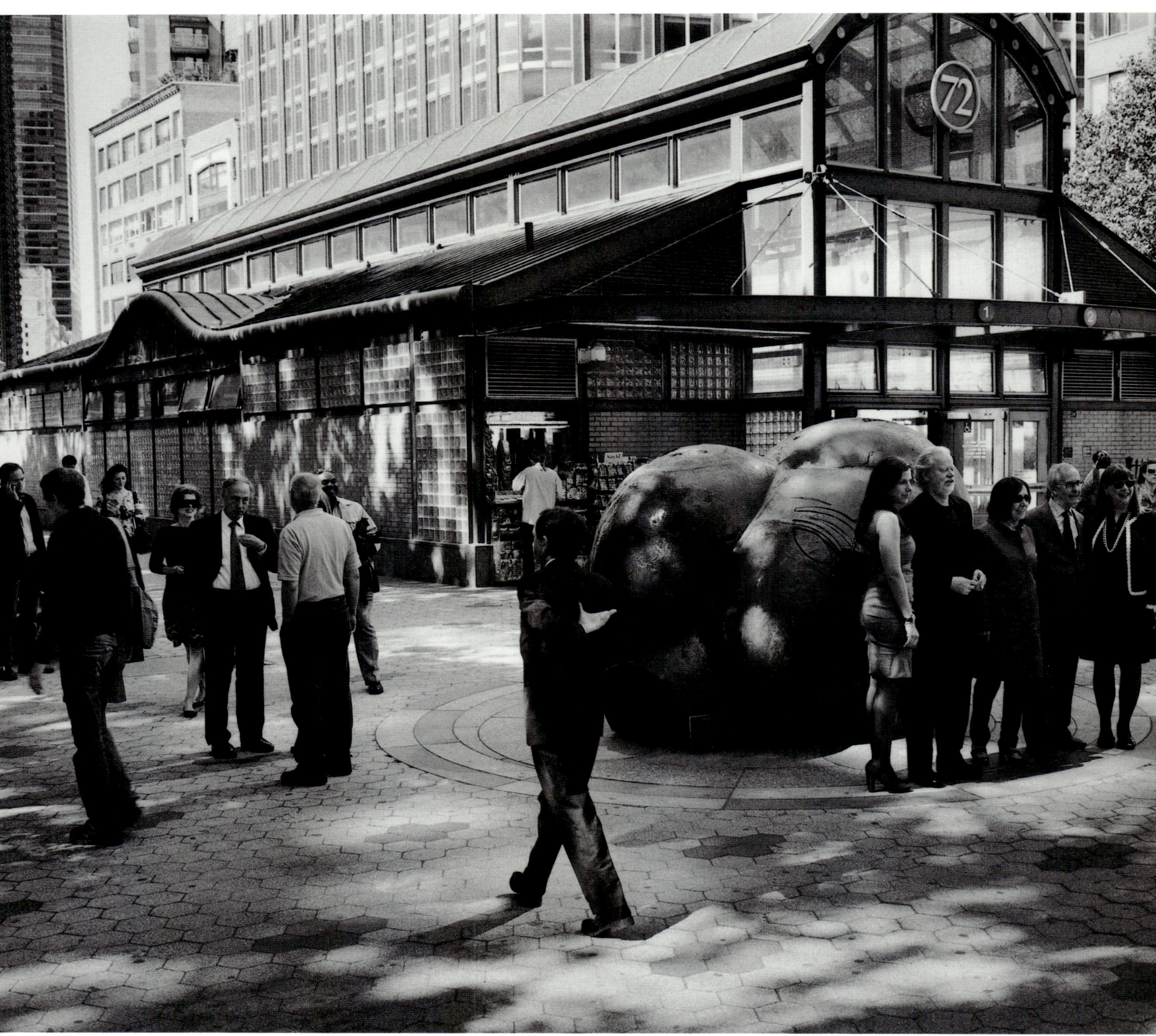

A photographic tour of Manolo Valdés's

sculptures in New York

Littered like castaways, pieces perhaps of a large ship, figureheads of some fabulous vessel that one day scattered these shards in the shape of heads. Traces of a bronze that became a male or female equestrian statue, volume and texture, a happy street accident. Large craggy rocks of silenced metal. Gourds for the automatic city. Meeting places. Escape points. Sculptures which perhaps ceased to be sculptures in order to become sidewalk tenants, eyeshades of the world against the summer sun. Awnings like mothers, acting as protection against the winter.

Art which divested itself on the asphalt of any evangelical
vocation in order to blend with the architecture, with the
palpitations of the day, with the sirens and the murmurs
that fill the metropolis of corners like sluicegates. They do
not know it, but they are also city and uncertain route:
from Dominican Harlem to Columbus Circle. This other
Manhattan on the route of the votive offerings..
Andrea looks at them. She came some months ago to meet
them, like someone who goes to a static hunting. Andrea
has her eyes as wide as saucers when the light beats
down on them and the world festival is different. Andrea
lives in the sculptures. They are her strange hospice of
anxieties. She is their unexpected tenant, and only thus
is she able to discover what takes place under the skin of
so much terrible majesty. In them are heard the bolt of
lightning and the requiem of every rainy nightfall. They
have a point of civilized melancholy. But above all they
do not explain why they are there..They are unable to say,
"New York, that is us." And at the same time they are
entirely that.
Andrea is watching them look. Andrea with her camera
hanging on her shoulder. A solitary woman with her
feverish harpoon to hunt for the secret, from these urban
successors who come from afar: from Velazquez, from
Botticelli, from Brancusi, from Memling, from Matisse,
from Holbein. She is aware that a sculpture can be

imbued with the terrible poetry of neglect and also the immense heat of a hitherto-unknown world, the sweetness of the mythical, the tension of a cataclysm, the passionate brilliance adopted by art in the avenue when the city makes of it an instrument.

She searches for the light that is still dissolved in oblivion, before dawn, so as to go out to meet it. The adventure involves the will of a geographer. Manolo Valdes's ladies trace a geological grotto in the upper part of New York. In each neighborhood that they occupy, in each perimeter, they establish a map, a stratum of fantasies to be resolved, a sedimentation of footprints and eyes, of hands and silences, of joys and sorrows. Because the sculptures are the people. Because the ladies are the faces of all those who stop within their orbit with the heavy palpitation of their existence, adding new life to each sculpture.

BROADWAY
166TH St

In the swarm of Dominican Harlem on 166th Street, beside the River Hudson, the route starts where metal and men, image and rumors merge together, creating fiercely human harmony. The first sculpture, *Irene,* is very *chic,* with a markedly twenties style and a headpiece of spheres that could easily be the rings of a far-off planet. Her elegance makes her more of a widow in the midst of this part of the world, embedded like a meteorite into a city park, somewhat hidden, almost furtive, slowly revealing the reason of her enigma. Or testing the attraction of her enigma for no reason.

Andrea approaches. She stretches out her hand until she touches her. Then she moves back, and shoots. *Irene* is alone. Blessed by aromas of fried chicken, by the sickly sweetness of Dunkin Donuts, by the hooting of children on the sidewalk, by the buzz of conversation coming from the Hispanic hairdressers, with their rise and fall of words of a Spanish that mutates, changes and floats expressions which are elusive, sometimes heart-rending and sensible. *Irene* does not negotiate with her status of art. In reality she would like to be a window, the top of a ship,

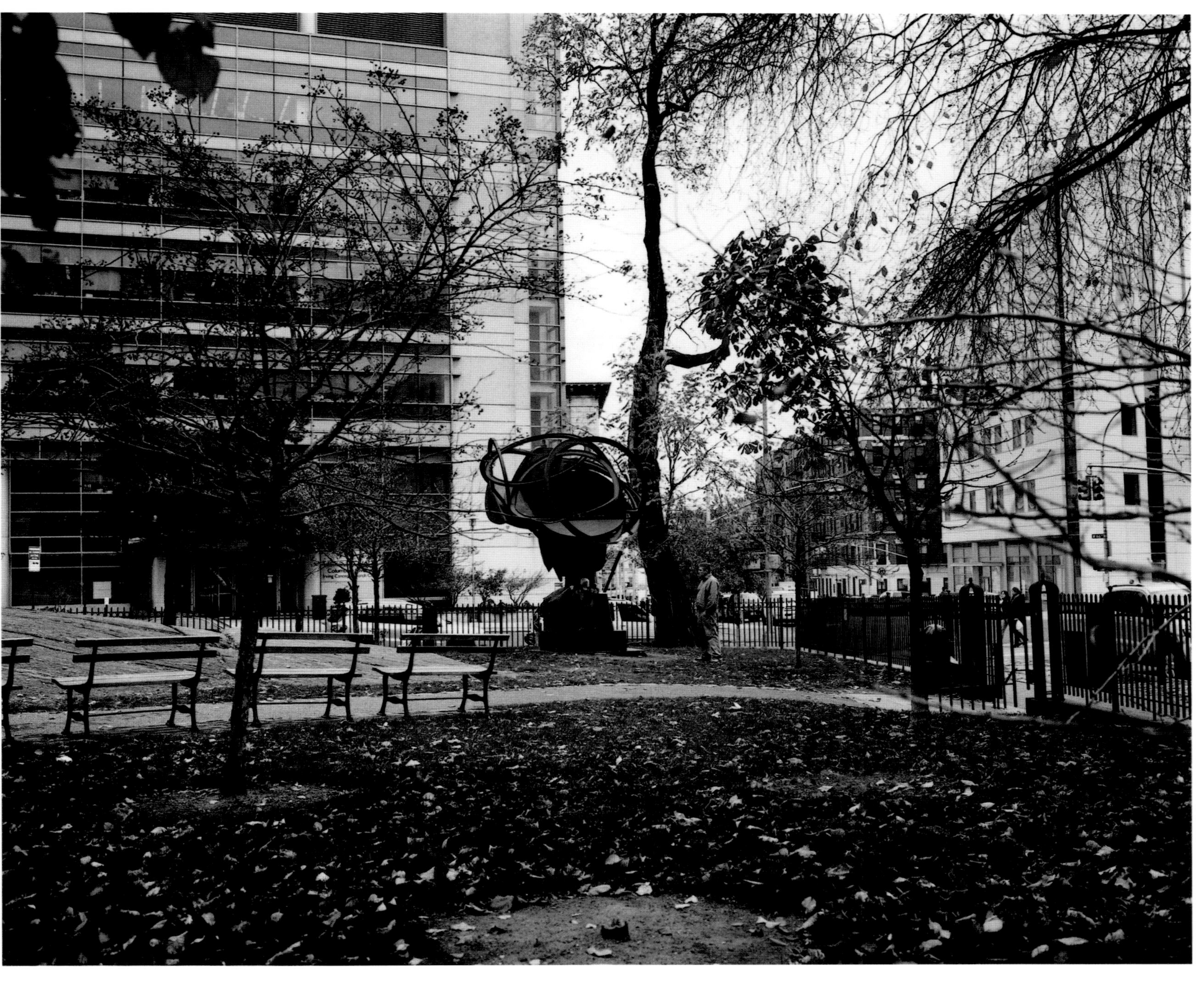

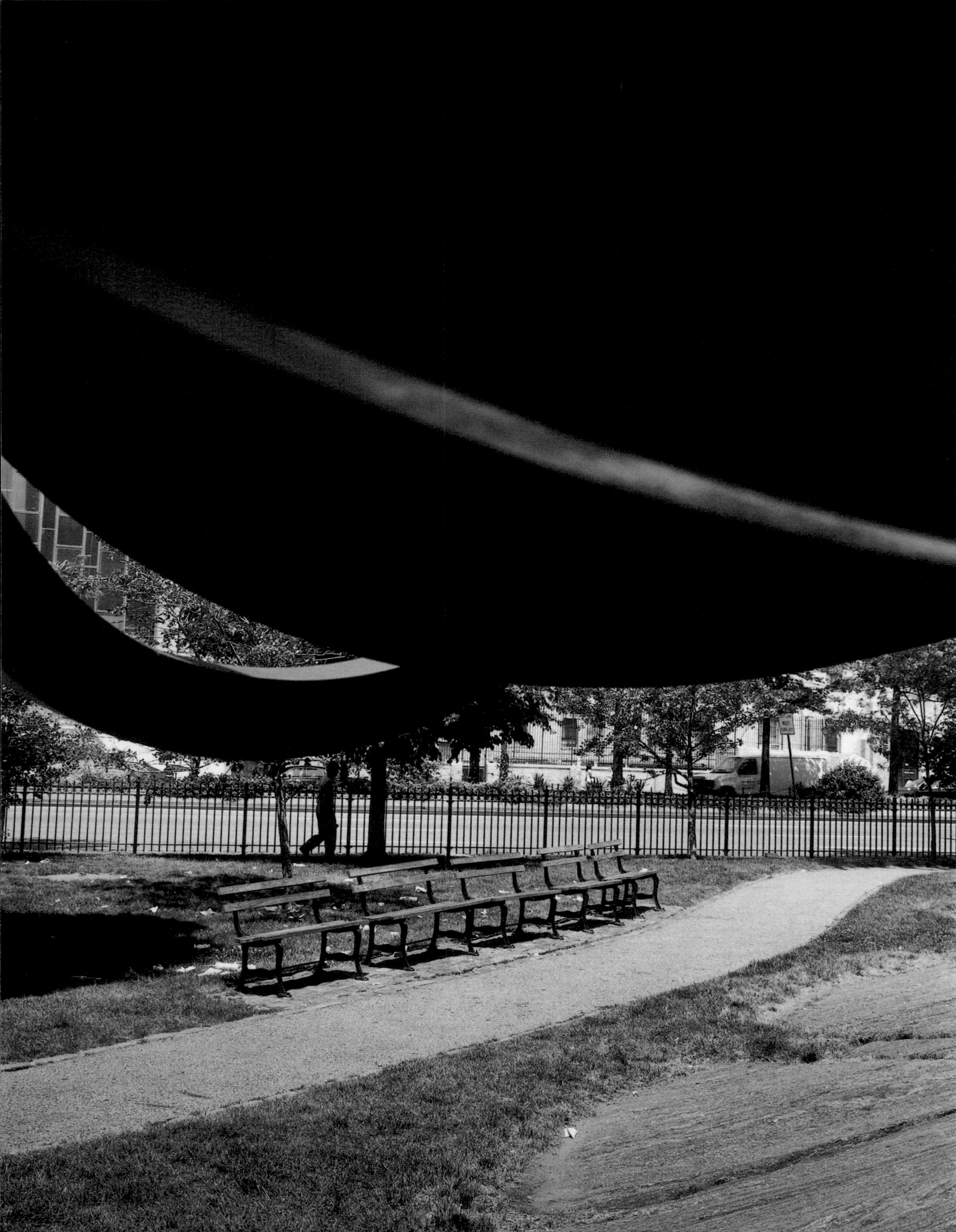

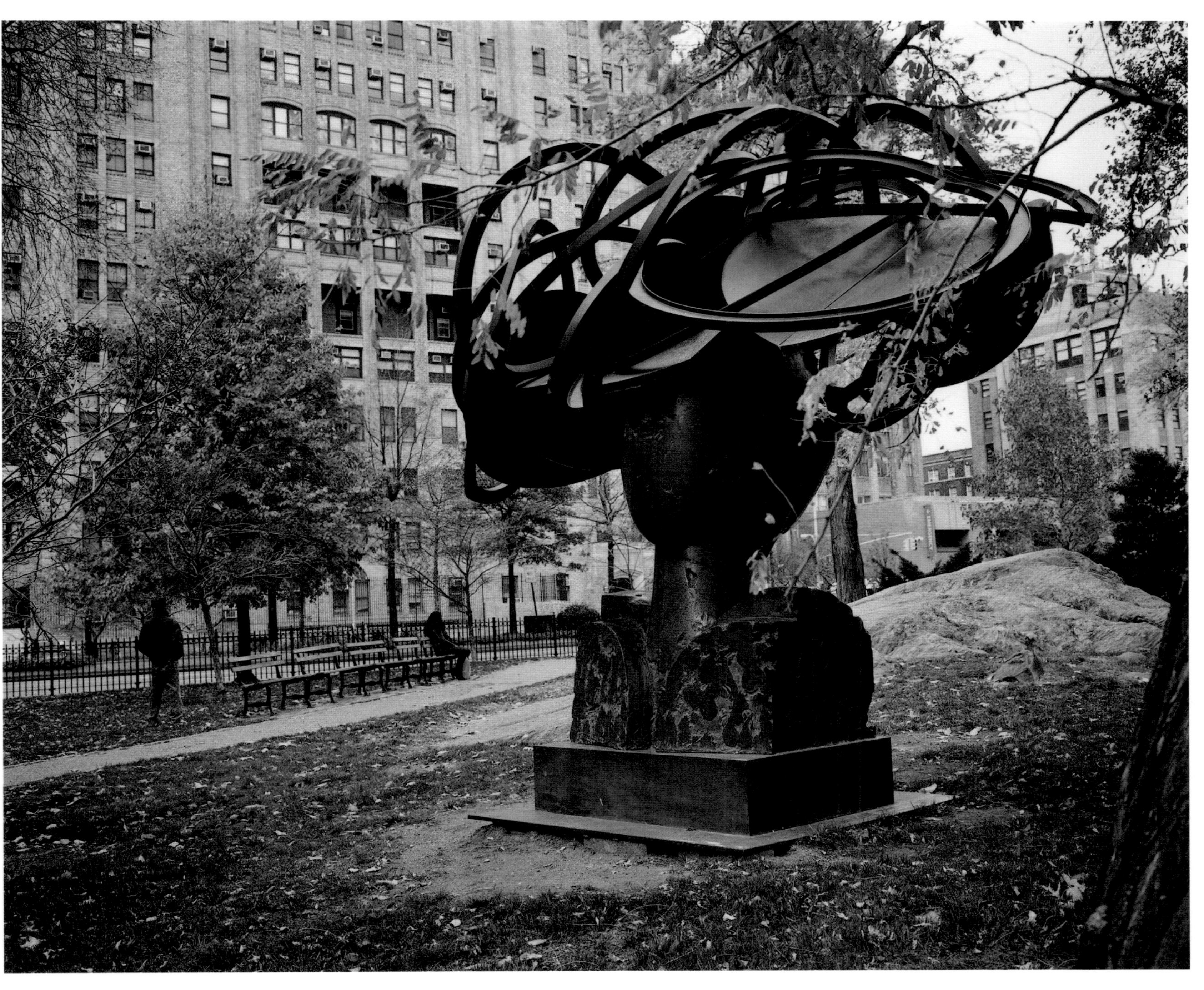

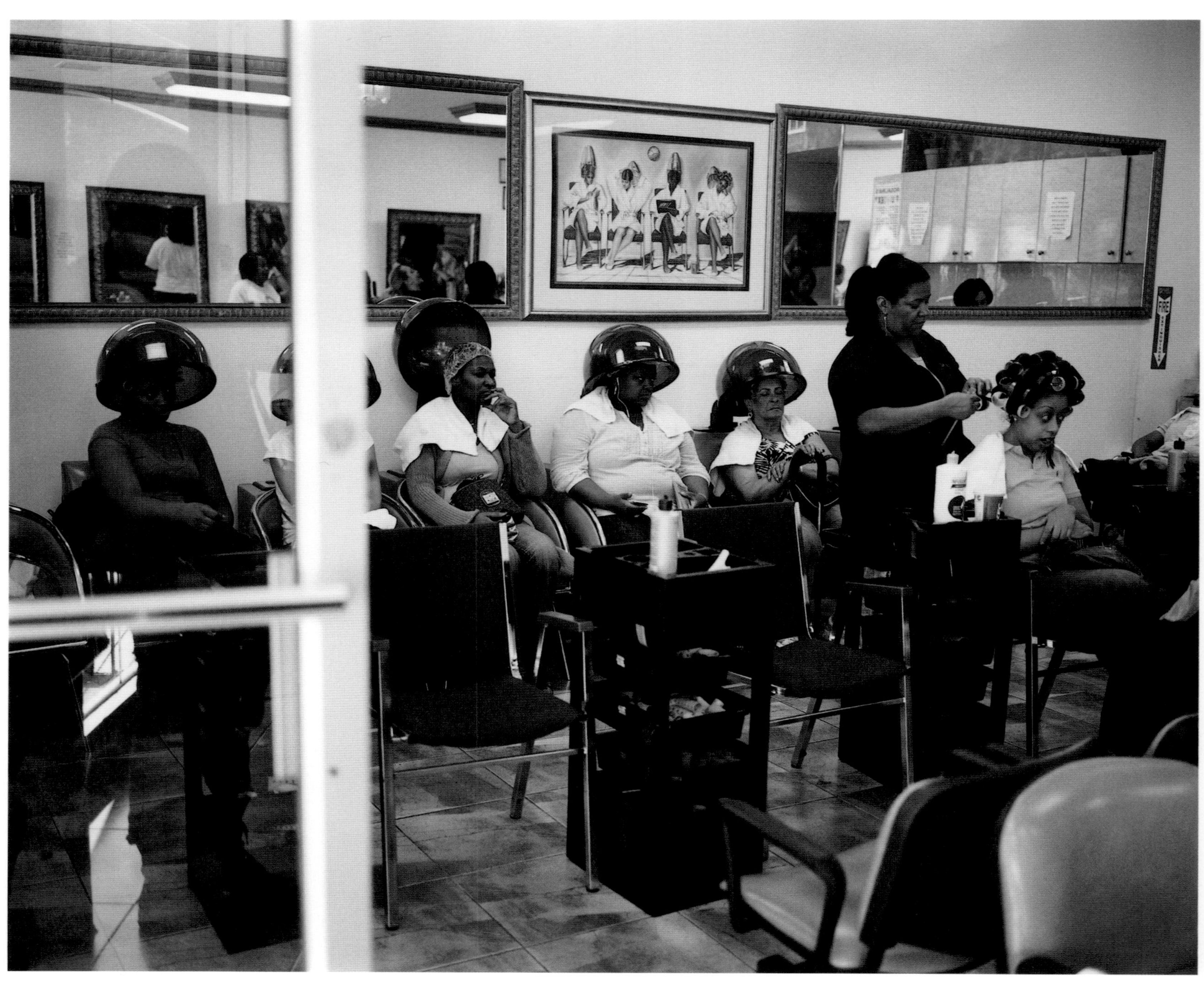

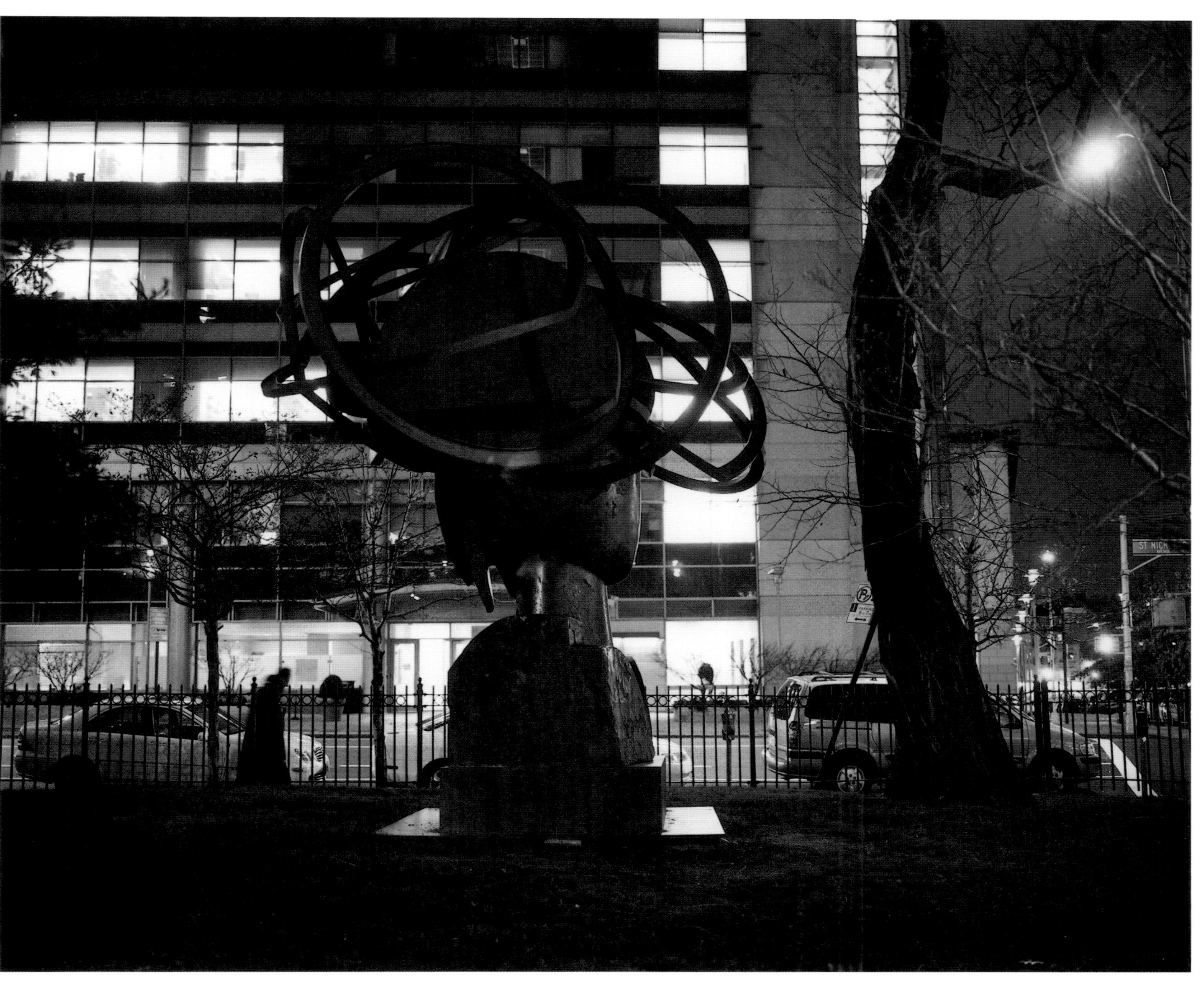

a viewpoint or a fragment that the traces of daily life have left up here, at the top of the island, where vanity has crumbled and everything is a transplanted town, an array of displaced lives.

The city through Manolo Valdes's sculptures acquires a sociology of very varied possibilities. It is the other New York, with the moth-eaten overcoat, with people who exchange glances of warmth and stupefaction. Observe the conflict that exists between *Irene* and *Caballero IV*. Taking photos is engaging in dialogue in an imprecise silence. Andrea knows that. Photographing is listening and guessing what other people are saying. A spectator gives his version of the piece in front of her. "They say that they made it with remains of the Twin Towers, with bits of iron rescued from their collapse. Only a few people know that. But it's true. Believe me." The lavish mechanism of the collective imagination has started up. And each sculpture shows off its lost legend, its tailoring of possibilities, the exaggerated phrases that provide it with identity, meaning and a motto.

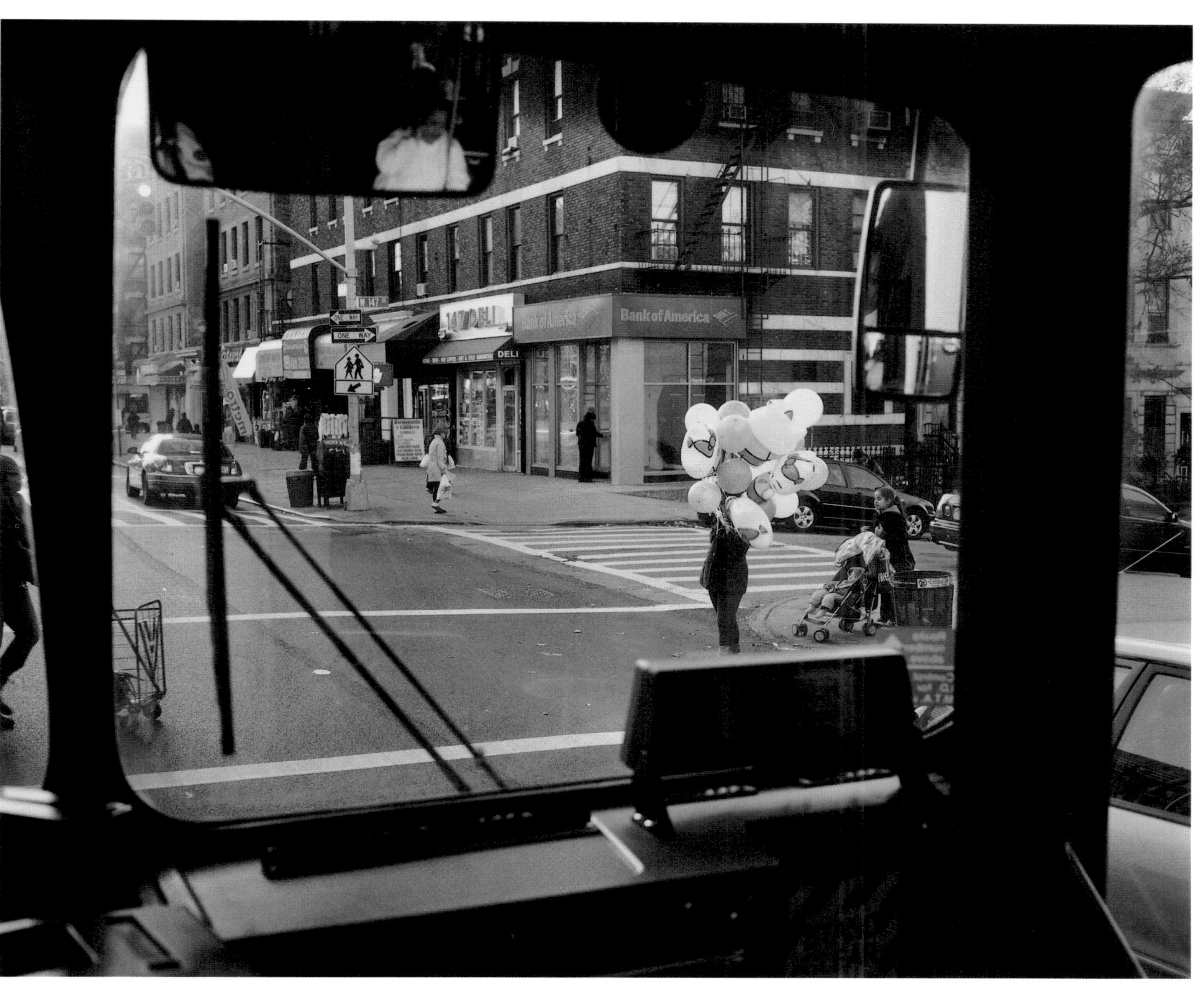

BROADWAY
157TH St

This horseman with his mount has a perpetual swarm of onlookers around him. New Yorkers from that other inland New York. They breathe life into the sculpture by accepting its presence as that of another participant in a literary gathering during the long hours of chatting in the street, breaking off anything else that is not letting time go by with the spiritual lucidity of he who perhaps leaves nothing behind him. That is where its grandeur lies. The city dwellers are part of the work – life applied to a sculpture made without them. Andrea seeks them out with her camera, like a water finder. She finds them between the light and the open air, in order to construct this hypnotized novel.

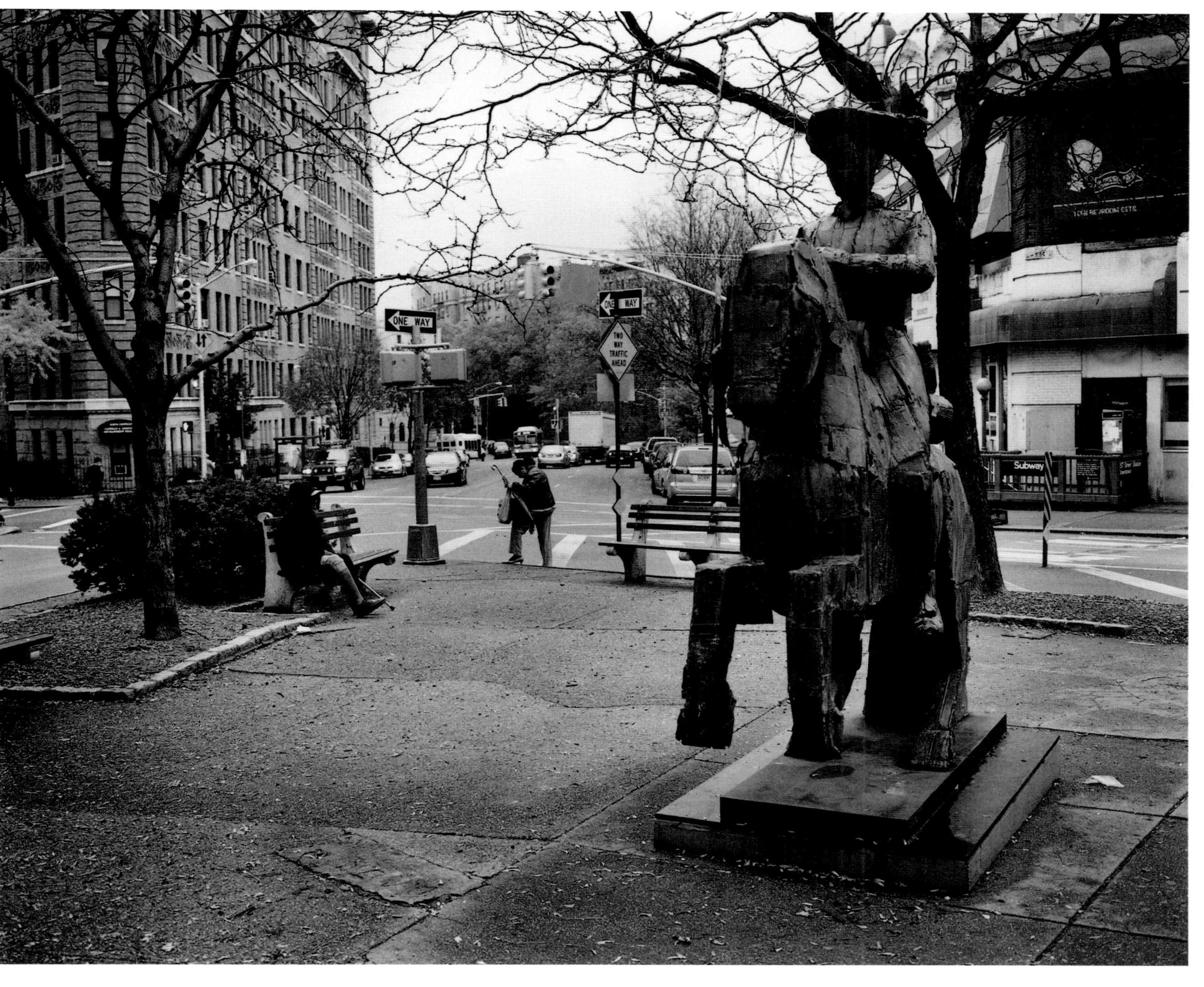

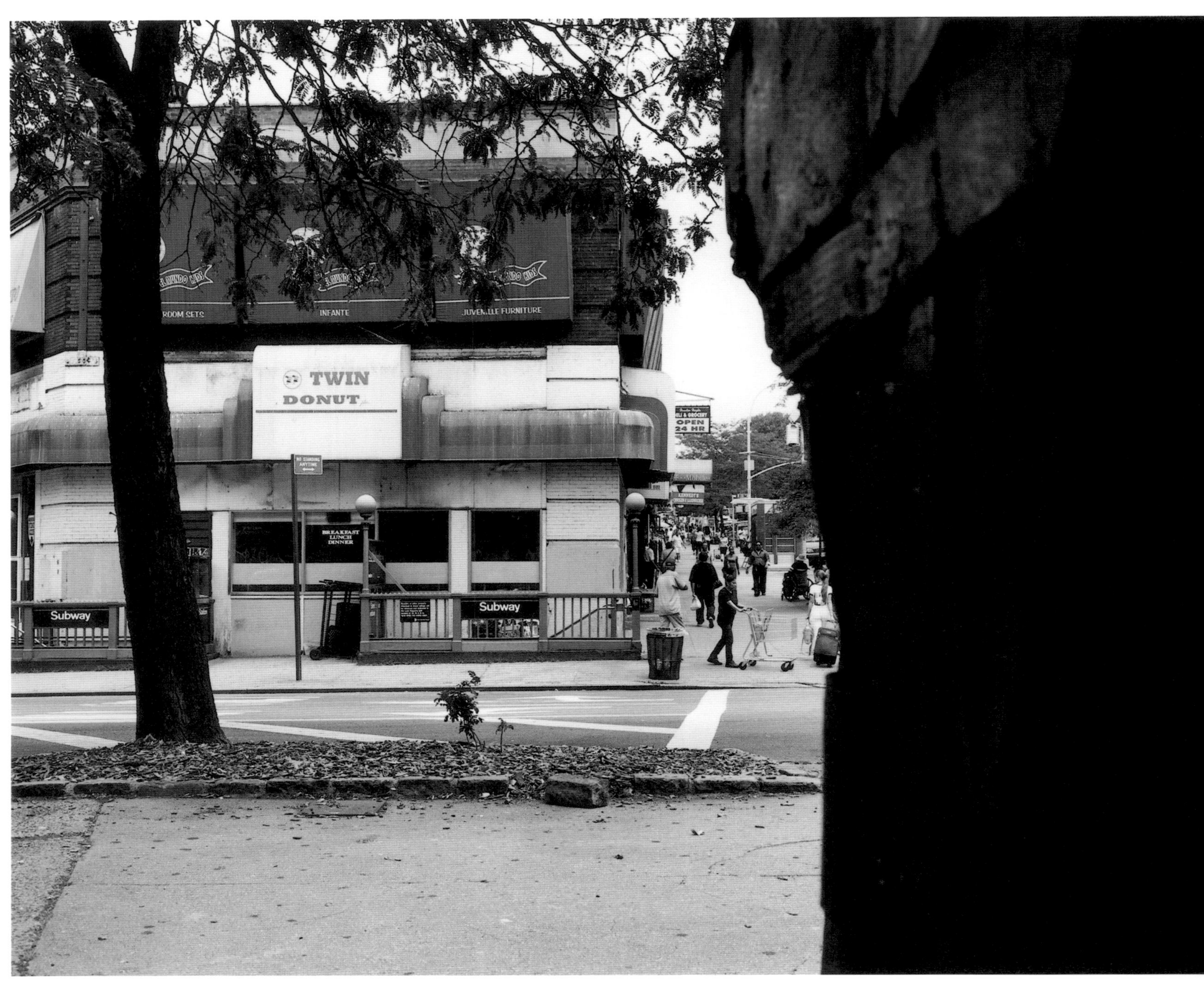

TWIN
DONUT
ROOM SETS   INFANTE   JUVENILE FURNITURE
BREAKFAST
LUNCH
DINNER
Subway
Subway
OPEN
24 HR

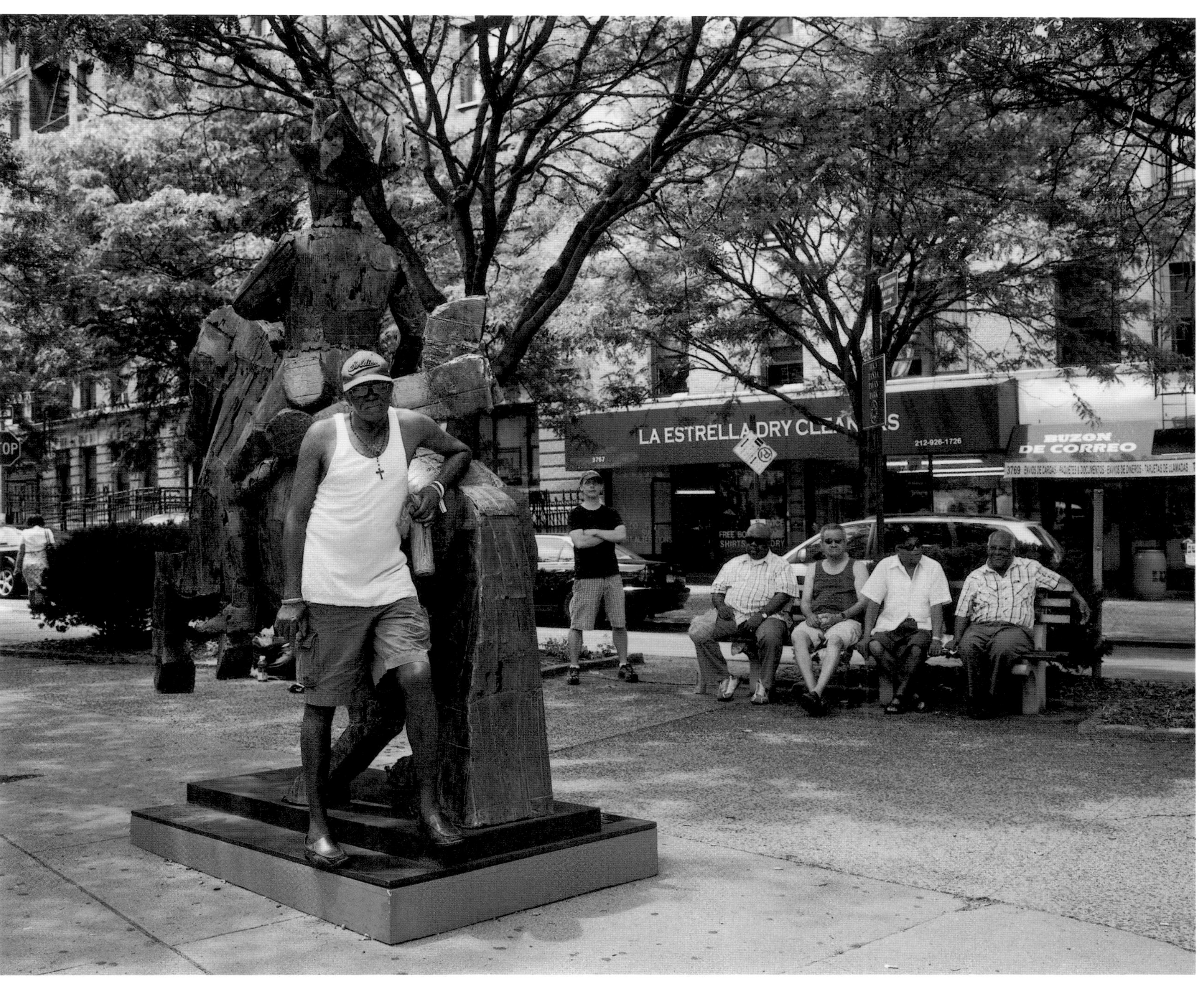

LA ESTRELLA DRY CLEANERS
212-926-1726
BUZON
DE CORREO

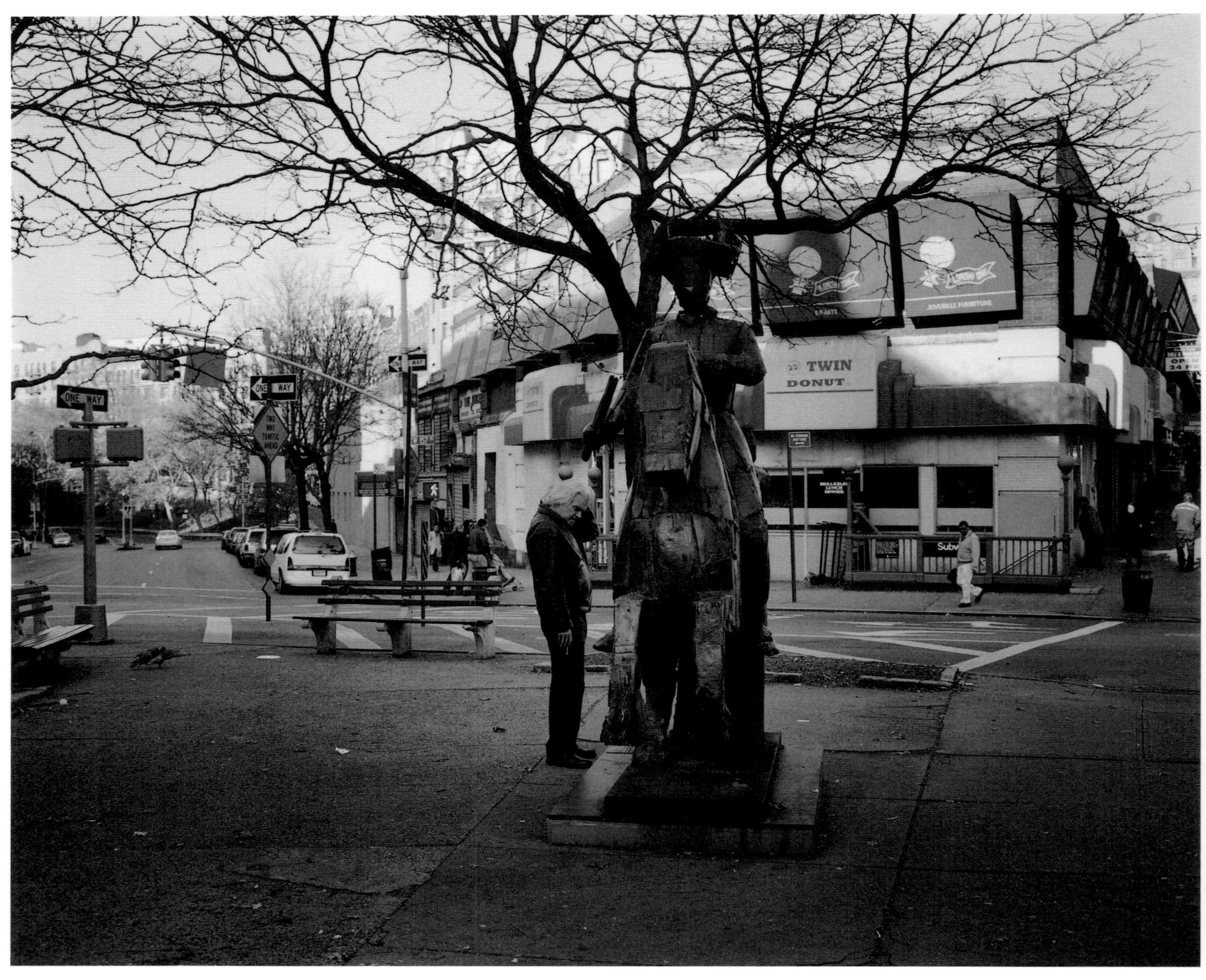

ONE WAY
ONE WAY
TWO WAY TRAFFIC AHEAD
TWIN
DONUT
Subway

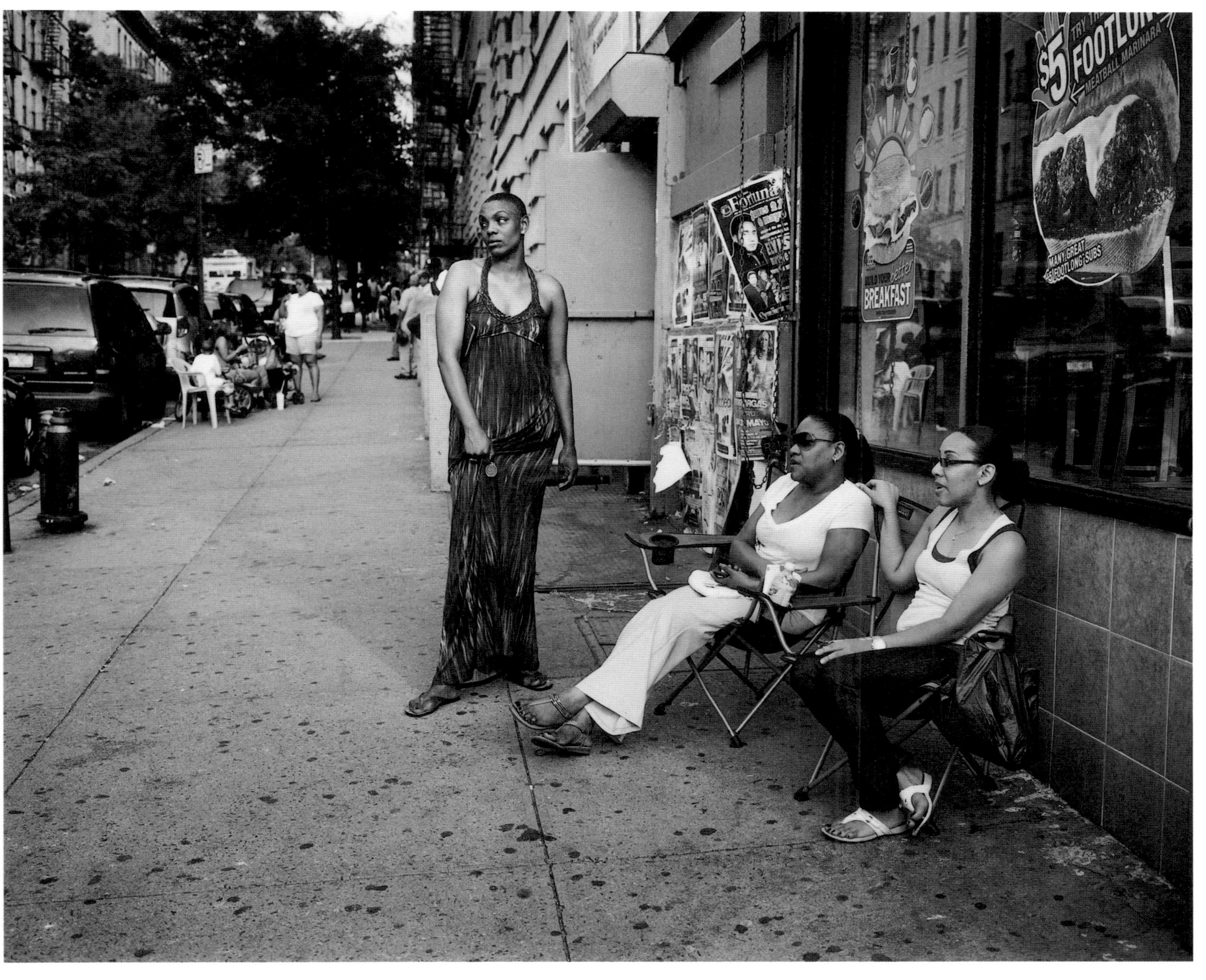
$5 FOOTLONG
TRY THE
MEATBALL MARINARA
MANY GREAT
FOOTLONG SUBS
BUILD YOUR
BREAKFAST
Fortuna

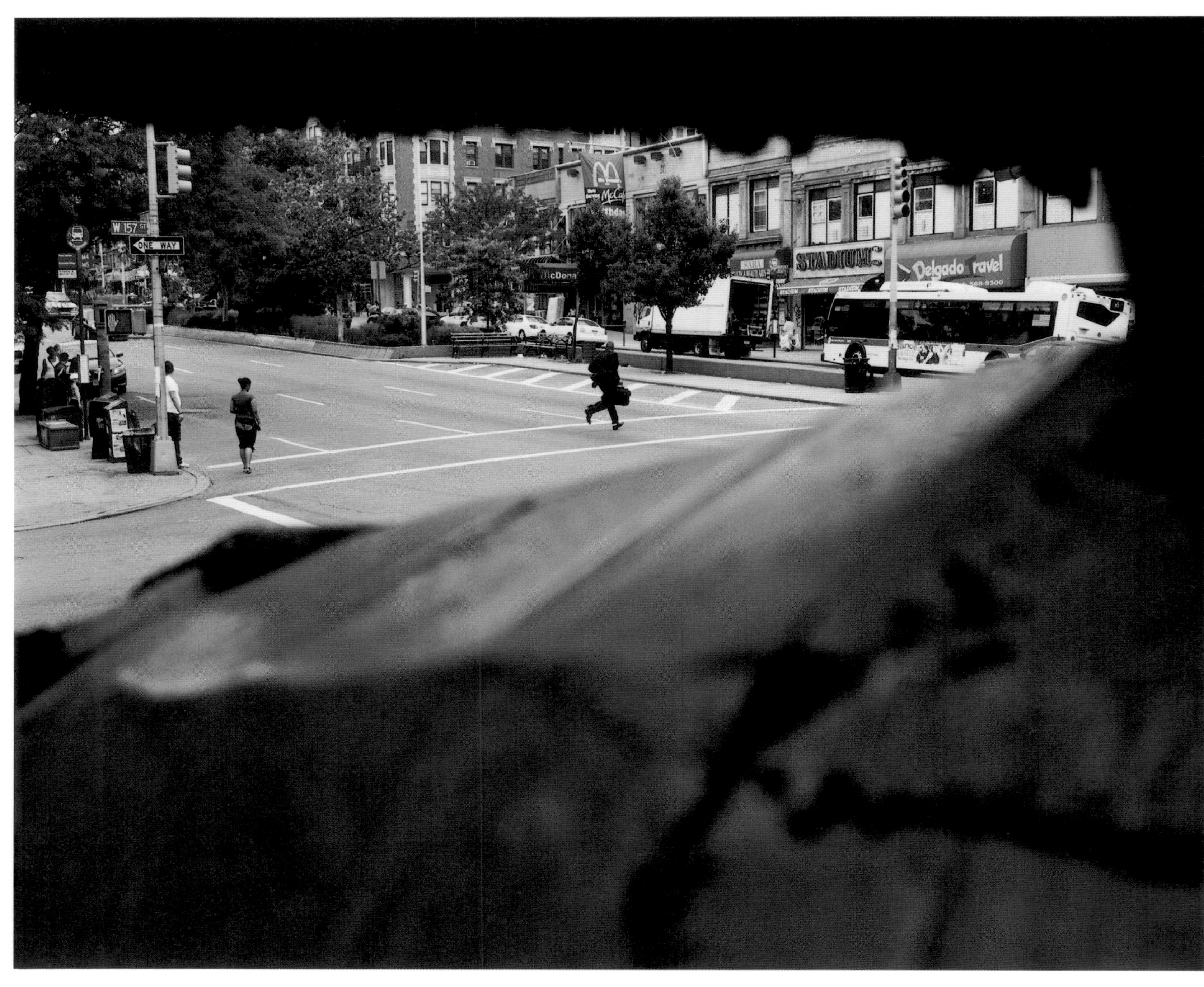

W 157 ST
ONE WAY
McDonald's
STADIUM
Delgado Travel
568-9300

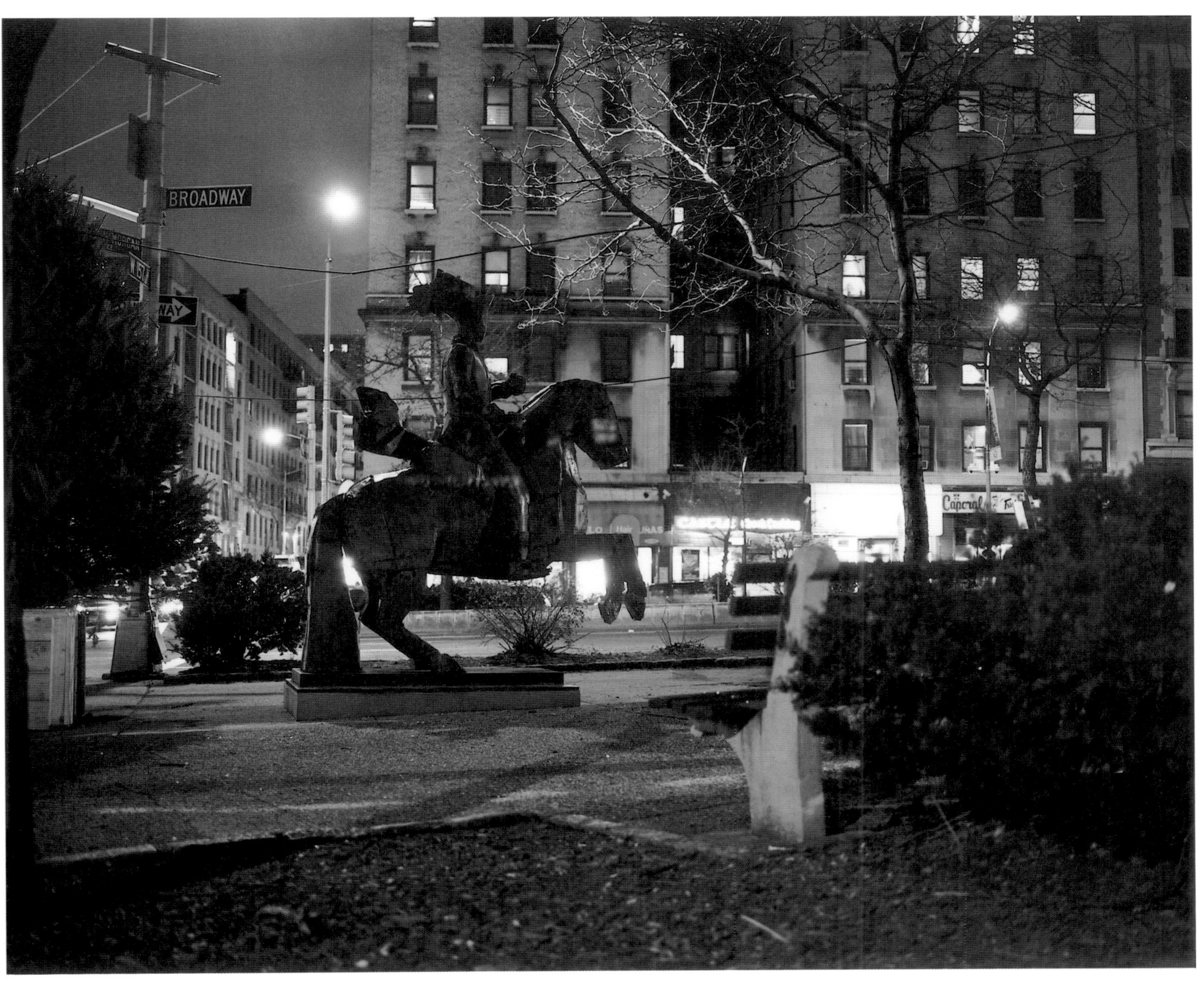
BROADWAY
W 157
WAY
Caprala

BROADWAY
148TH S_T

[DAMA III]

There is a cemetery between *Caballero IV* and *Dama III*.
A graveyard separates them. A Morse code of corpses
and prayers for the dead between the open sea that
divides the passageway from 157th Street to 148th Street.
On going down the avenue, the landscape consists of a
combination of fruiterers and infernal barbacues at the
foot of doorways. Life on these paving stones is something
else. It is a state of jubilation under the dark black skins
which contrast with the off-white of the false teeth of
those who live here, who laugh, shout, love, wander about
and die. *Dama III* is in the center of the boulevard, with
her long hair of Matisse-like acanthus leaves, with her
carder of "marijuana leaves", as the parishioner of the lost
afternoons at the feet of the statues asserts. Because here
they talk to them, they appropriate the works, they are a
sudden treasure, a parasol, an accomplice in the long gulps
of beer, and a shelter from the short sips of bitterness.
But what are you looking for Andrea? Which seed, which
galaxy, what alarming fervor among the sculptures? Which
live dimension in their bronze? What conversation in the
faces without a face? What words have come from these

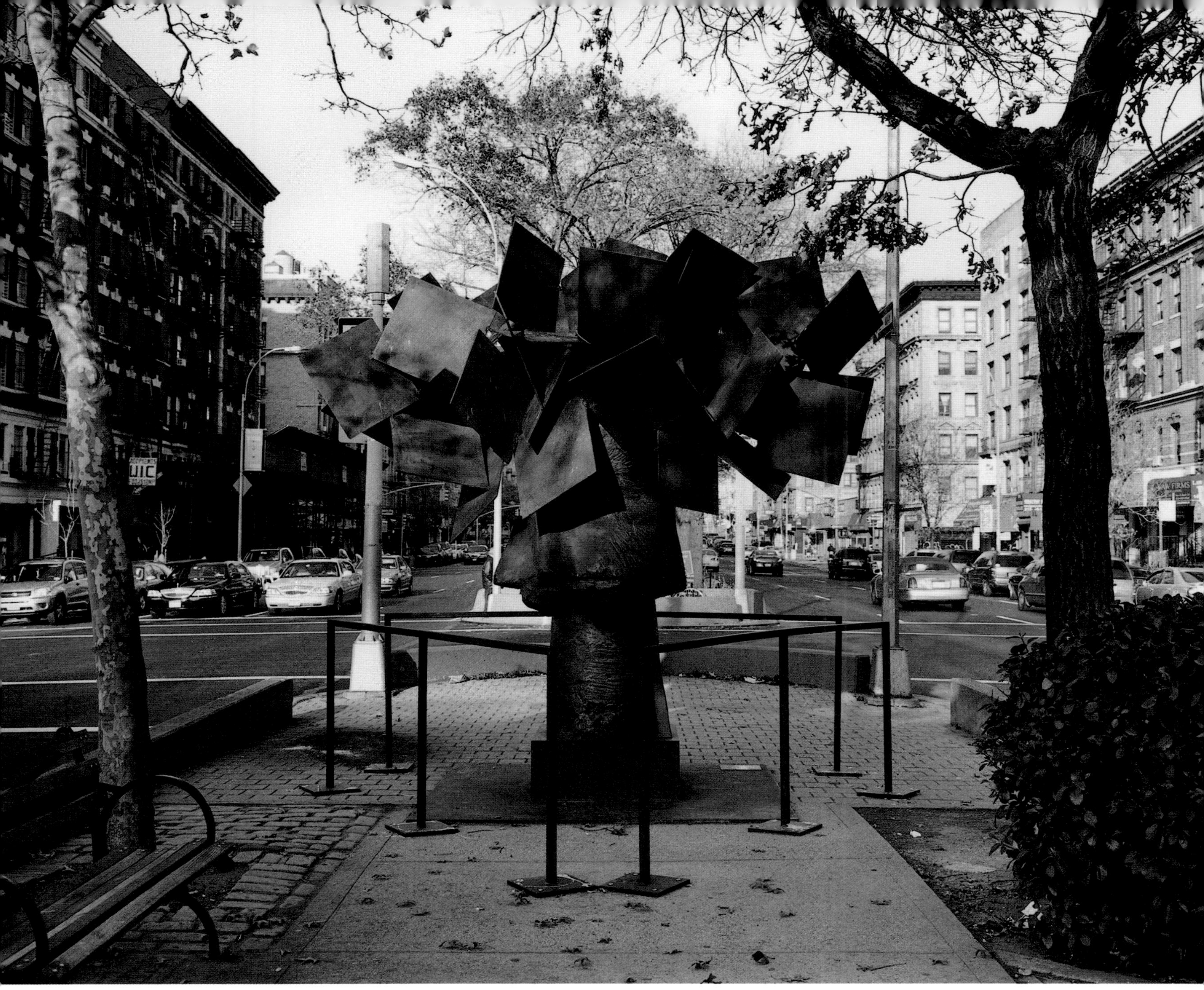

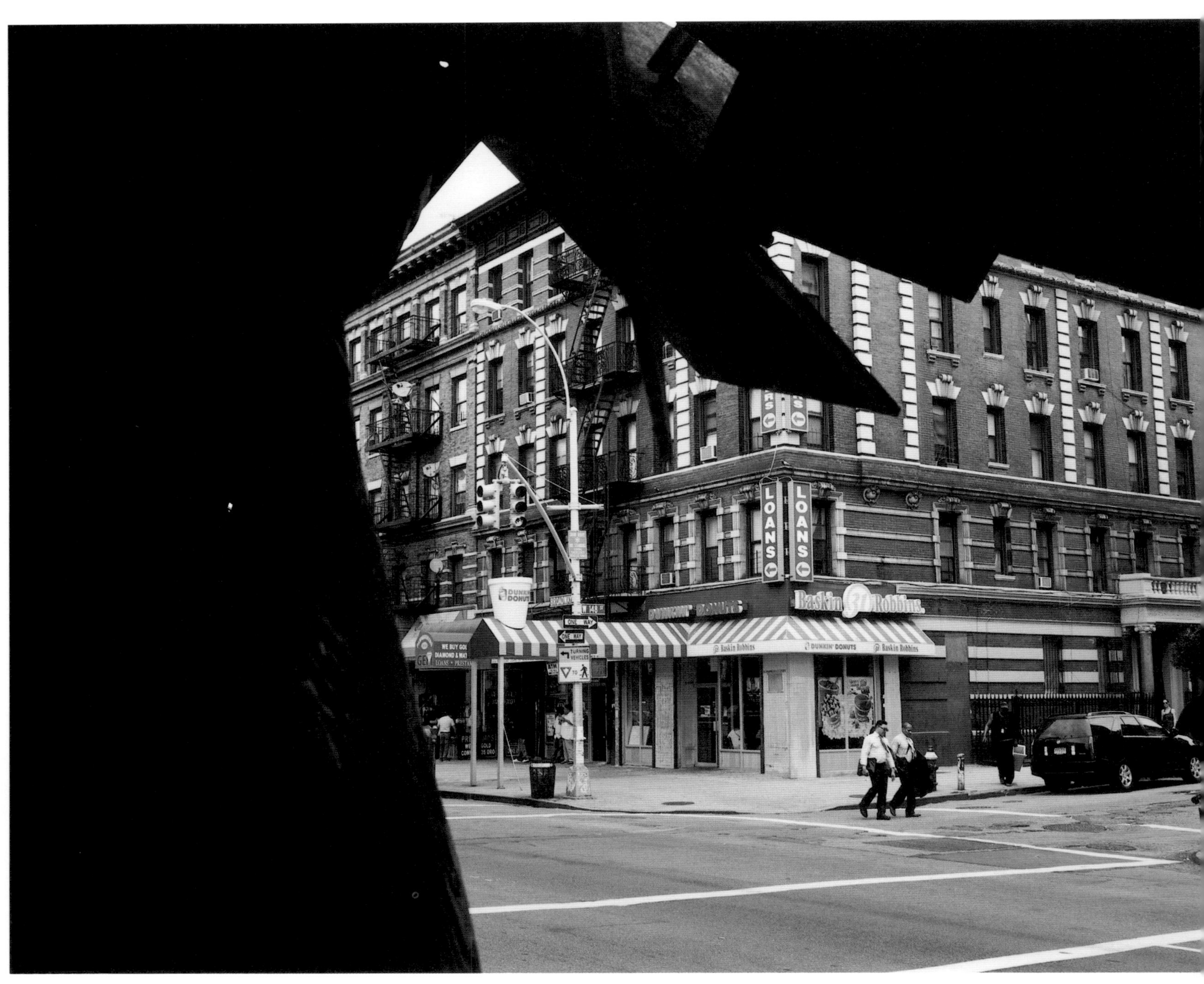

LOANS
LOANS
Baskin Robbins.
DUNKIN' DONUTS
WE BUY GOLD
DIAMOND & WAT
LOANS • PRESTA
ONE WAY
ONE WAY
TURNING
VEHICLES

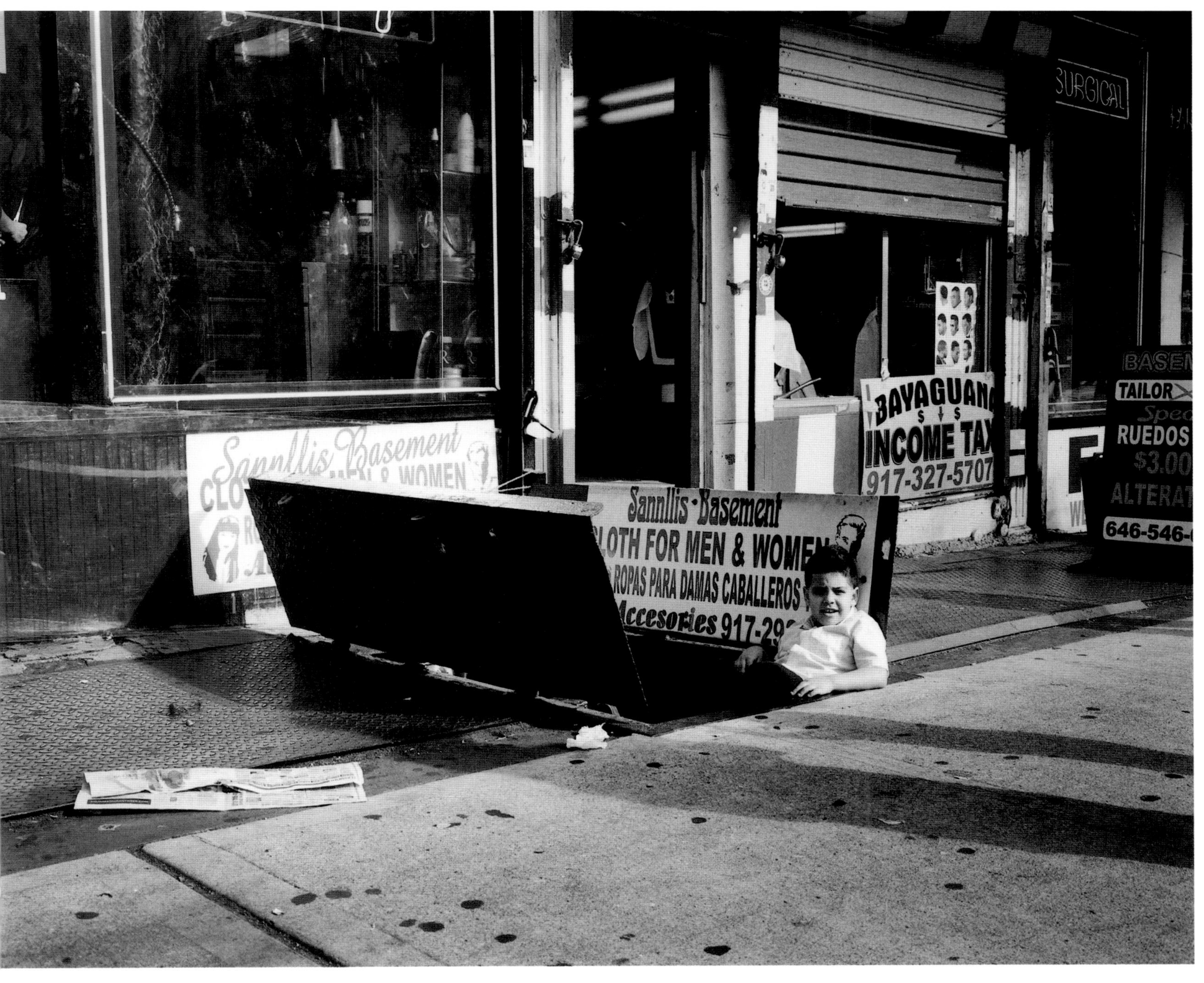
SURGICAL
Sannllis..Basement
CLO... & WOMEN
Sannllis · Basement
LOTH FOR MEN & WOMEN
ROPAS PARA DAMAS CABALLEROS
Accesories 917-29
BAYAGUANA
$ $
INCOME TAX
917-327-5707
BASEM
TAILOR
Spe
RUEDOS
$3.00
ALTERAT
646-546-6
W

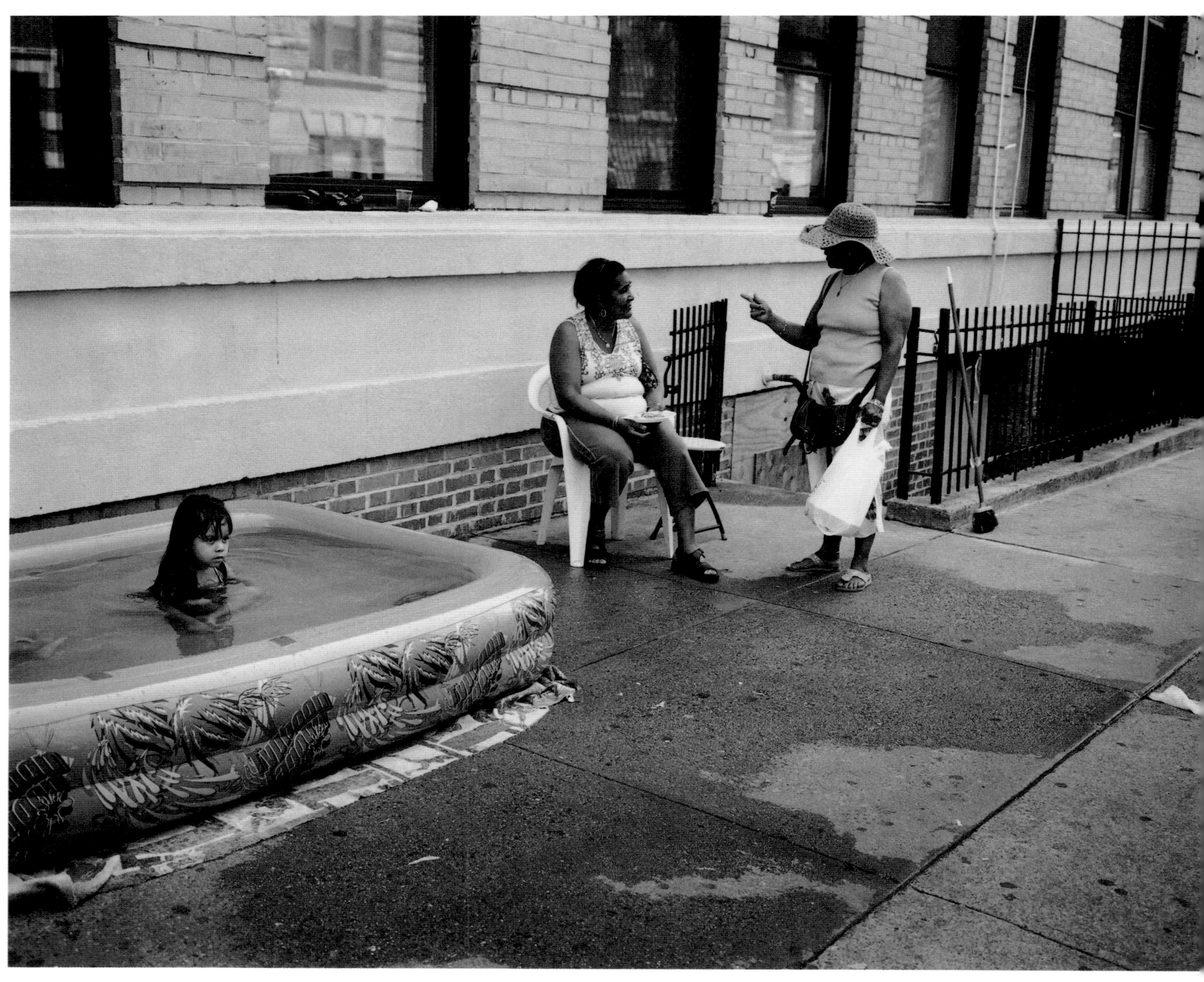

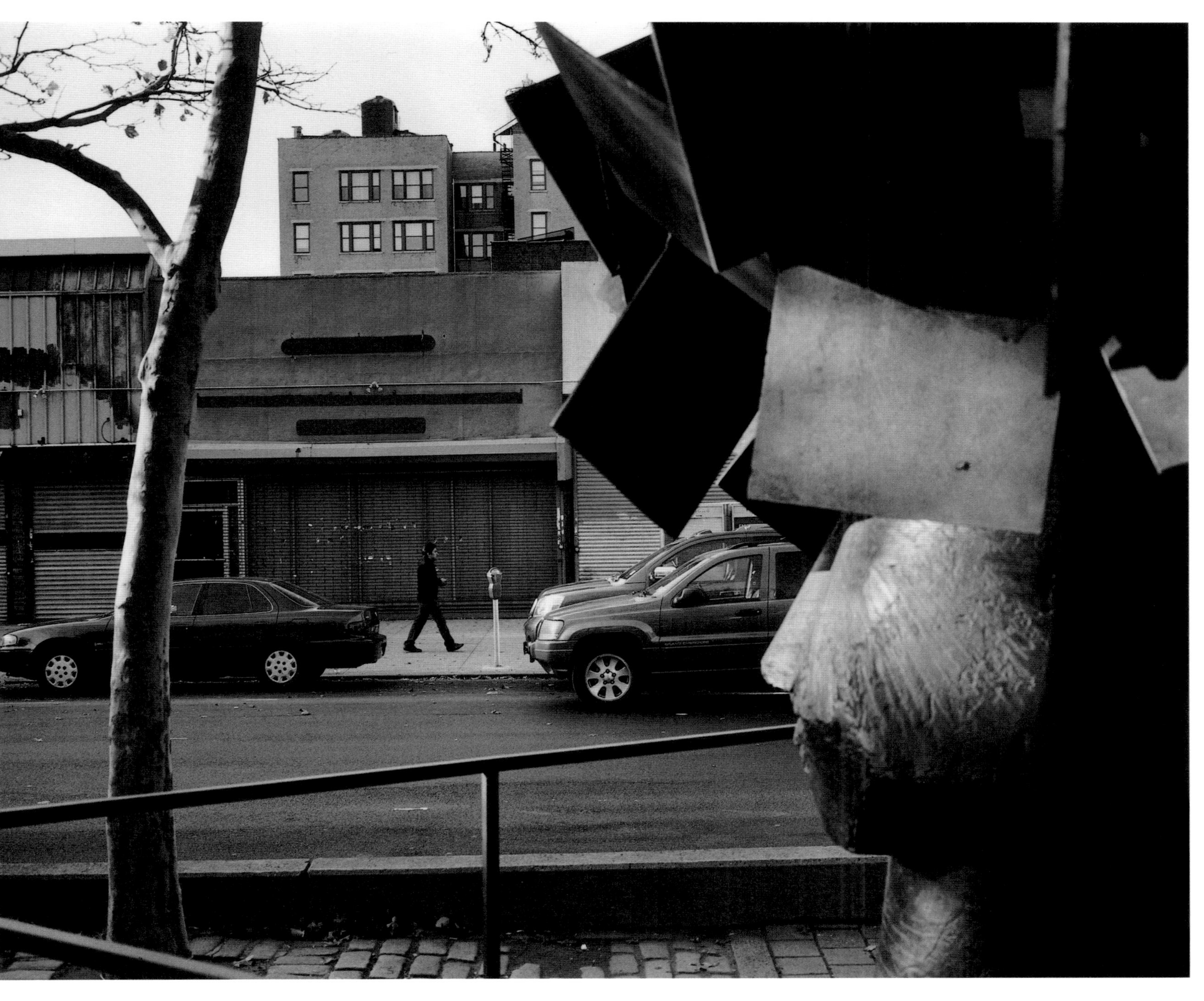

mouths without lips, from this frost worked
like a song with a female face? What do you
feel of which we still have no premonition?

–Design, architecture, life. New York
differently. The construction of people and
Valdés's sculptures. All one. The city invaded
by this fabulous family of ladies who come
from the old plumage of art in order to
re-invent themselves in this space; to invent
us with it. I come to see the blood dancing
in the hyperbolic, populous or sad shade
of these sculptures which have created new
instantaneous horizons that are punctual
and soluble according to how they appear.
Andrea talks about Mr. G., the cousin of
Miles Davis, with his impeccable Sunday
suit, bi-color shoes and wide-brimmed hat.
His eyeballs reflect arrogance and suspicion.
Andrea photographs him when he walks
around *Ada - Ada* in the Cubist ardor of her
hairstyle of cubes, of her winged geometry.
She seems the closest to an apparition where
apparitions are certainly improbable. She
also teaches us to look, with her austere
fascination that is so remote. She fled from
the workshop to mix with the passers-by.

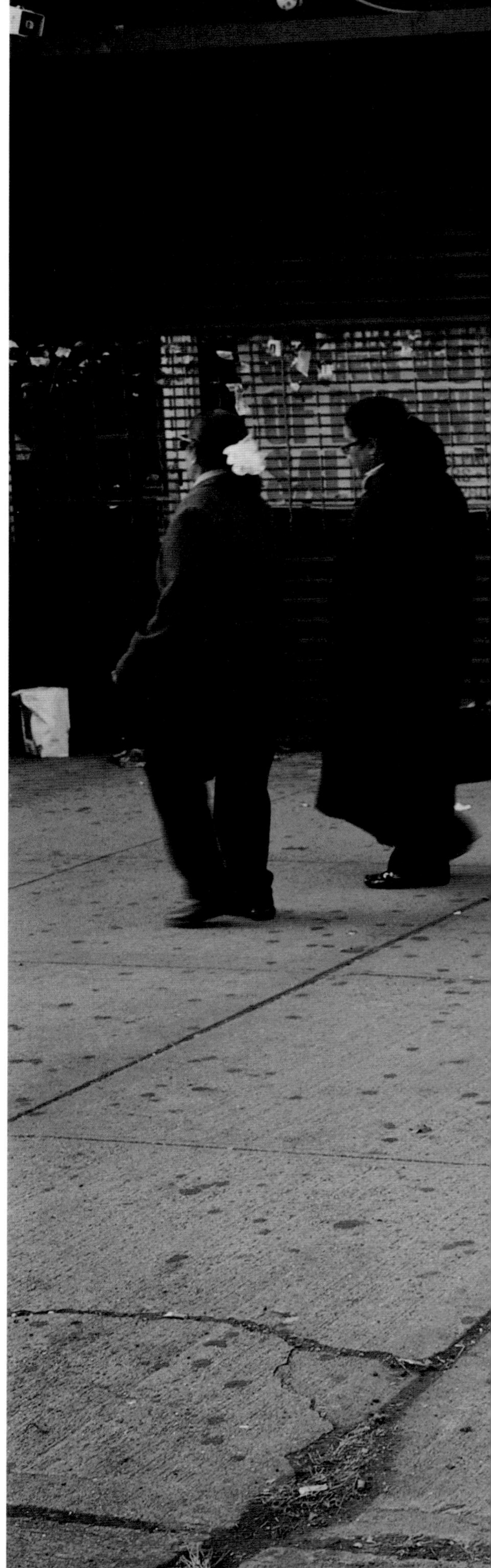

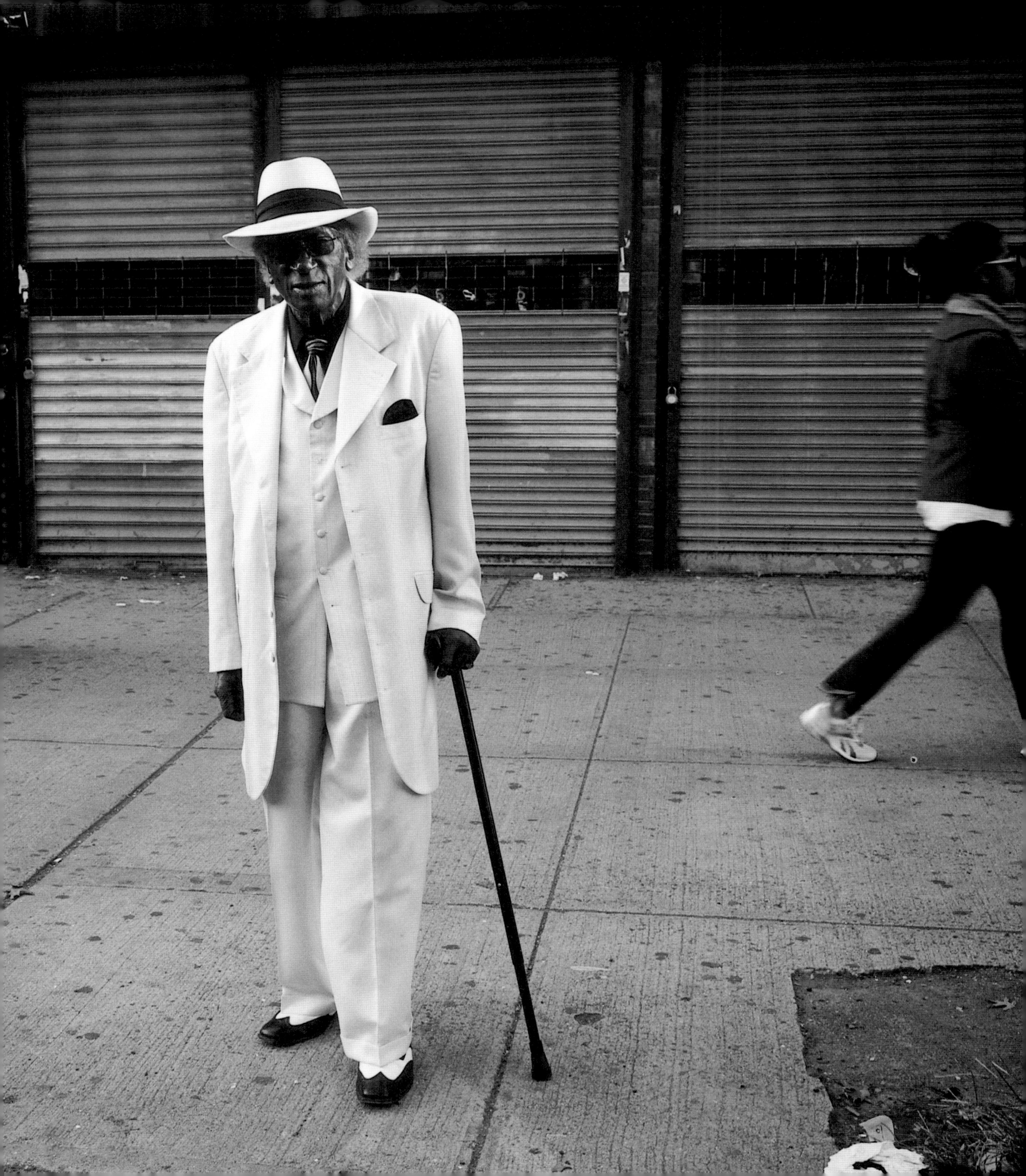

137TH S_T

[ADA]

We continue to go down through New York, with its
meticulous archeology of neighborhoods of Latinos,
of gangs of blacks, watched over (and cheered on) by
indefatigable storekeepers in the arcades of the brown
stones, these old buildings of copper-colored brick, with
their fire-escape ladders resembling skeletal structures.
At this side of the river there are tenement houses. In
the shade of Mr. G. *Ada* gets a blast of jazz, an aesthetic
solemnity of antiquated modernity which protects her
from the autumn. This is the adventure of rediscovering
the city, from groups of laborers to caryatids with an air
of fatigue as a result of exile and aspirations many times
fulfilled and so many others betrayed. Art formed with the
harmony of an accident, with the luck of the fortuitous.
On 137th street, the flow of people does not stop. A child
fantasizes, sitting on the edge of an open hatchway that
leads to an underground market. Everything here takes
place with the same exuberance outside and underground.
The camera catches every incident, every minimum event,
successively revealing fragments of existence, the shock of
what has been certain and at the same time is the summer

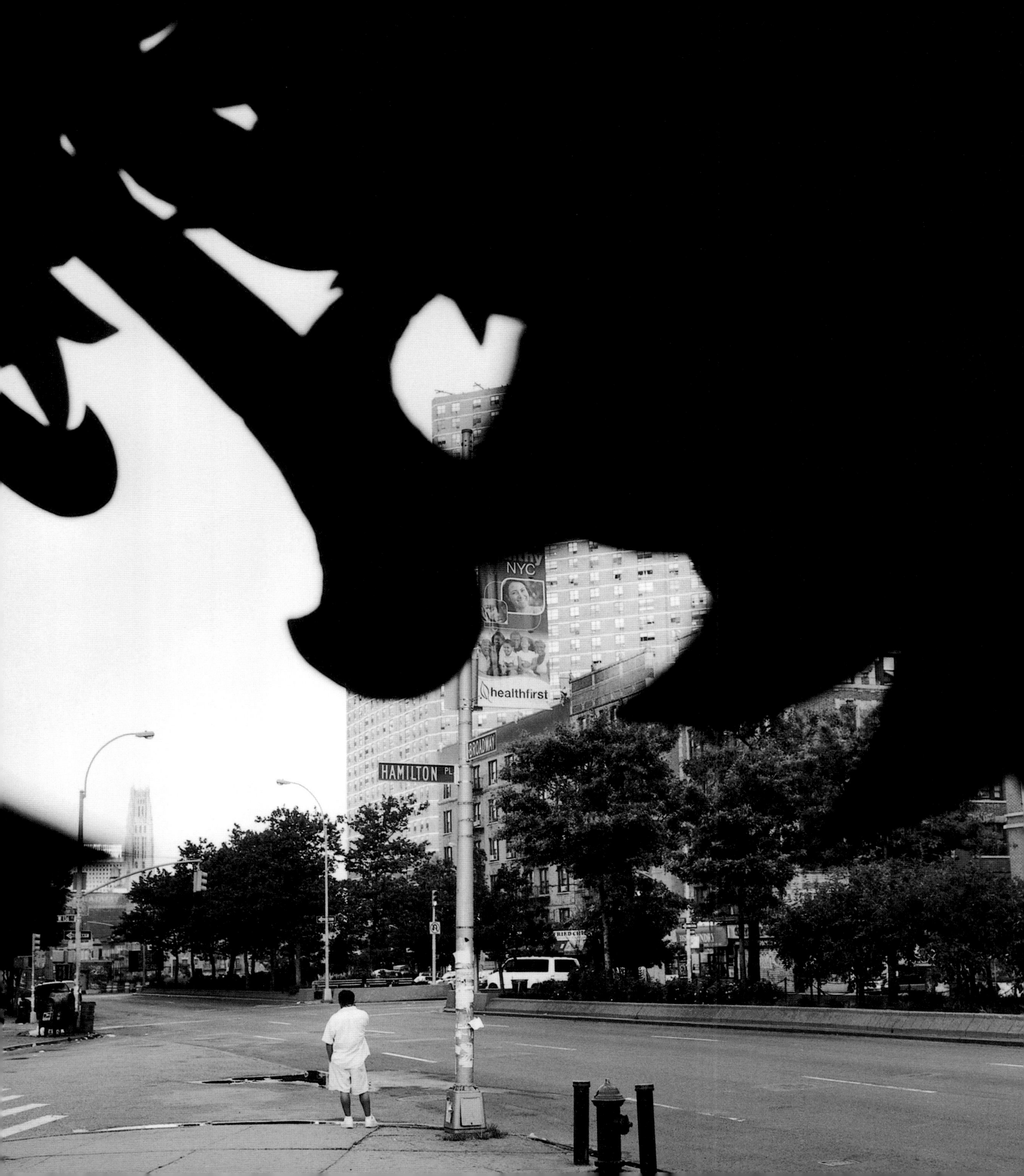

NYC
healthfirst
HAMILTON PL
BROADWAY

derived from a dream. The camera catches an elegant and dilapidated world. Andrea creates a reality that takes shape as she goes down Broadway. Already "order and disorder are the same thing"[1]. It is life as it is. The day in New York is seen through the lens, with the only drive axle offered by a set of works arranged at the sides of Broadway like a seam of old bronze, of combinations of Neolithic materials. The works are correspondents from another age, fire and forge that is compacted, and they assume the speculative diction of mythological metamorphoses. Although in reality they come from the experience of the artist in his wandering through the history of art, through the happy tensions of better times. And they are not here on account of a sudden impulse, but rather are aware of being an enriched vestige of lava or slag --like a harmonious collection of minerals, travelling from who knows where.

[1] Poem from the book *Los países nocturnos* by Carlos Marzal. Tusquets, 1996.

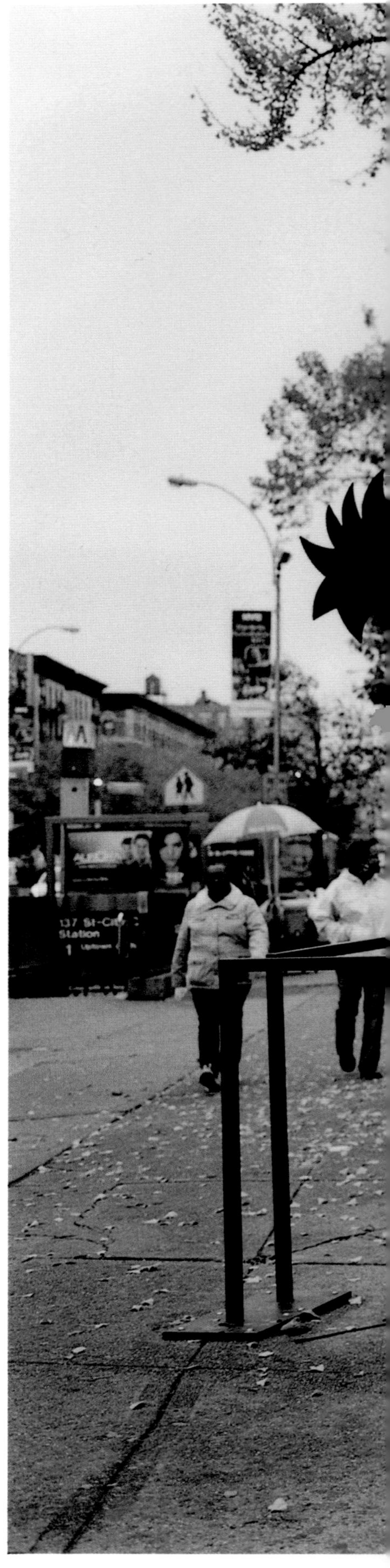

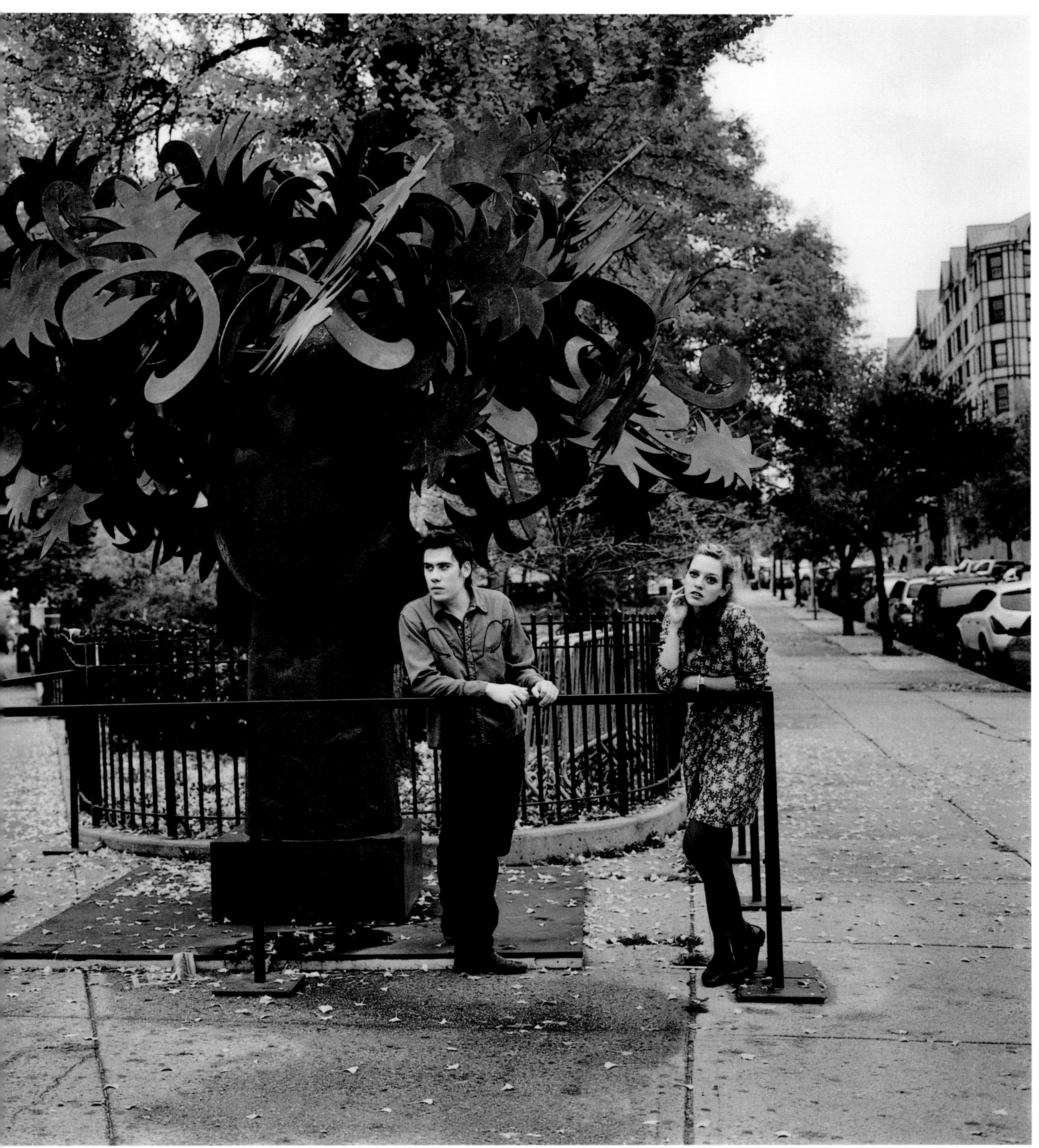

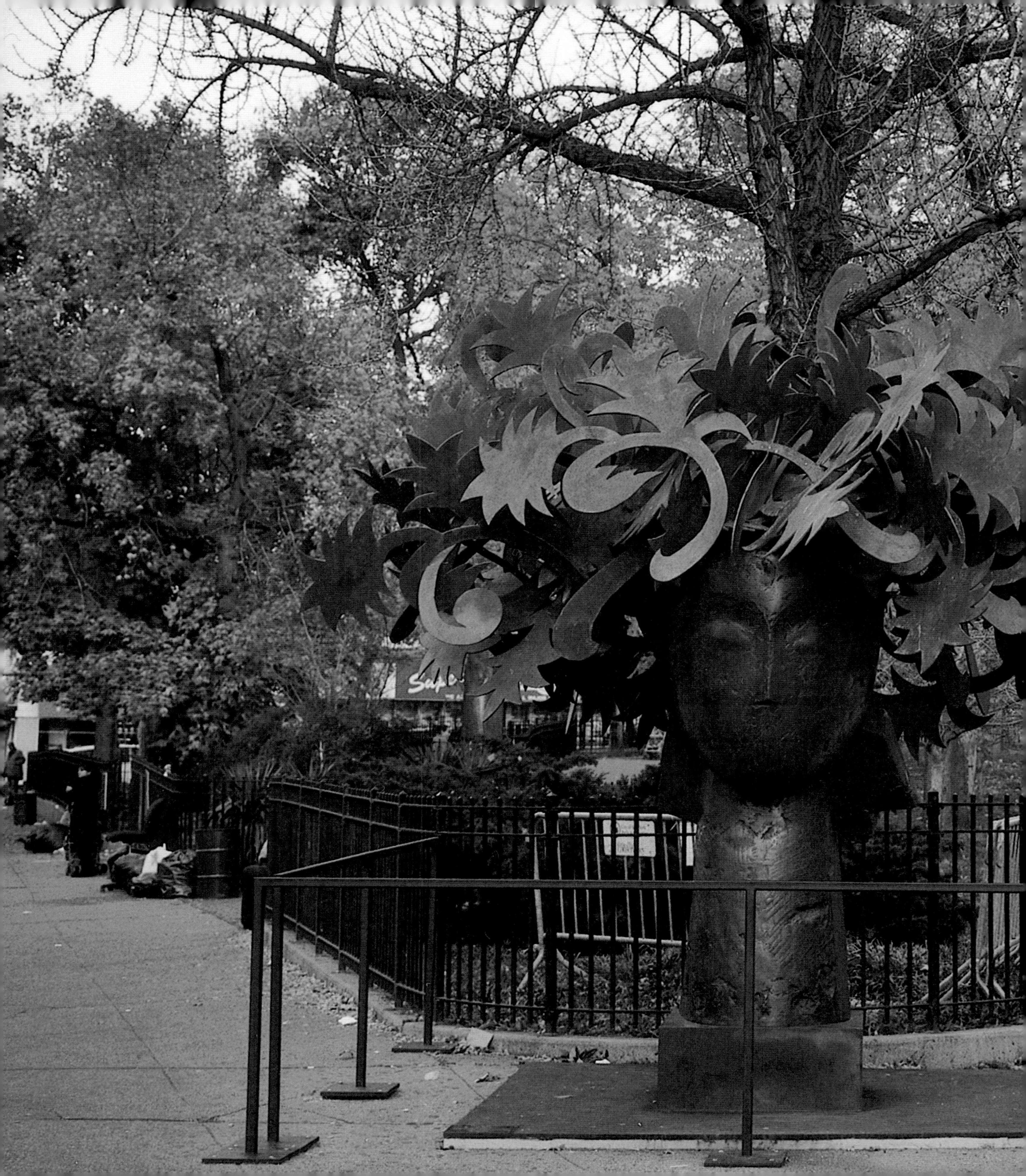

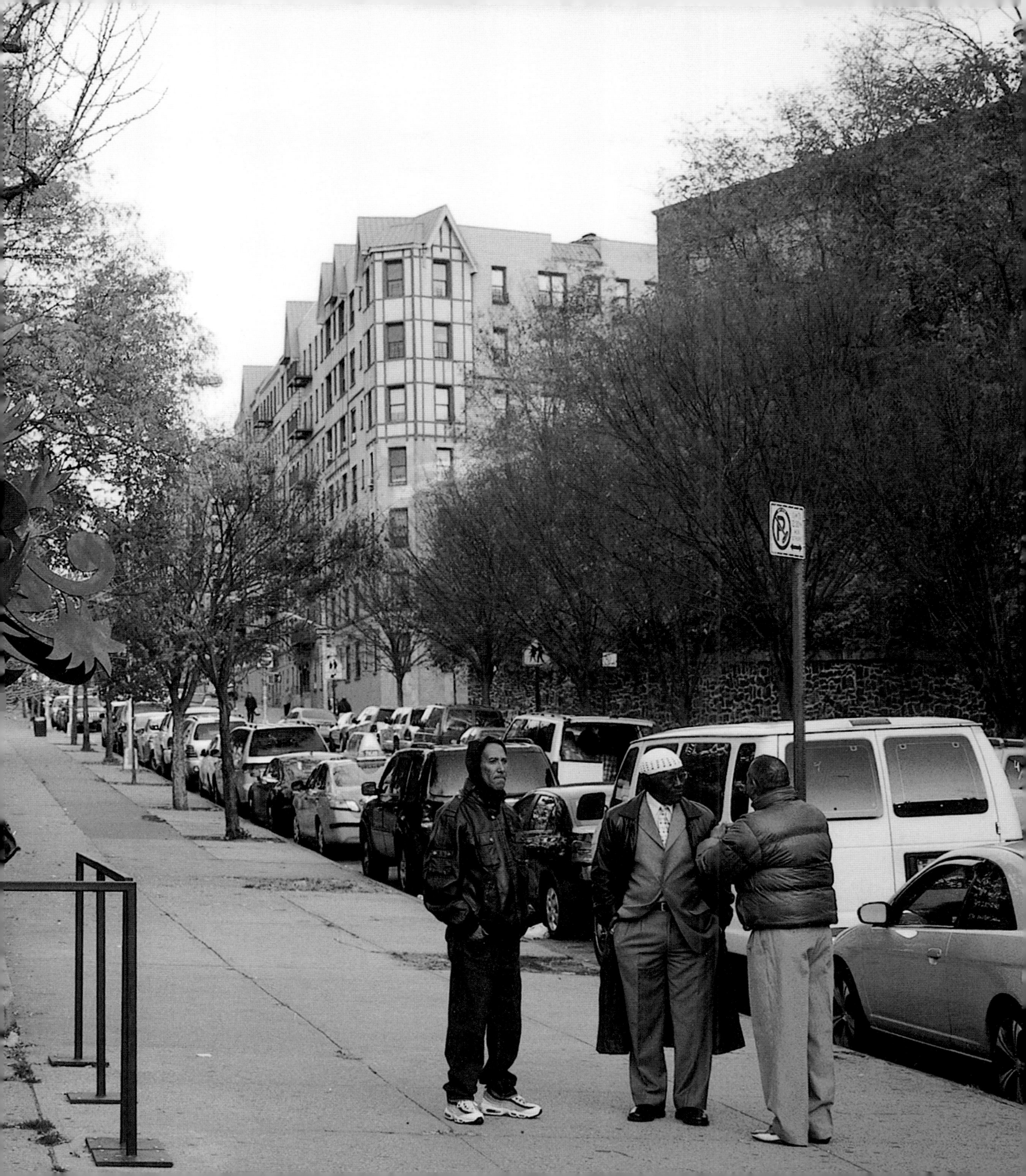

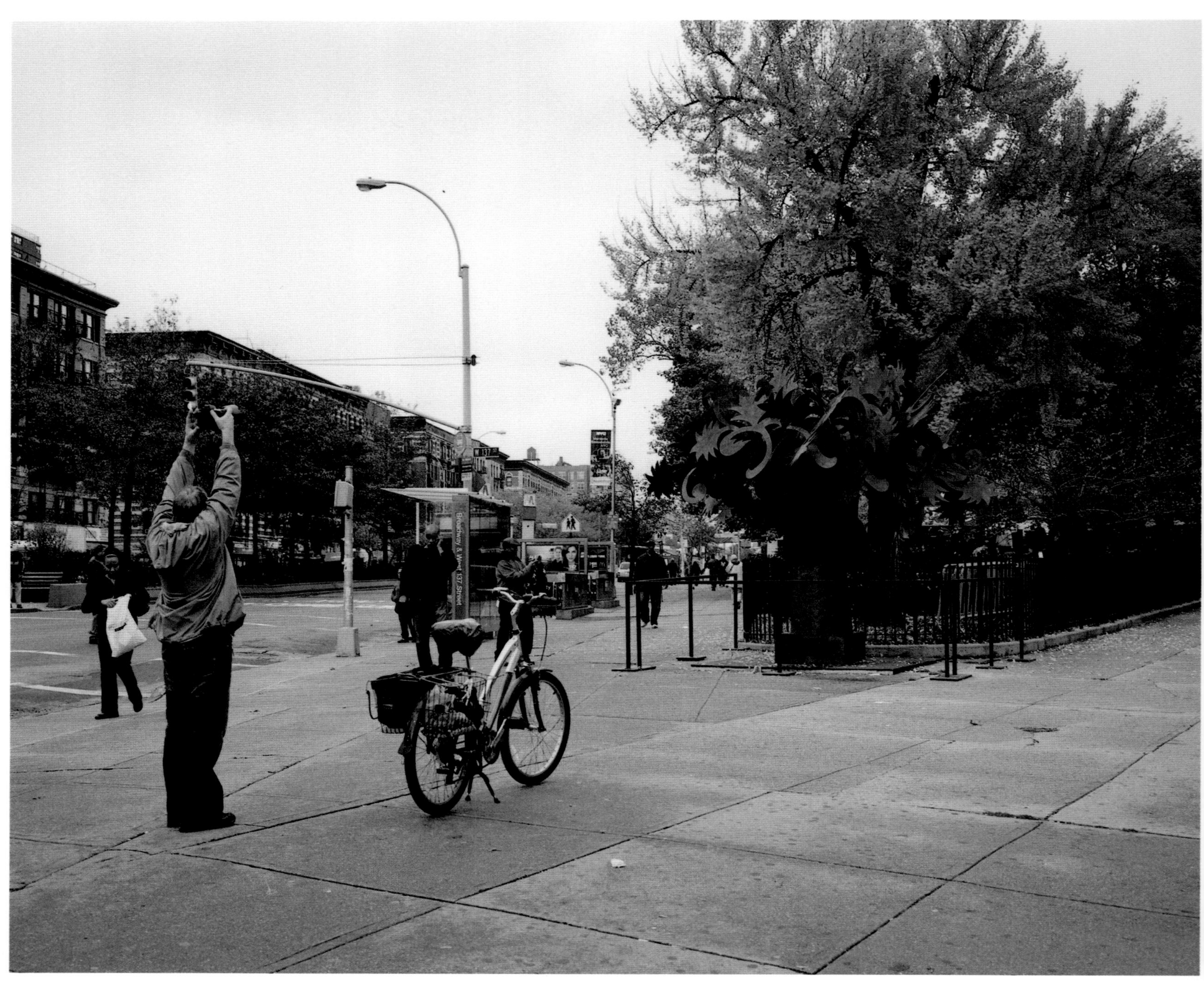

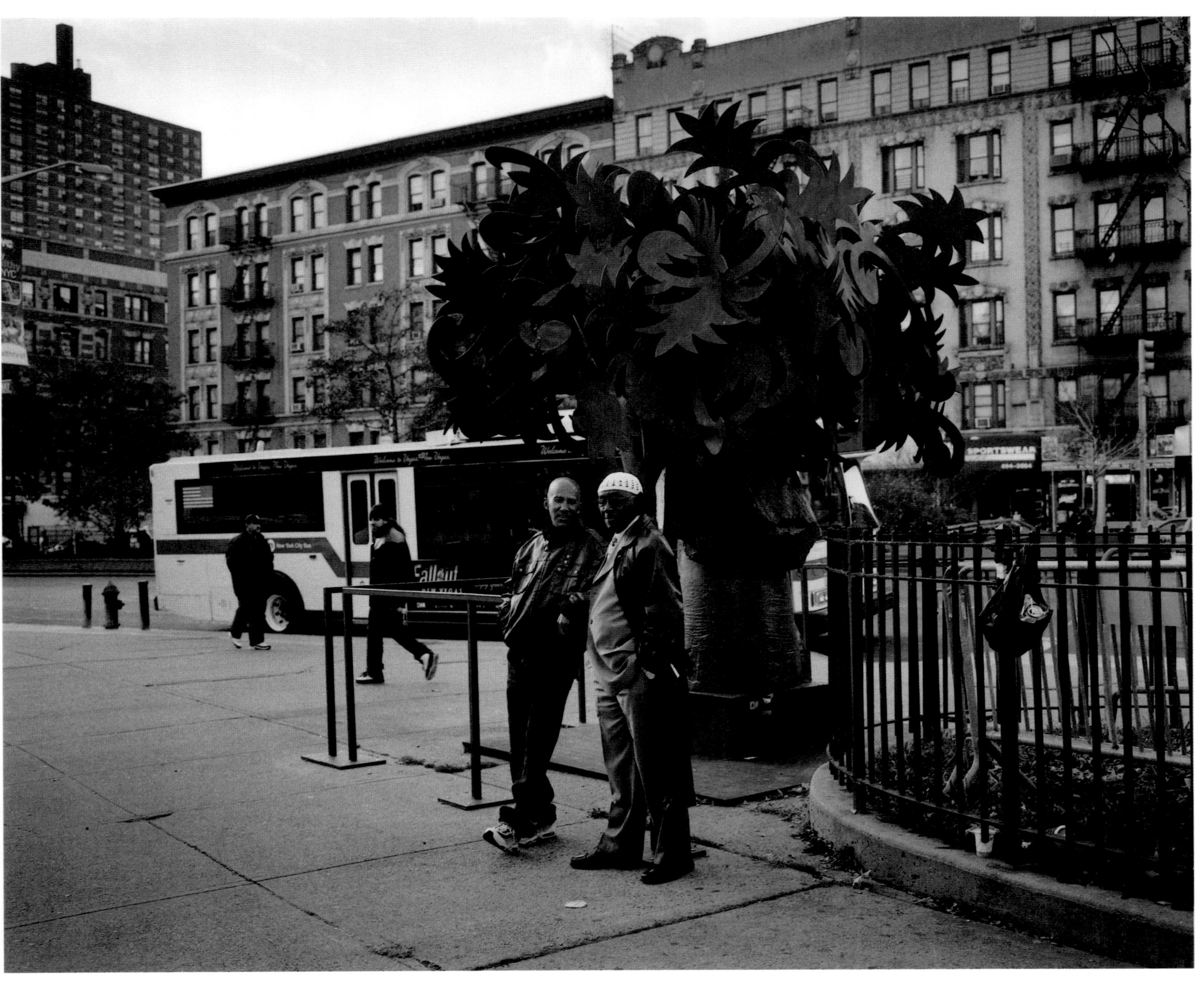

Everything happens differently according to whether it is day or night. Andrea confirms this once again. She searches in the daylight hours and delves deeply in the dark of the early hours (here there are still a lot of people around). That is because the ladies differ according to the light. There is nothing so unreal as the frozen reality of the sculptures, nothing is as senseless as attempting to clarify their mission in the avenue. They appear with an authority of permanence, but also of the immediate. Even with the inexactitude of what is known, that in a few months it will be only a memory, a fleeting story. That is why these works are, simultaneously, what is there and what is due to disappear. They did not come to remain.

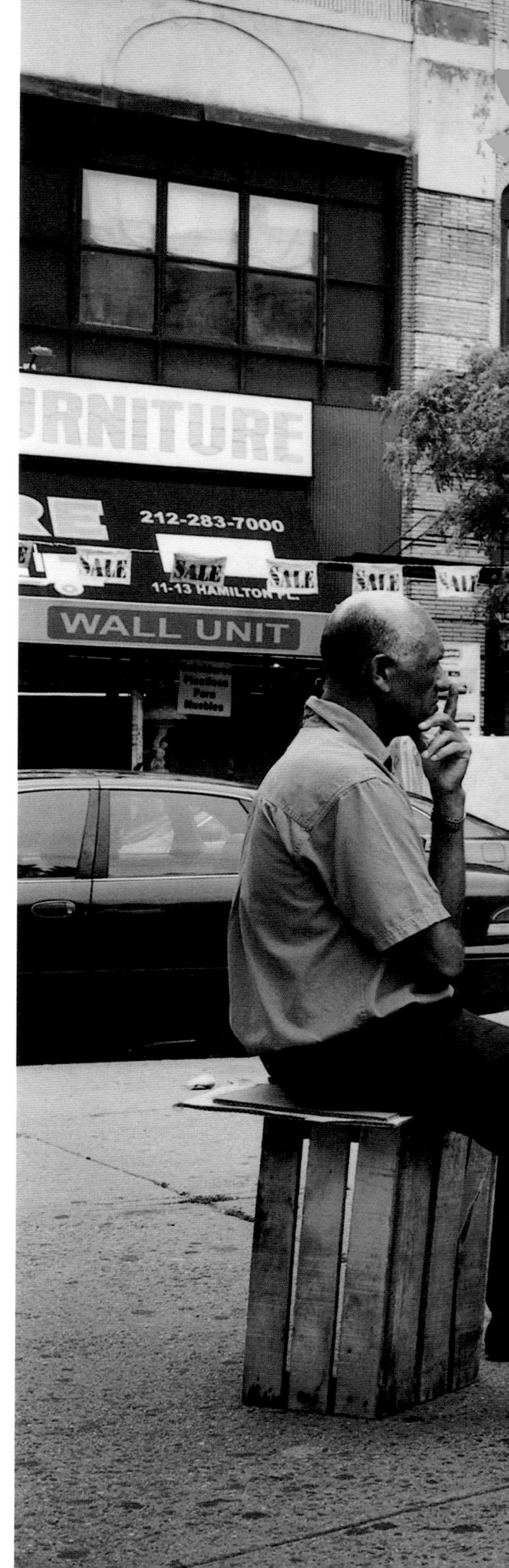

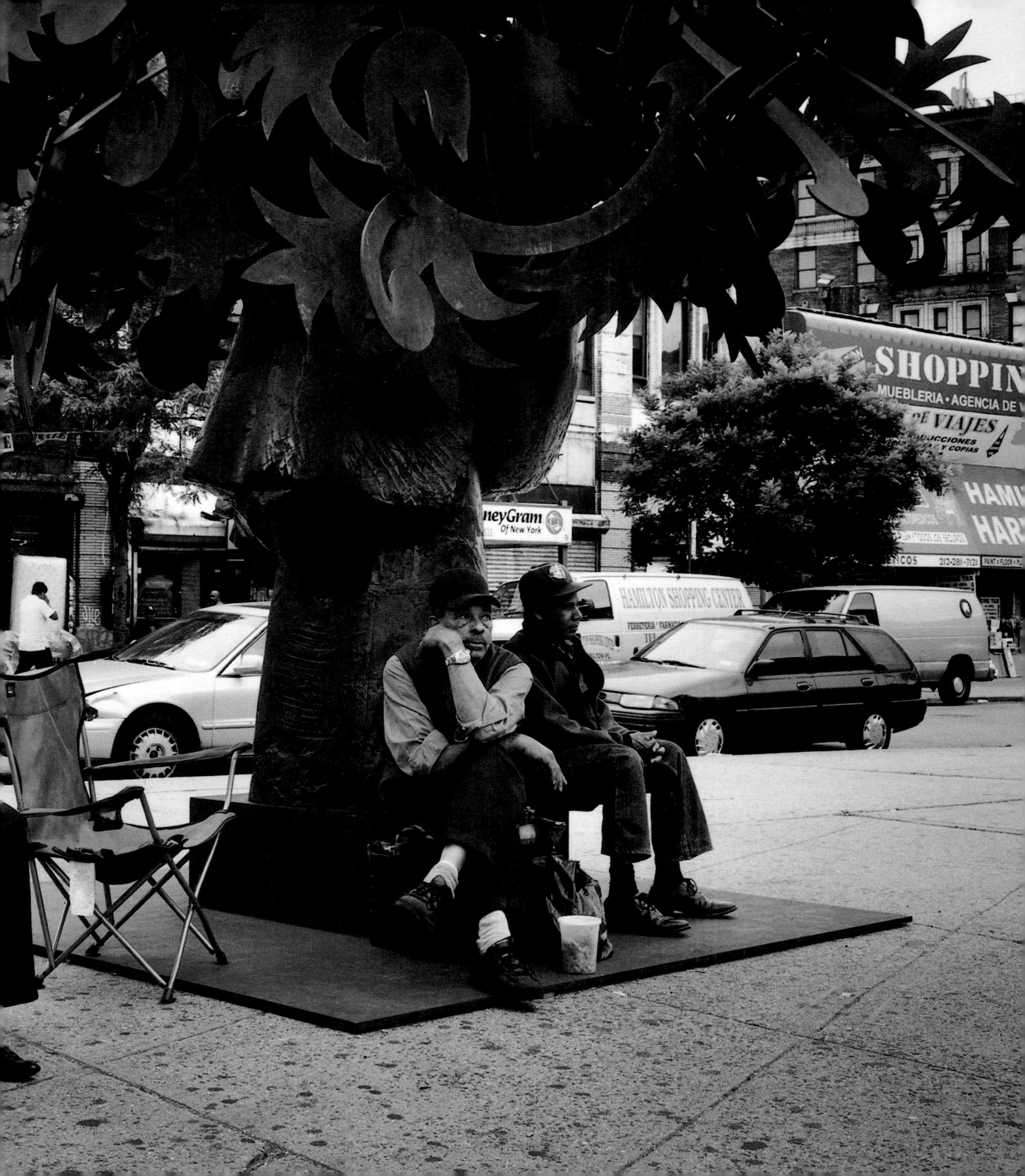

SHOPPIN
MUEBLERIA · AGENCIA DE V
DE VIAJES
ADJUCCIONES
Y COPIAS
HAMI
HAR
neyGram
Of New York
212-281-7121
HAMILTON SHOPPING CENTER

BROADWAY
103RD S_T

Andrea explains the itinerary with that combination of the mechanical and the passionate of someone for whom this route has given meaning to her days. We have already left Broadway and are In Upper West Side, 103rd Street, with *Regina* ahead of us, next to Columbia University – there where the bare-footed girl embraced the sculpture while leaning on its compact bronze shoulder. Do you remember? She seemed to be supported by a "fury the color of love, love the color of oblivion"[2].

Because the works by Valdés do not dissimulate their vocation for being eroded by a thousand hands, gazed at by so many eyes, brushed against by the bodies of all these divine beings who lean on them while the afternoon goes by. They want to be in themselves a public square, a place of exchange, a moving finishing line, which does not demand to arrive anywhere. Andrea catches this quiet, fleeting life with her camera. She records it in its greatest intensity, taking each instant as if it were the moment *in flagrante*. Adding abundance to what lacks gravitation if nobody comes near to look at it, if nobody appropriates

[2] From the poem by Luis Cernuda, "La canción del oeste", in the book, *Un río, un amor* (1929).

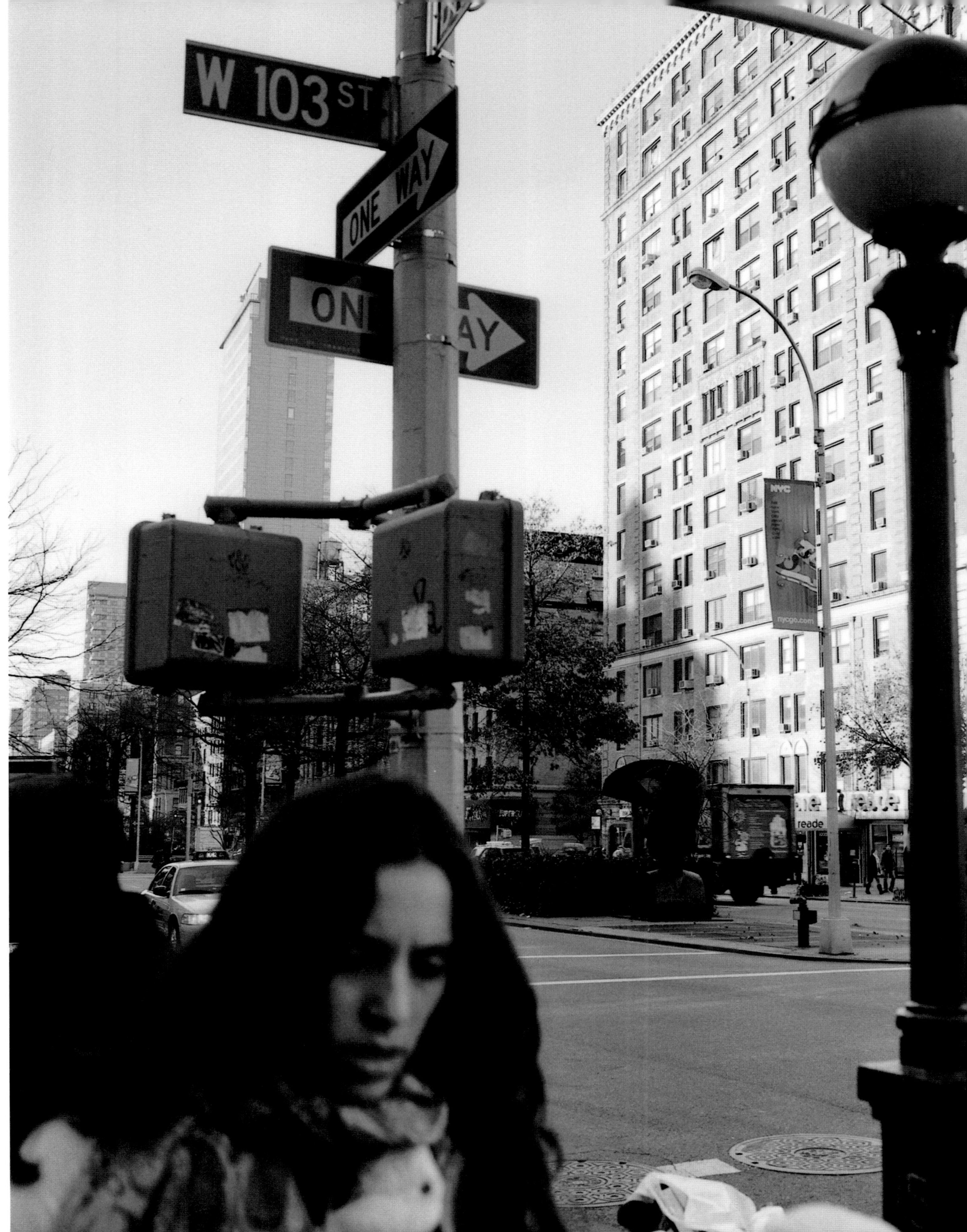

W 103 ST
ONE WAY
ON
AY
NYC
nycgo.com
reade

its volume, its posture, its presence. Almost as in a rescue.

Each sculpture has been placed to form an extravagant longitudinal checkerboard like a backbone of suggestive images. The impression prevails that they were transplanted exactly there in order to facilitate the short haul flights of solitary people.

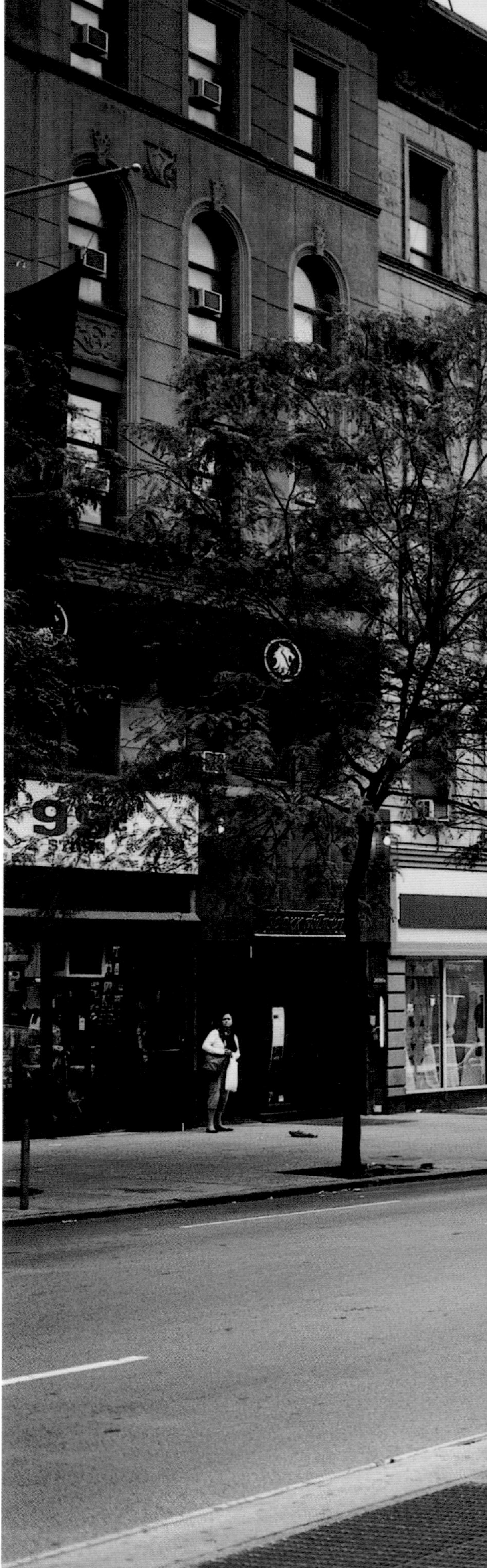

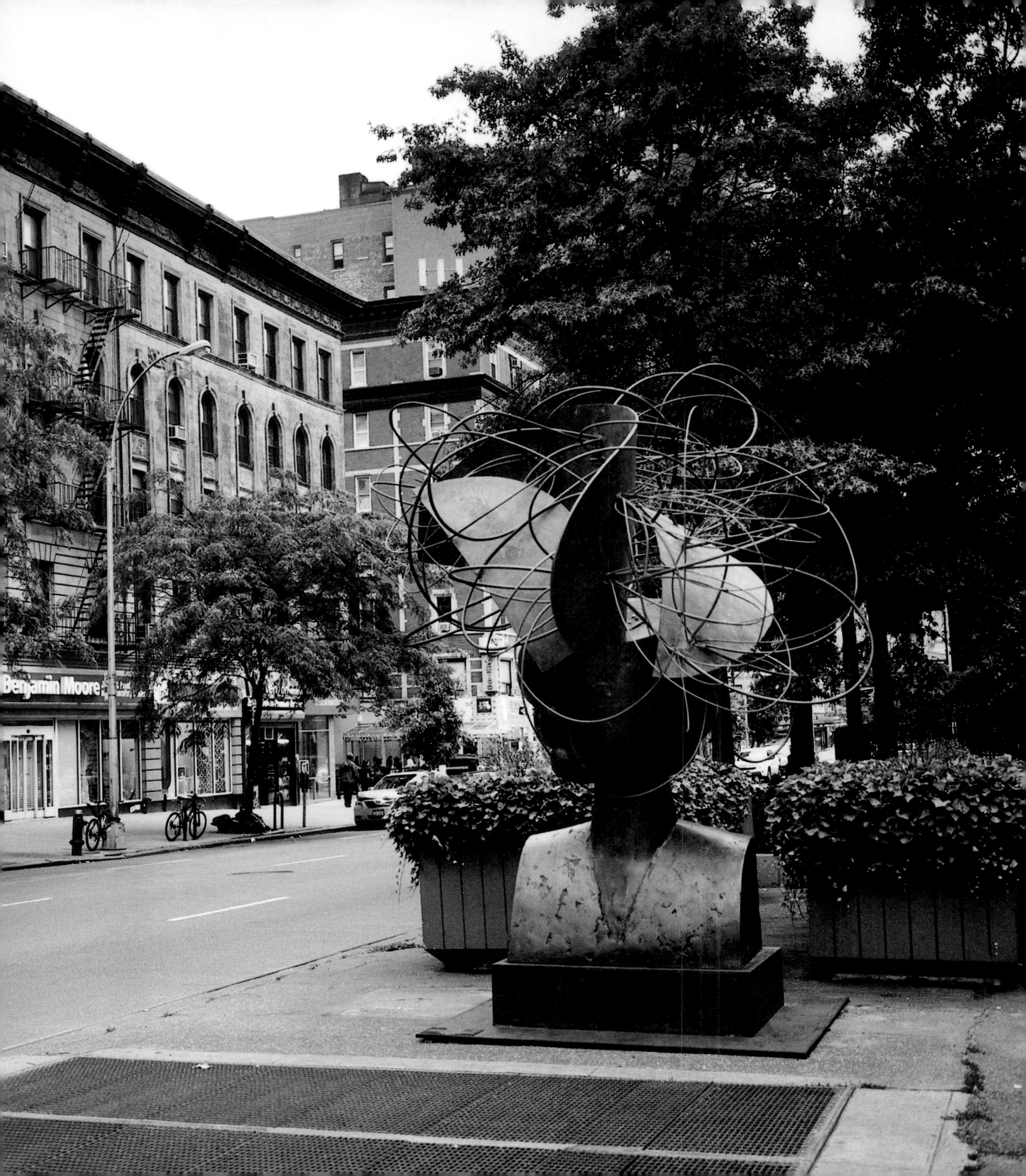
Benjamin Moore

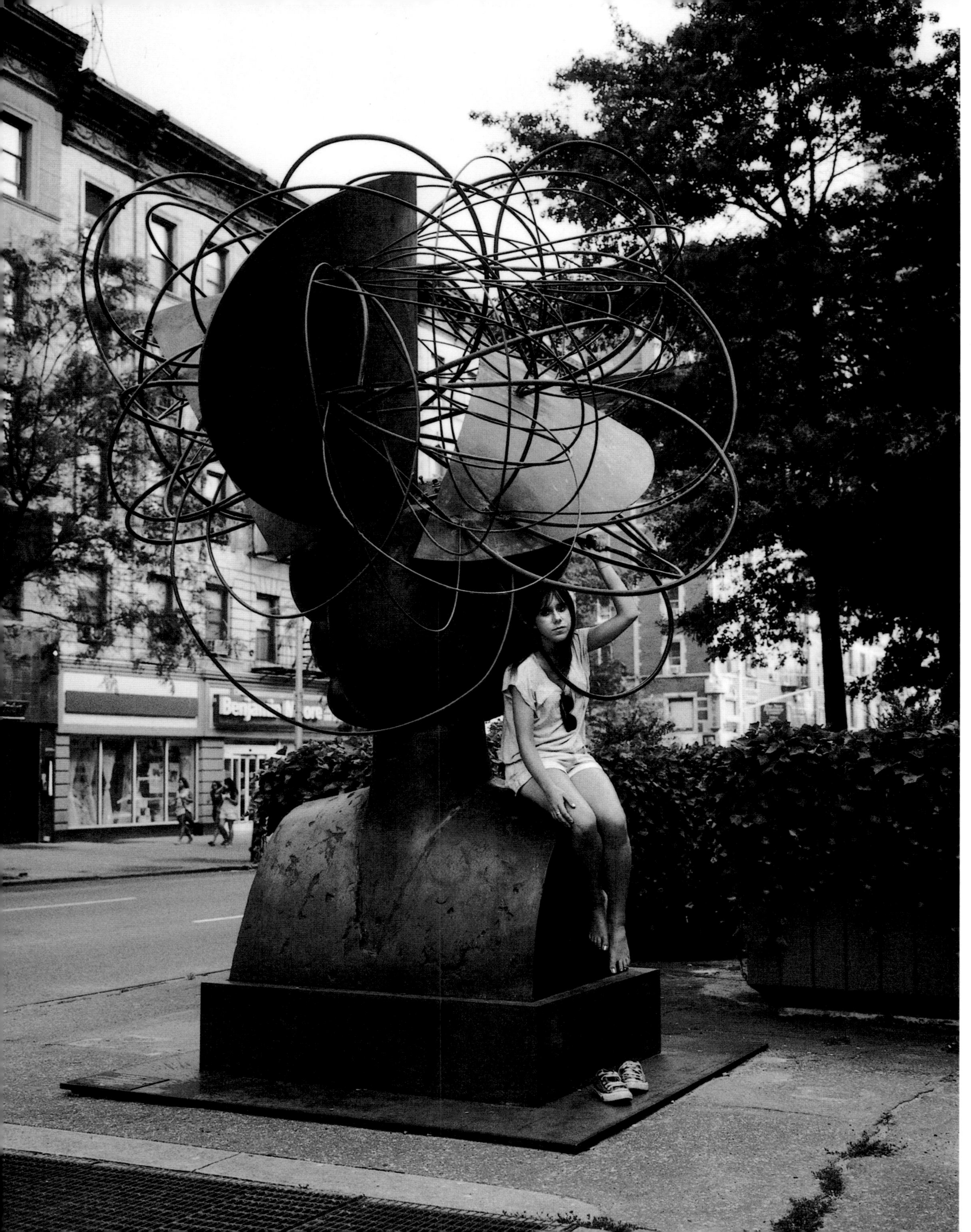

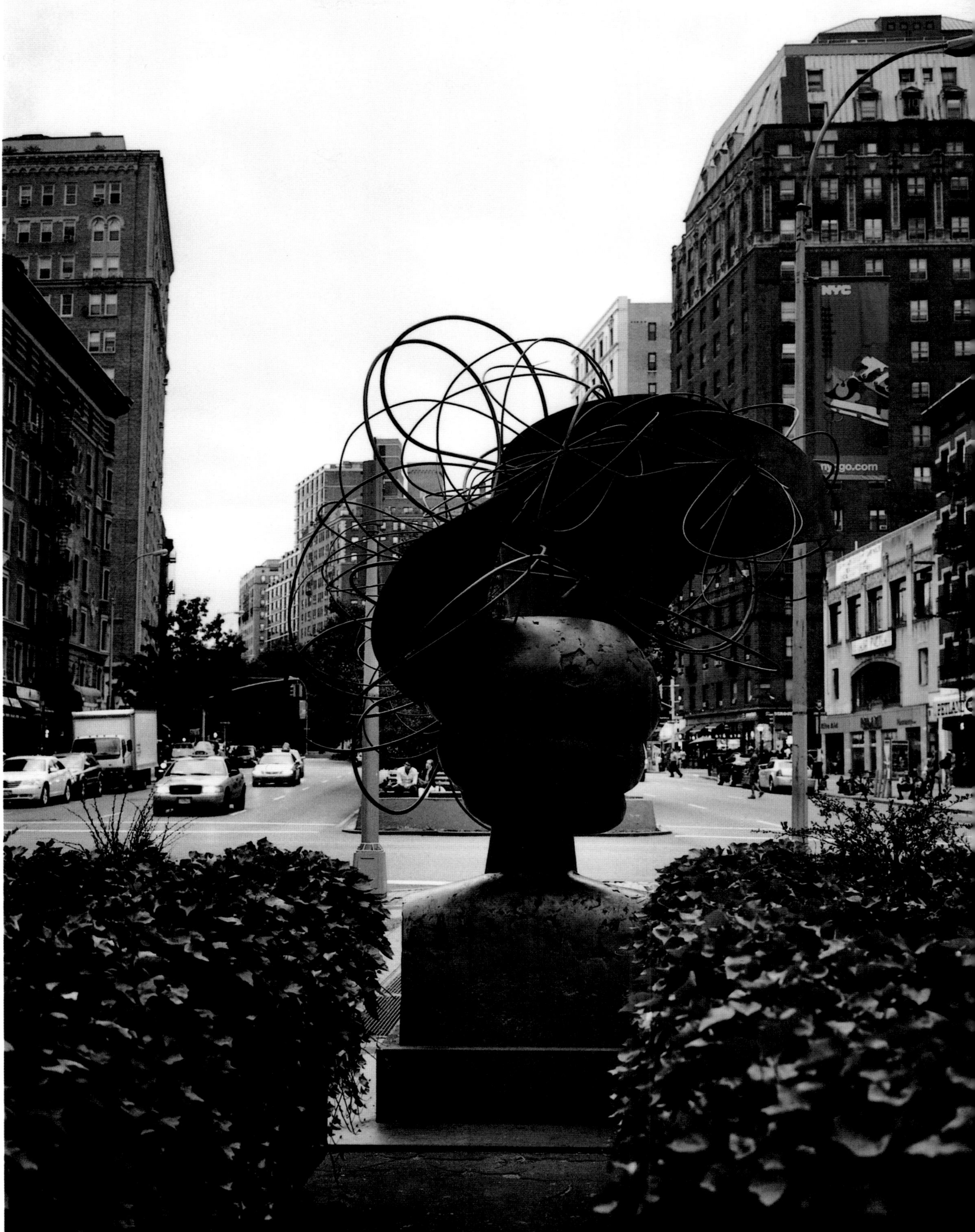

BROADWAY
96TH S_T

Ivonne is set in no. 96. Around her, students and passers-by are eating their lunch. Others merely stop to look, to contemplate a fixed point in the city. In front of her and her storm-swept look -- that arpeggio of waves that crowns her, each person thinks of his own business and goes "from his heart to his affairs".

Andrea tells us what *Ivonne* is saying. It is almost like an imaginary story. "If you look closely, each one breathes and gesticulates. There are even nights when you leave Lower Manhattan behind and come to meet them, when you hear soft singing, like a metallic ringing. They are natural exhalations that change according to the days. On calm early mornings, they give off stirring, wild music that lasts like damp ash: a kind of strong north-west wind that starts to die down when the first lights flash against the window panes. It is strange. And that is also in *Ivonne*." Andrea holds curious conversations with the sculptures and their inhabitants. She has discovered that they have different personalities, connected with their surroundings, their neighbors, their fleeting observers, even with their tenants: some shelter people, as we have already said.

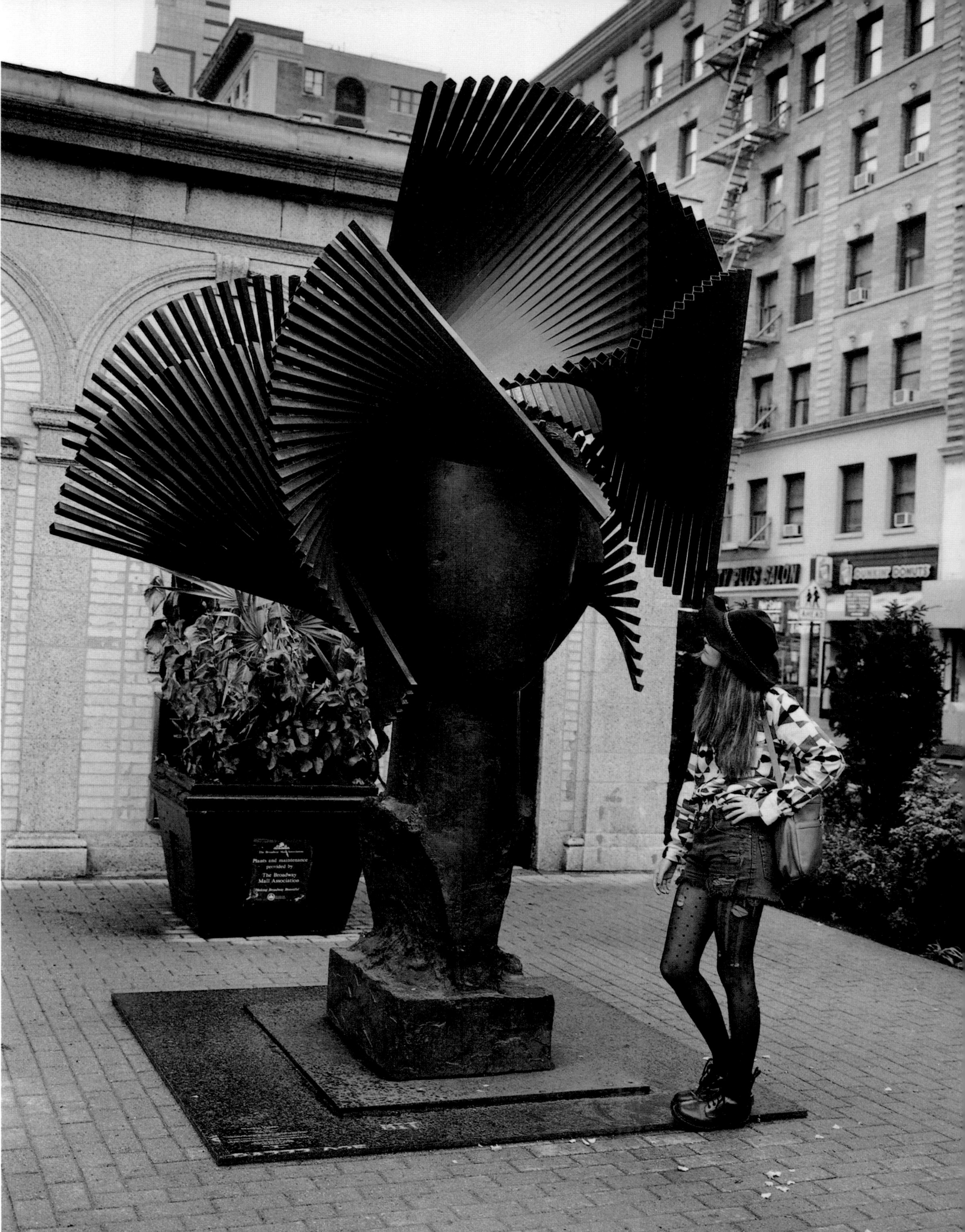

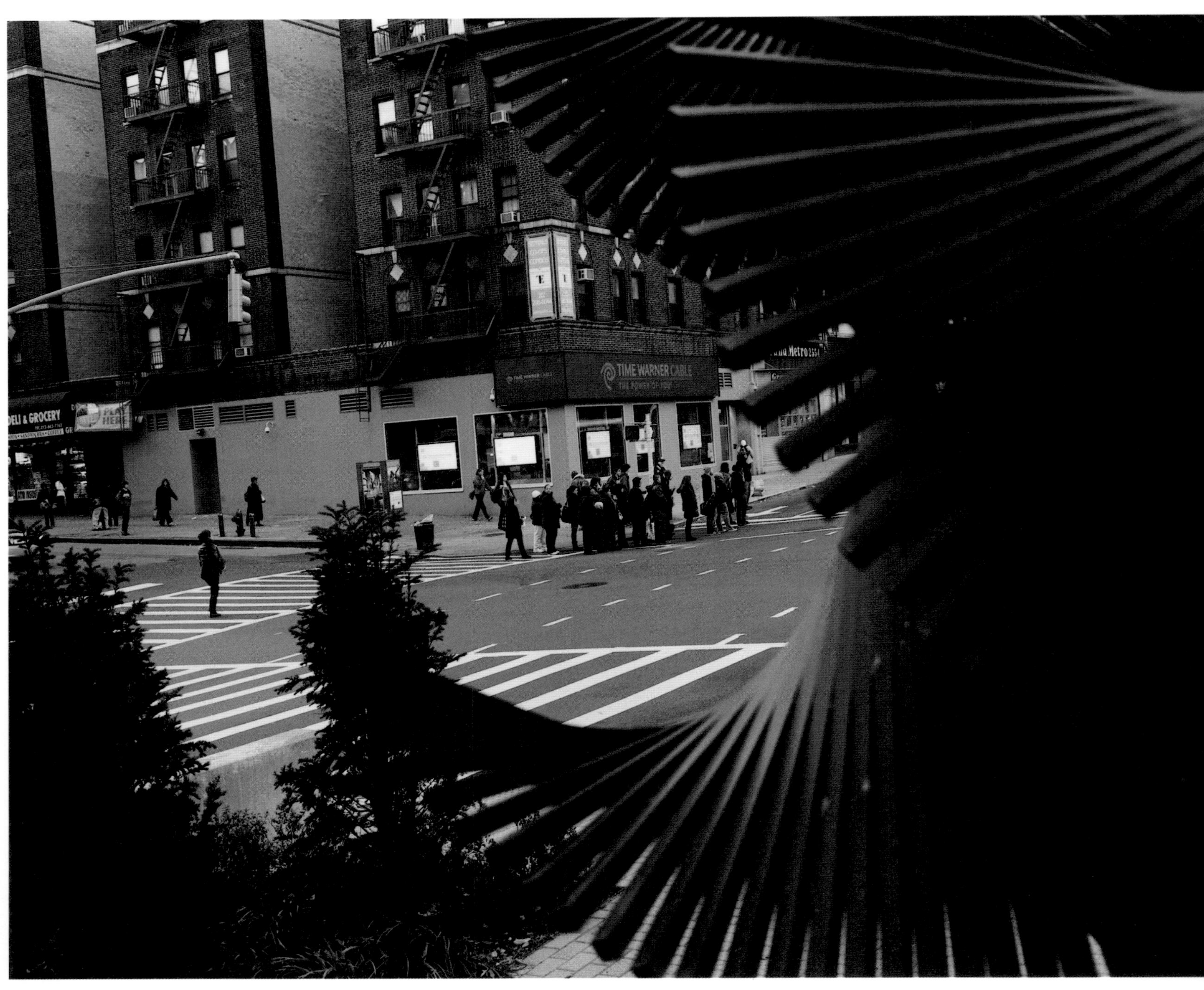

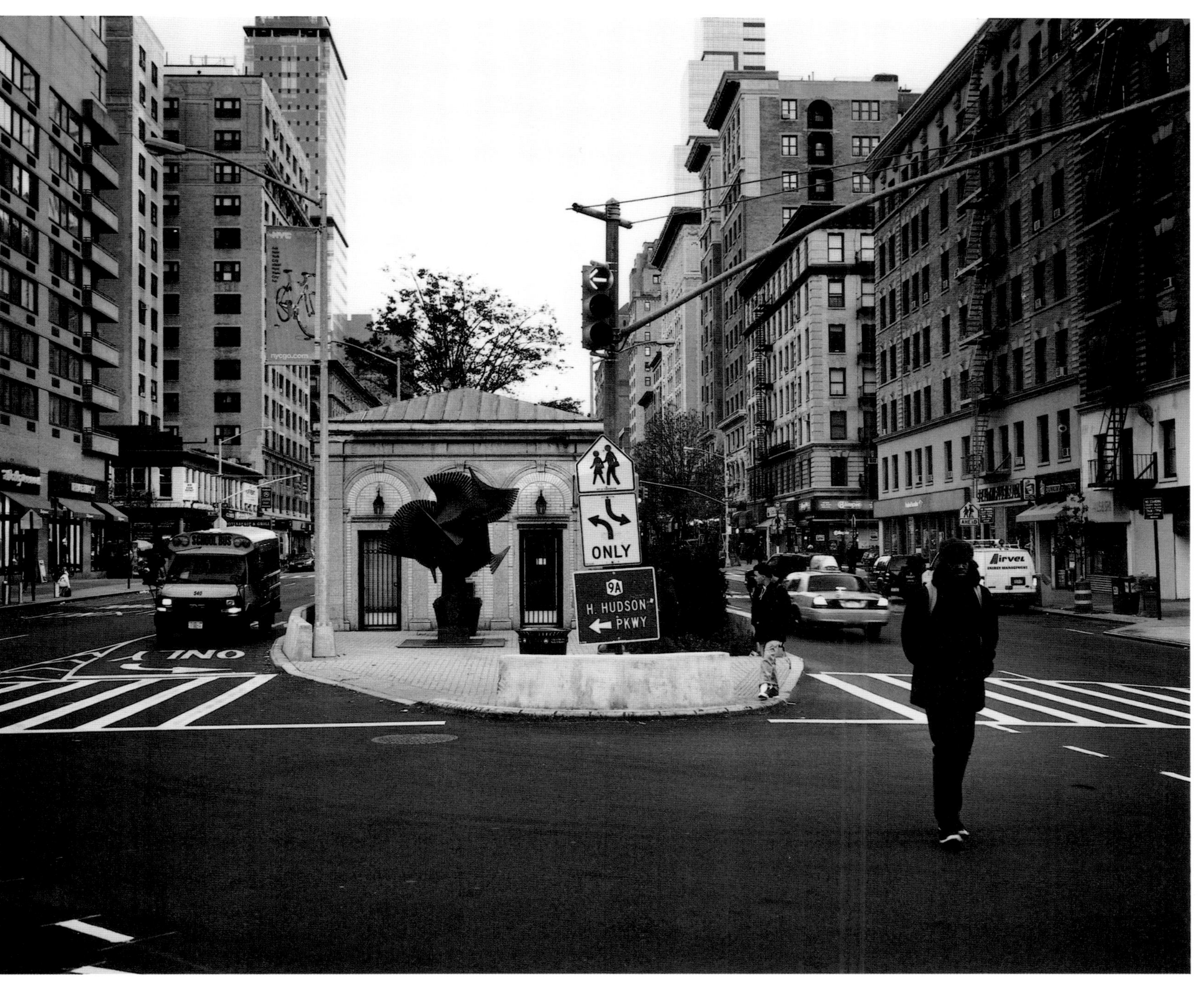

ONLY
9A
H. HUDSON
PKWY

She has seen them dozens of times and
only thus has she been convinced that they
contain an enigma that transcends the
general judgments of art, the expectations
of works embedded in the sidewalk, far
from that state of mind that needs theories
obsessively in order to explain to themselves
something that has no form nor fits into
any form. Now we are speaking about how
photography constructs a story, a narration
as slow as the course of a river. Perhaps it
reinvents each one of the works according
to the instant in which it was shot. And
in each piece, New York is concentrated
– an unharmed cataclysm of appearances
that the city imposes on man. That is why
Andrea portrays each of the works as if it
were an island that injects more truth into
the general truth of the world. What takes
place on the perimeter of each pieces is quite
magnetic at times, at others unfathomable,
but always impossible to transfer from
one to another. The character is in the air,
in what surrounds them, in extraordinary
solitude accompanied by whoever suddenly
crosses the sidewalk.

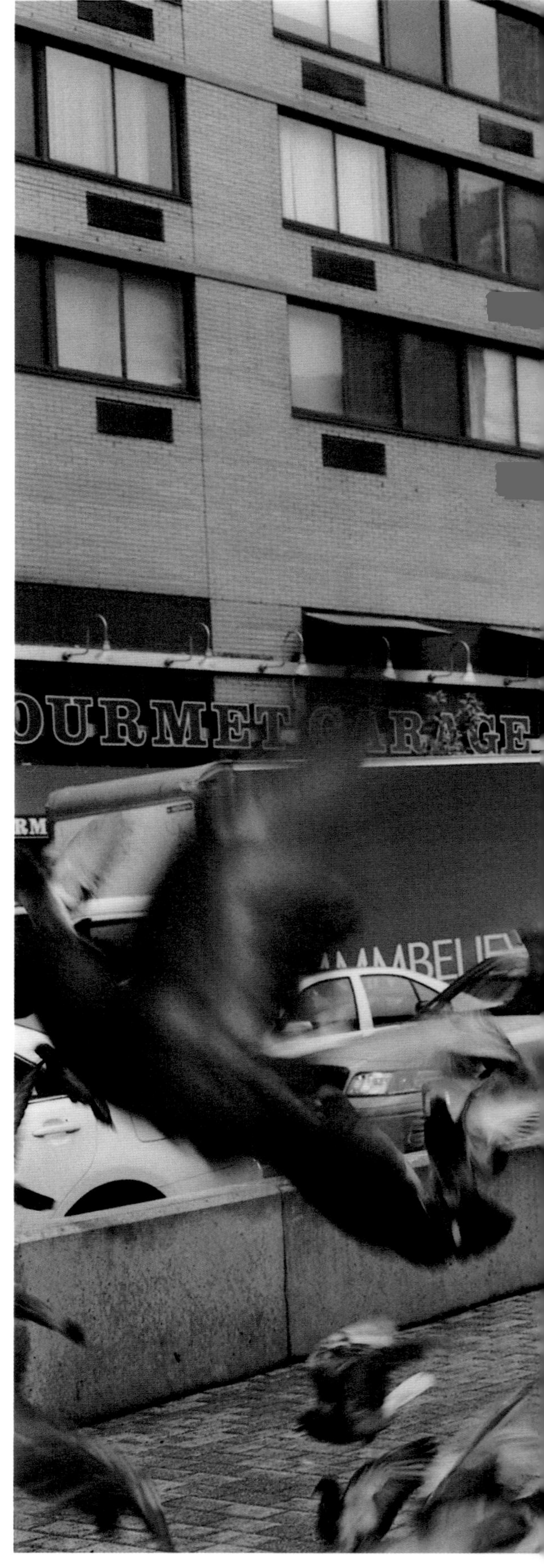

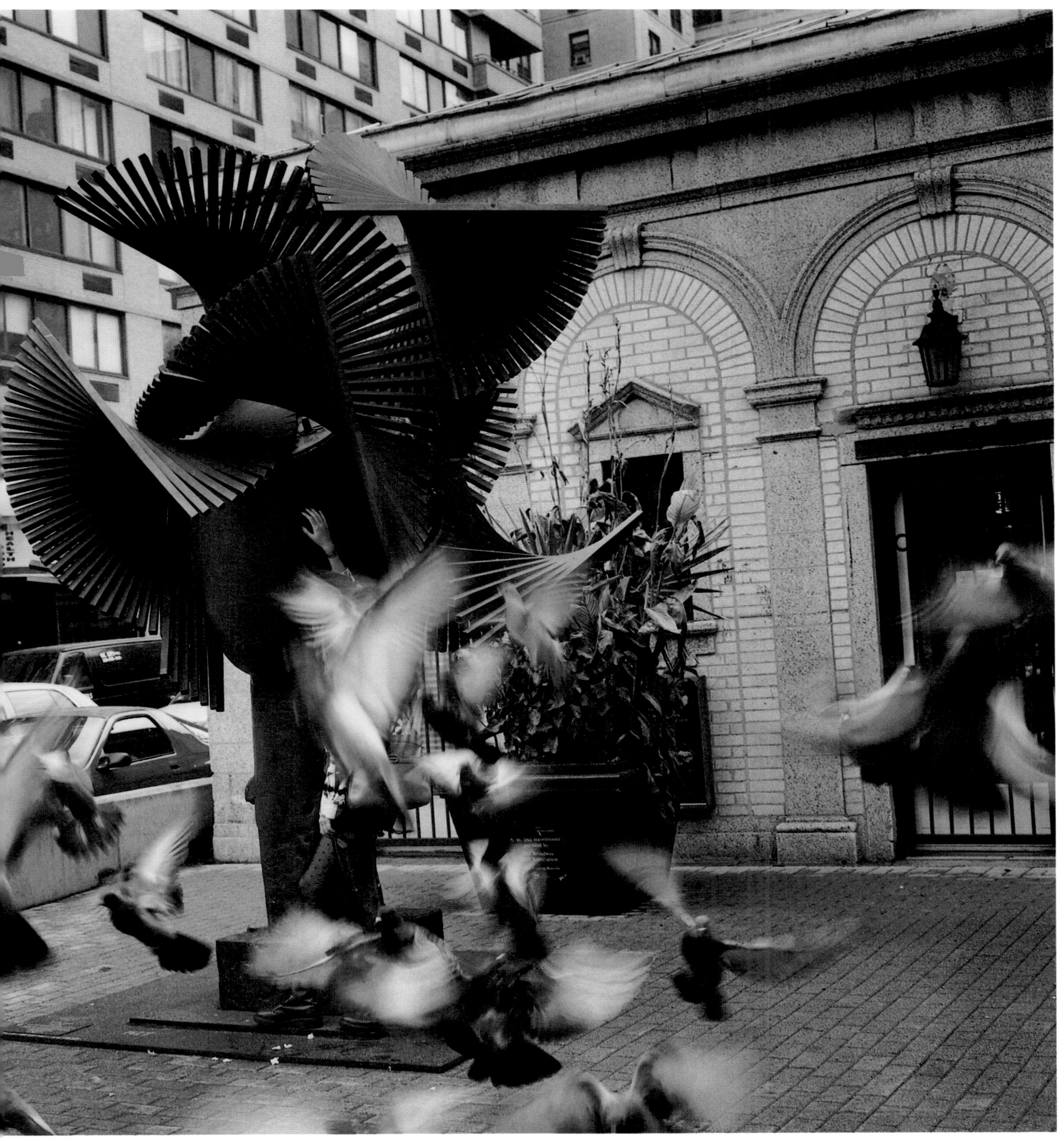

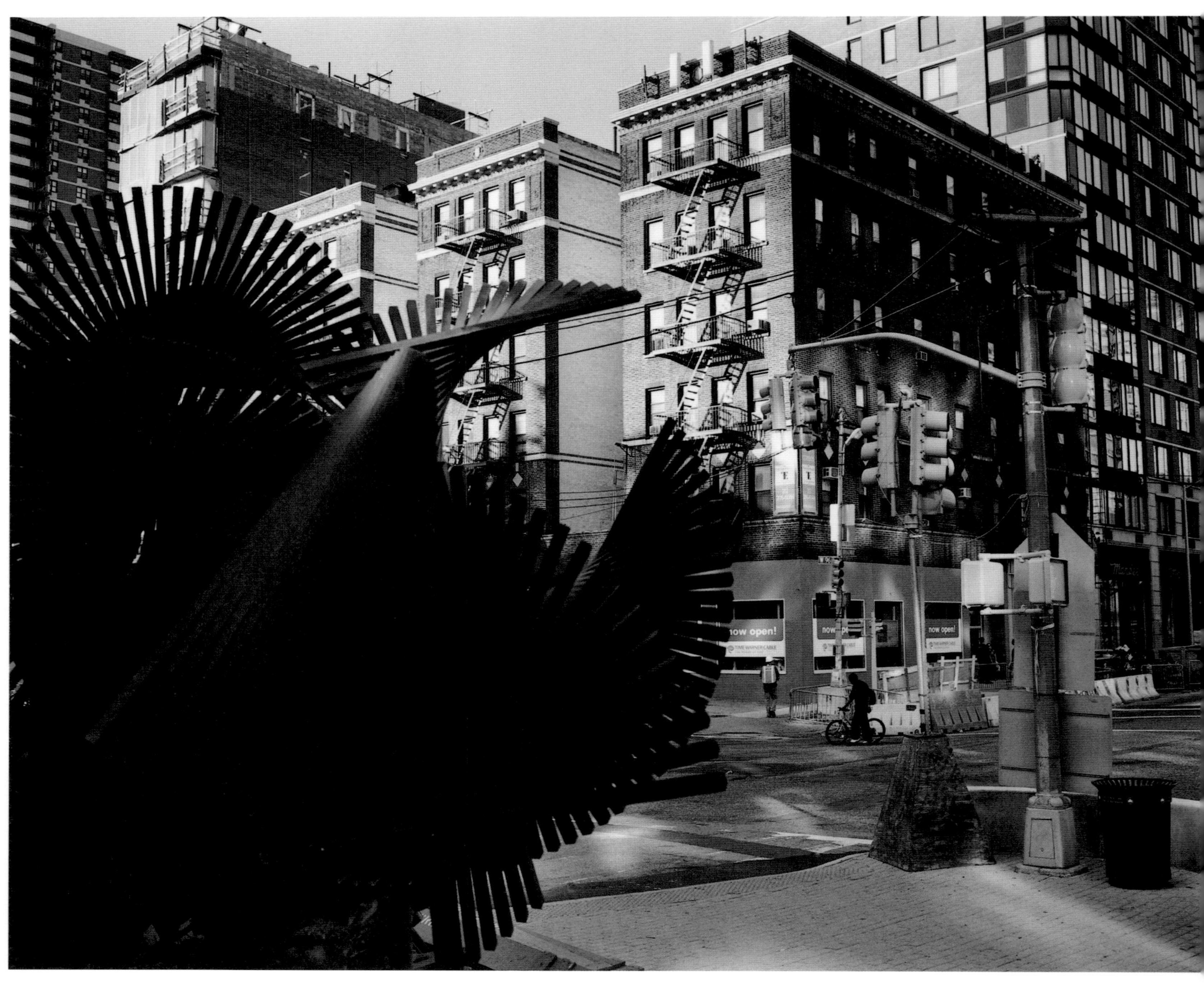

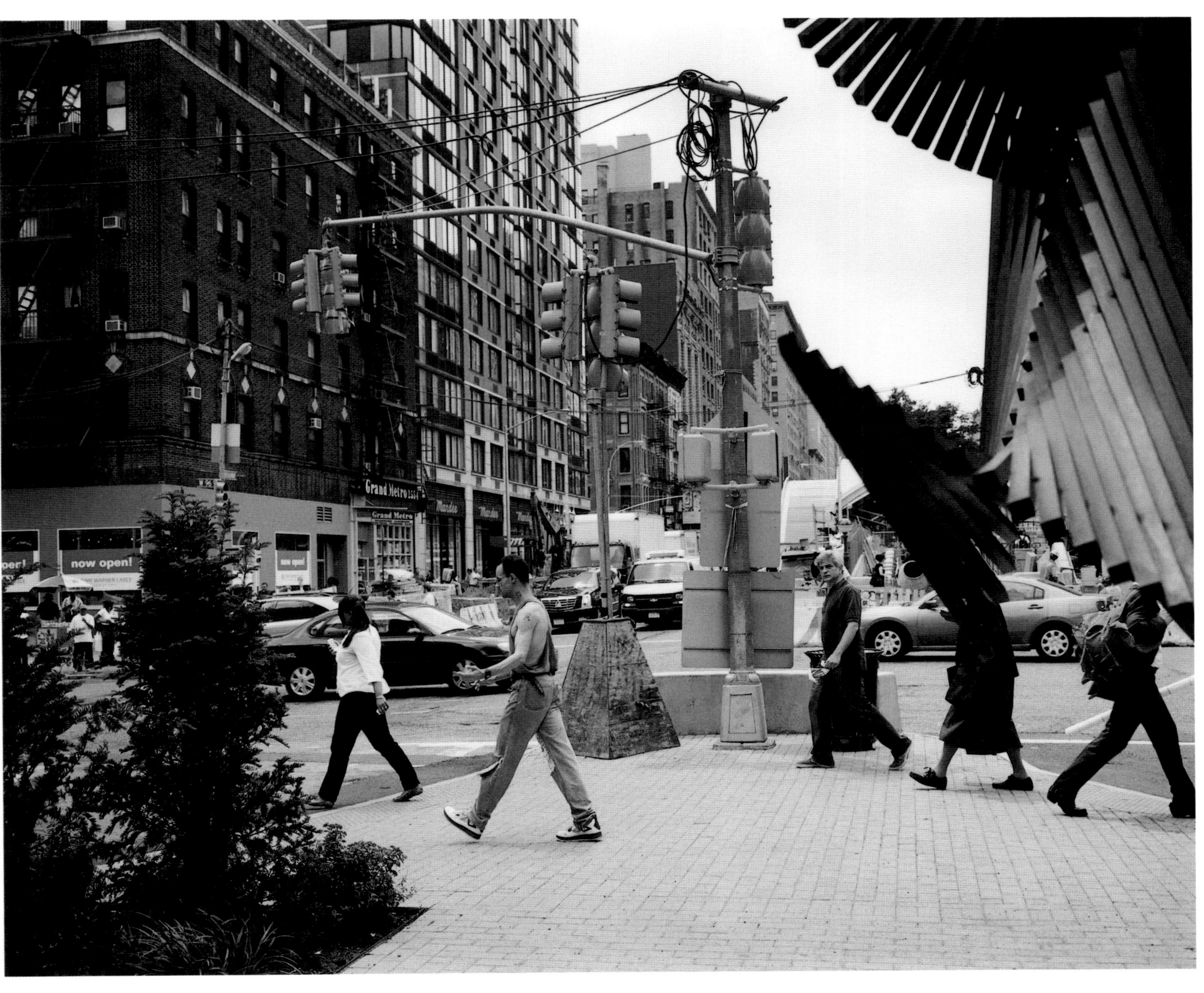

BROADWAY
79TH St

Look at what happens to *Lydia* when, on this expedition you reach 79th Street – so close to where Miles Davis lived. *Lydia* is ready to be observed in the little boulevard in which she was left. *Lydia* is like a little bell. *Lydia* in front of the benches where pedestrians linger while she turns her back on them. It is a head on which Matisse and Modigliani collided. It has the accidental velatura of compacted bronze that has been dissolved haphazardly The first Baptist church in New York was built at the right

    – And this one, Andrea?

    – It is delicate. It is rotund. The sun impacts it and makes it suggestive. It is even more attractive if we look at it from behind. So serene, so bereaved, like a rocky cliff where one stops to listen to voices and echoes. And if you wait quietly, you come close to that feeling of lack of reality that the autumn north-west winds bring to the

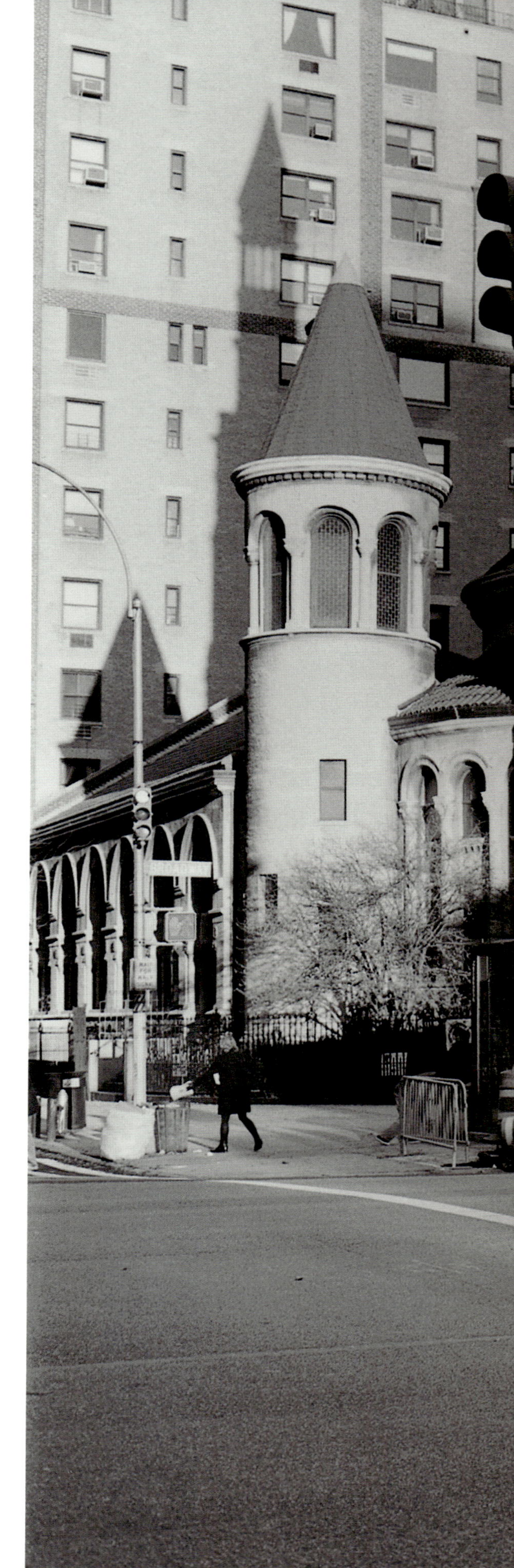

"

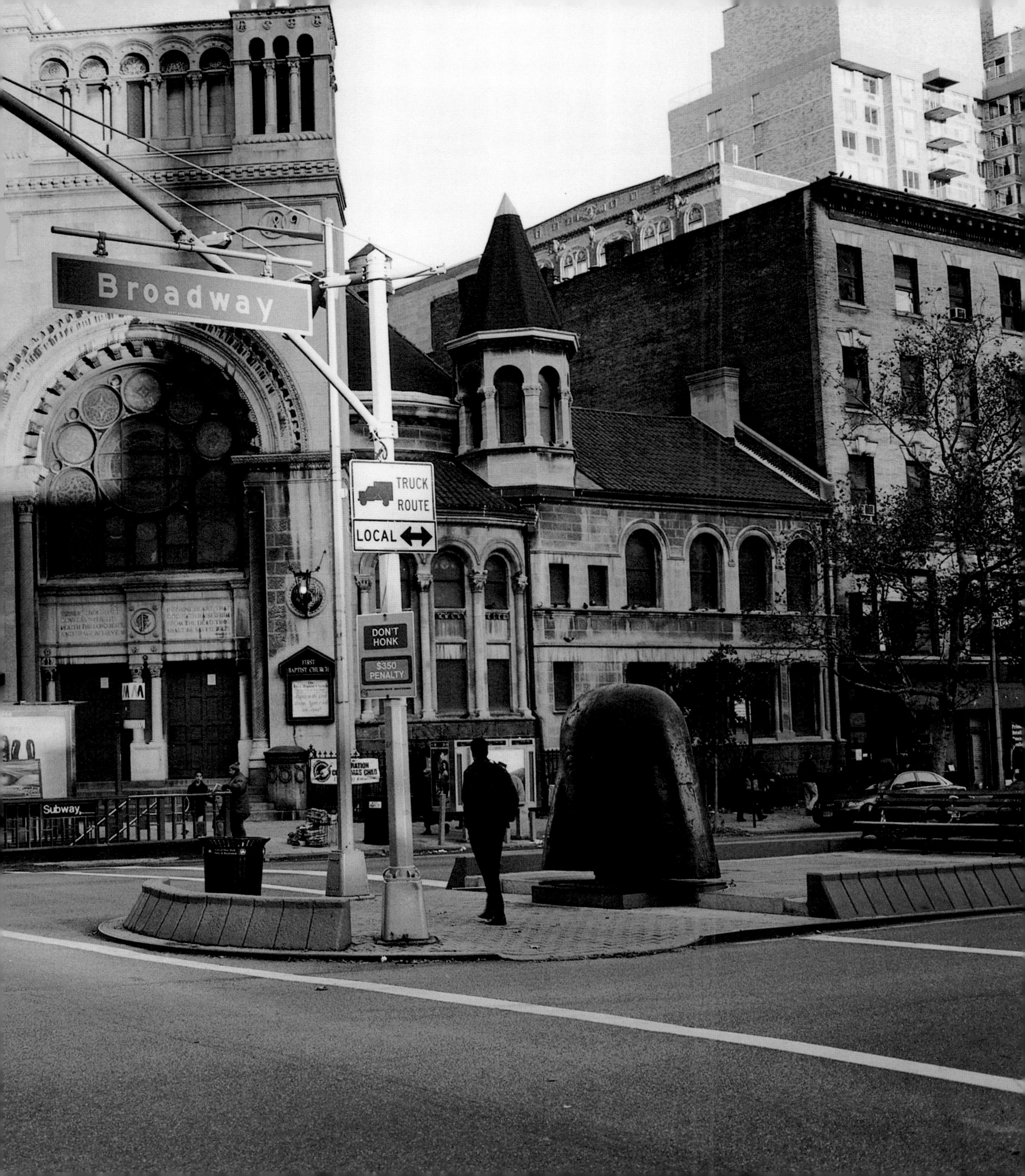

Broadway
TRUCK ROUTE
LOCAL
DON'T HONK
$350 PENALTY
FIRST BAPTIST CHURCH
Subway

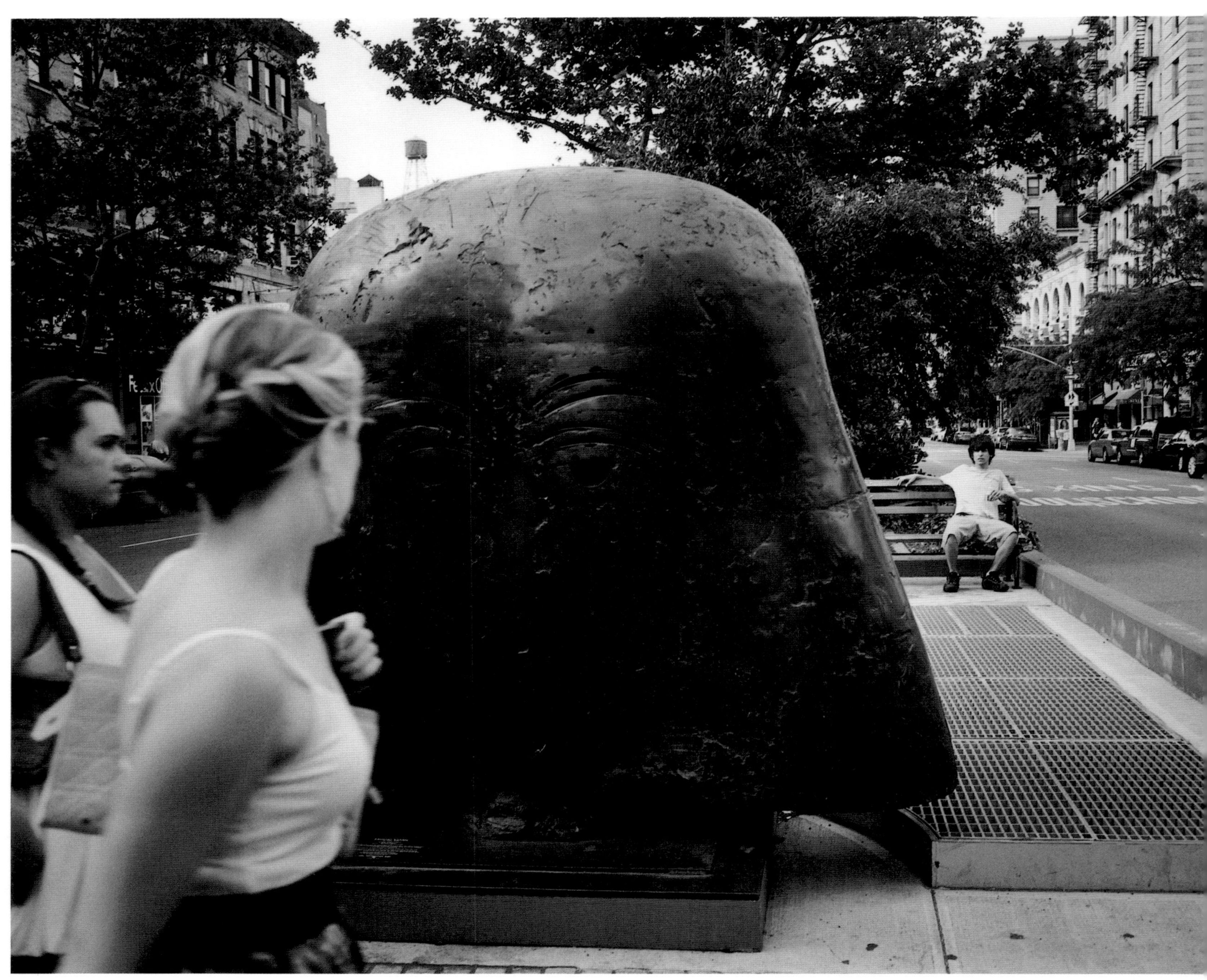

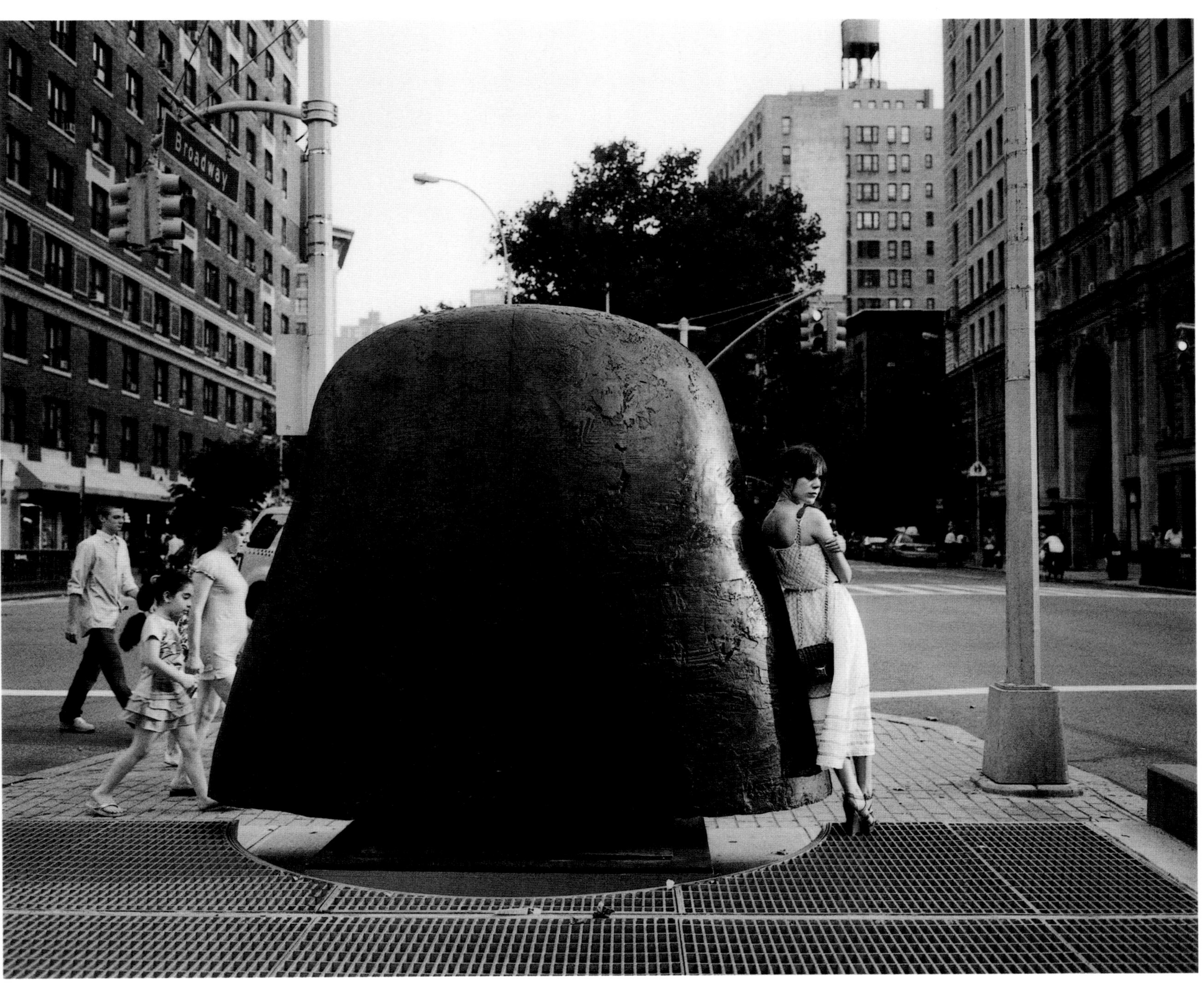

Broadway

city, the cold of winter in New York. Everything that happens around the sculptures is supposedly true, sharply attacking our sensitivity. There is the scene of the woman who lets herself fall, bent over, on *Lydia's* head and looks at the lens enquiringly, with the "sparkling" lust of the naked man, as coined by André Breton in a poem. This dispersed sculptural group by Manolo Valdés could be the culmination of his fantasizing in the traces of the history of art, by means of the spectral iconography of the masters. And we add a mop of red hair on leaving a body on its surface, a scratch, the eccentric wink of embracing each one of these "lighthouses" that live peacefully like discreet celebrities, events buried in the normality of the metropolis, almost fossils in the longitudinal section of the map.

New York opens up as you continue to go down. The generalized laziness and the endless showing-off become urgent and your gait quickens.

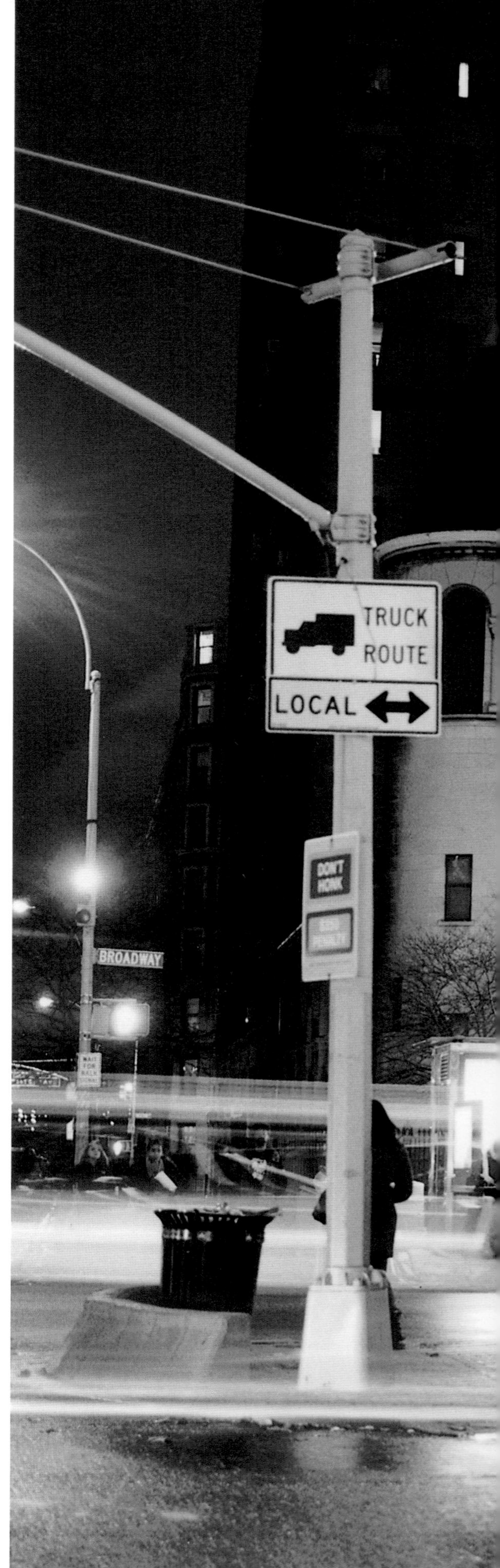

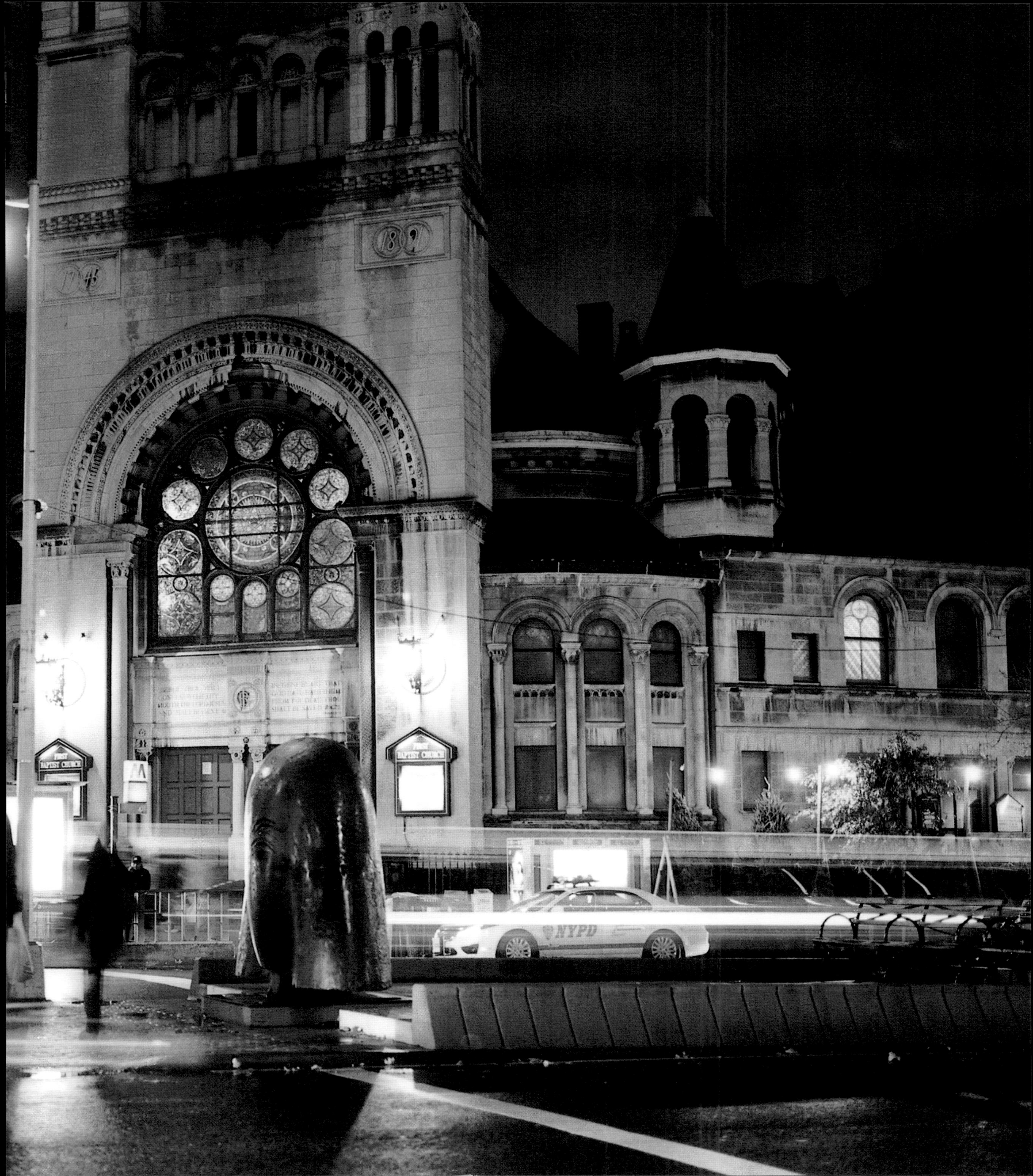
189
FIRST
BAPTIST CHURCH
FIRST
BAPTIST CHURCH
NYPD

BROADWAY
72ND St

Odalisca is in this area, where everything that is going to happen loses the minted personality of the lower-class neighborhoods in order to become a rush, places of transit to other forts and frontiers. Nobody comes to stay in the square where the subway of 72nd Street is located. Perhaps some beggar looking for shelter. And there is the *Odalisca* with the reclining head. This nodule of beauty in no-man's-land.

"You know", says Andrea, "she is the most abstract of all of them, and perhaps the most suggestive, constantly accompanied: the kiosco behind her never closes. Something is always happening in this square. At every point from which you observe her, she is different, and also the same. She has an unprecedented resonance. She is the most talkative of all the "creatures" that Valdés has

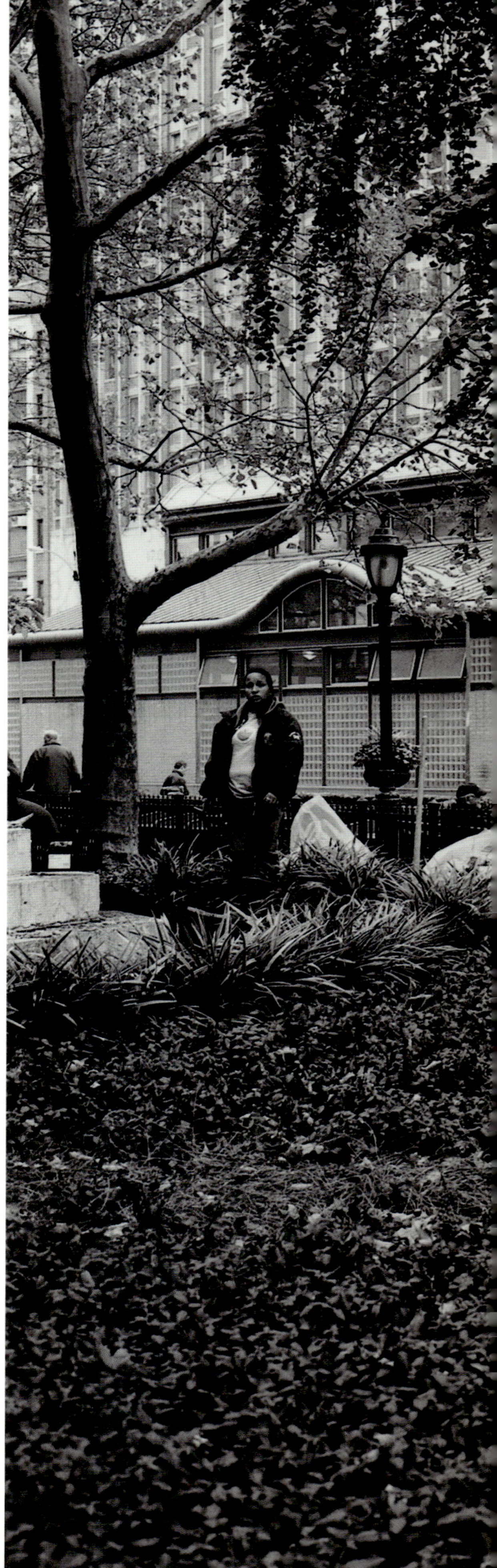

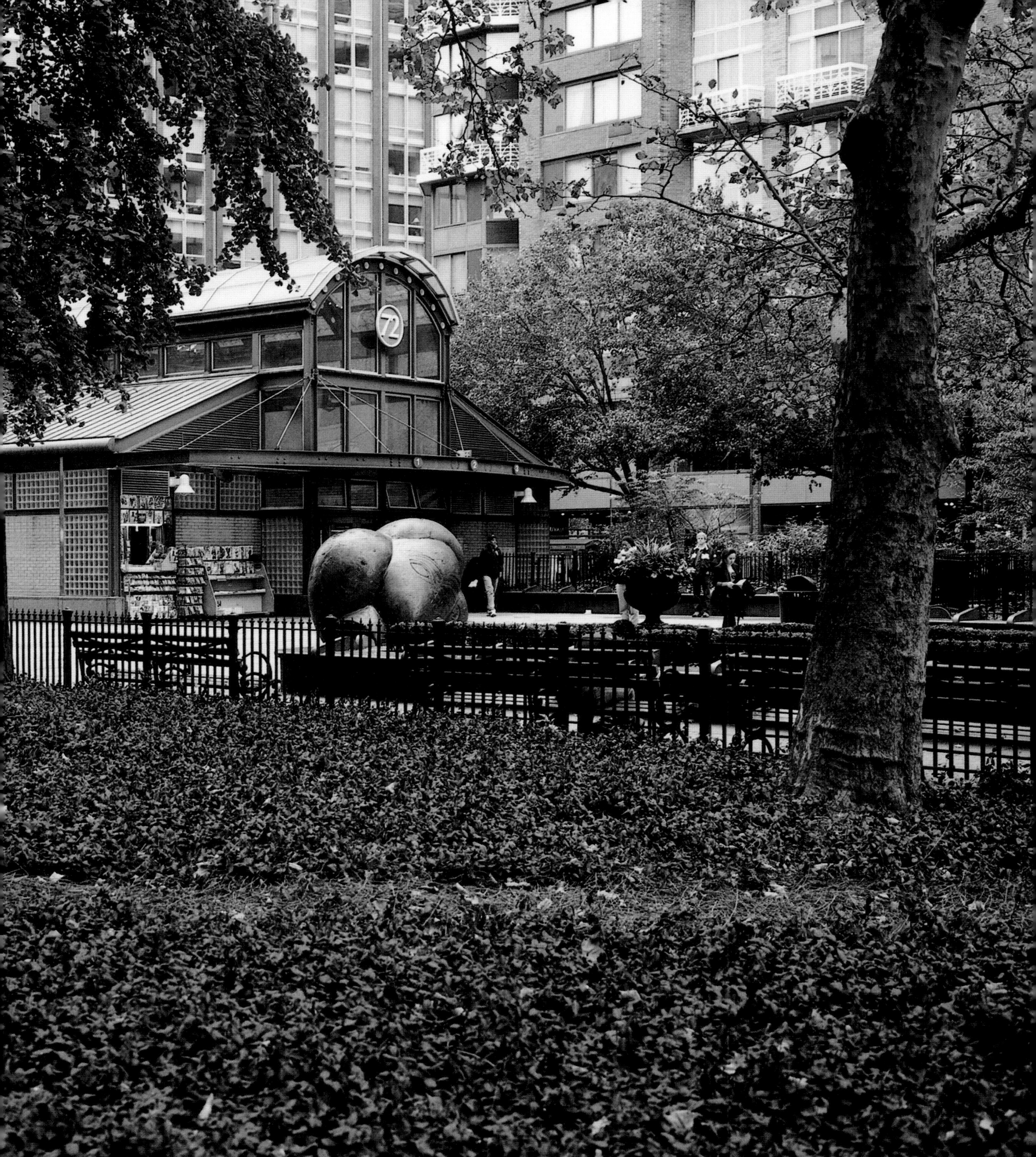
72

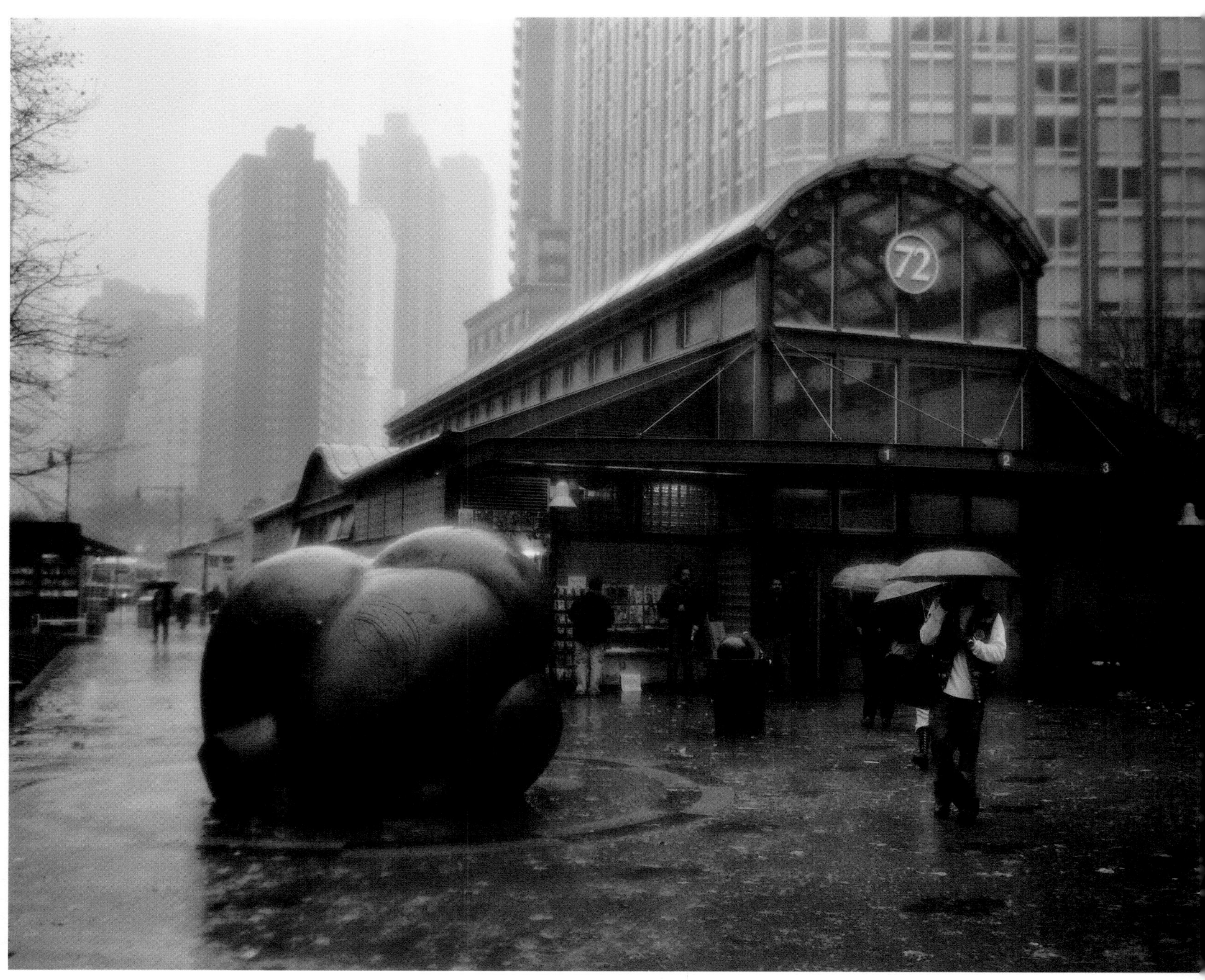
72
1
2
3

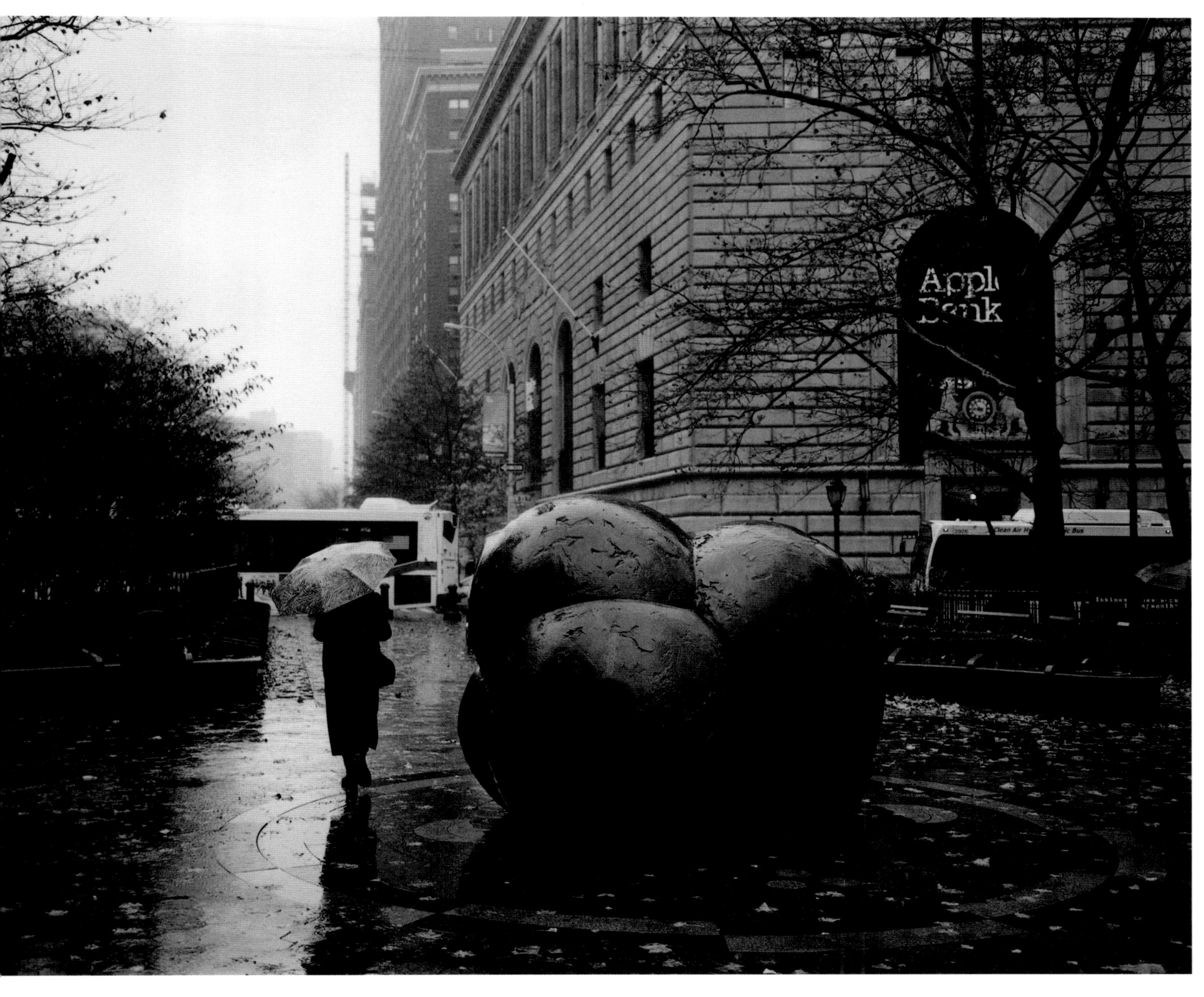
Apple
Bank

scattered around, like tesseras on an imaginary road. The skyscrapers begin to take definitive shape. Not afraid of this dance of heights, the *Odalisca* observes. Andrea is aware that it is not possible to capture an emotion that is really only our astonishment. Therefore she approaches and then draws back. She waits patiently like a *sioux* for the shades of color in the sky to soak the sculpture, replacing the mid-day rigidity by the magnetizing reverberations of the early evening, of the imminent night. It rains and changes. It snows and changes. Later comes the clean light of dawn and we see the concentrated brow of this bronze placed in a roving space of office buildings where perversity is rampant. She is hidden from those who do not want to see her. She is already on the final stretch before the league stone.

And not very far off the two *Marianas* appear, flanking the entrance to the subway in 72nd Street, a few steps away from the Dakota building and the start of Strawberry Fields (already in Central Park). At this stage of the "tour" nothing is what it seems. Or everything starts to be that New York that we have previously seen, that they have insistently told us about. That which, if you ever visited it, remained within while you were living for ever outside. Andrea seeks a frame from behind the camera. The precise second that Cartier-Bresson talked about, that prodigious spark, the fleeting gesture

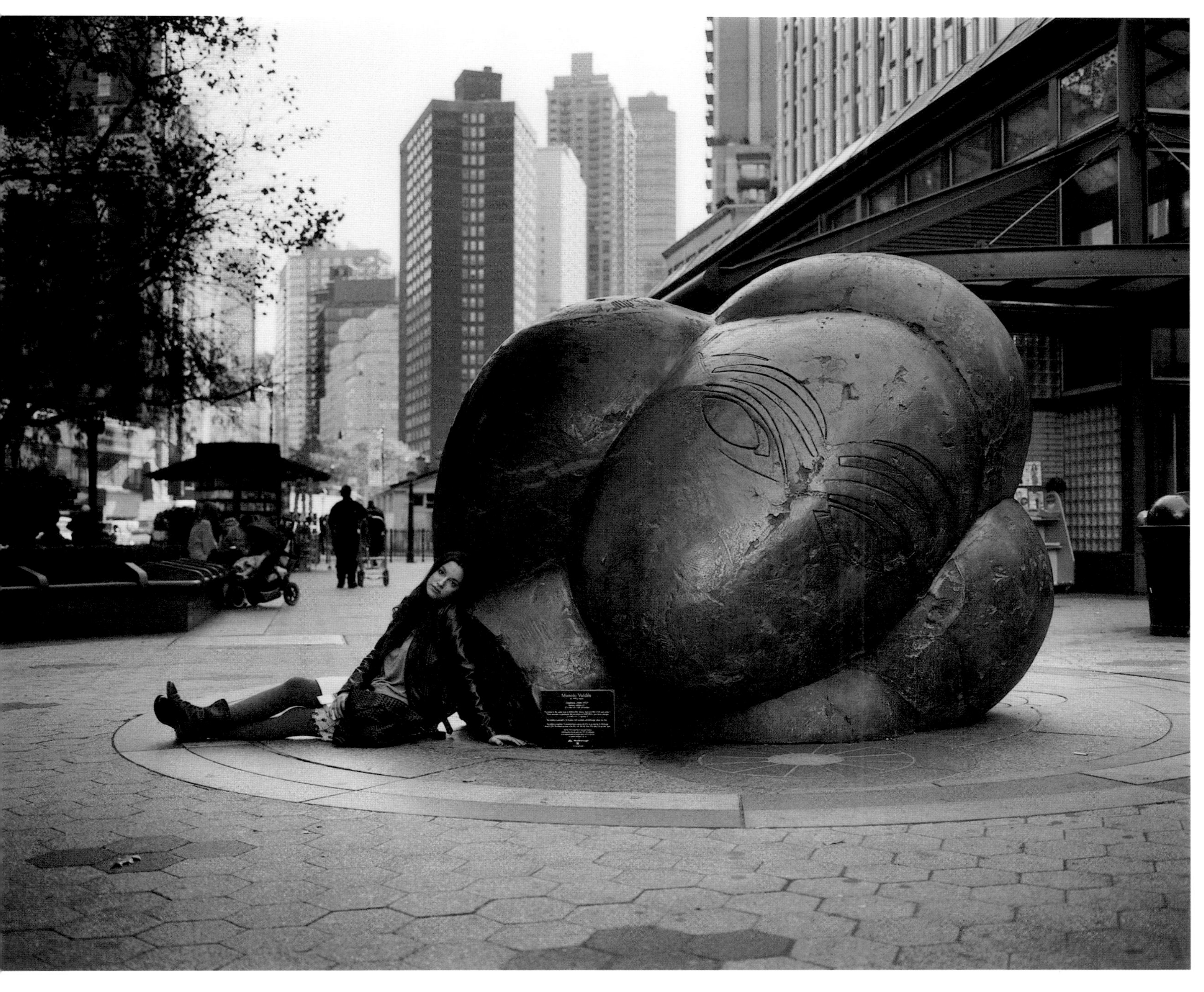
Manolo Valdés

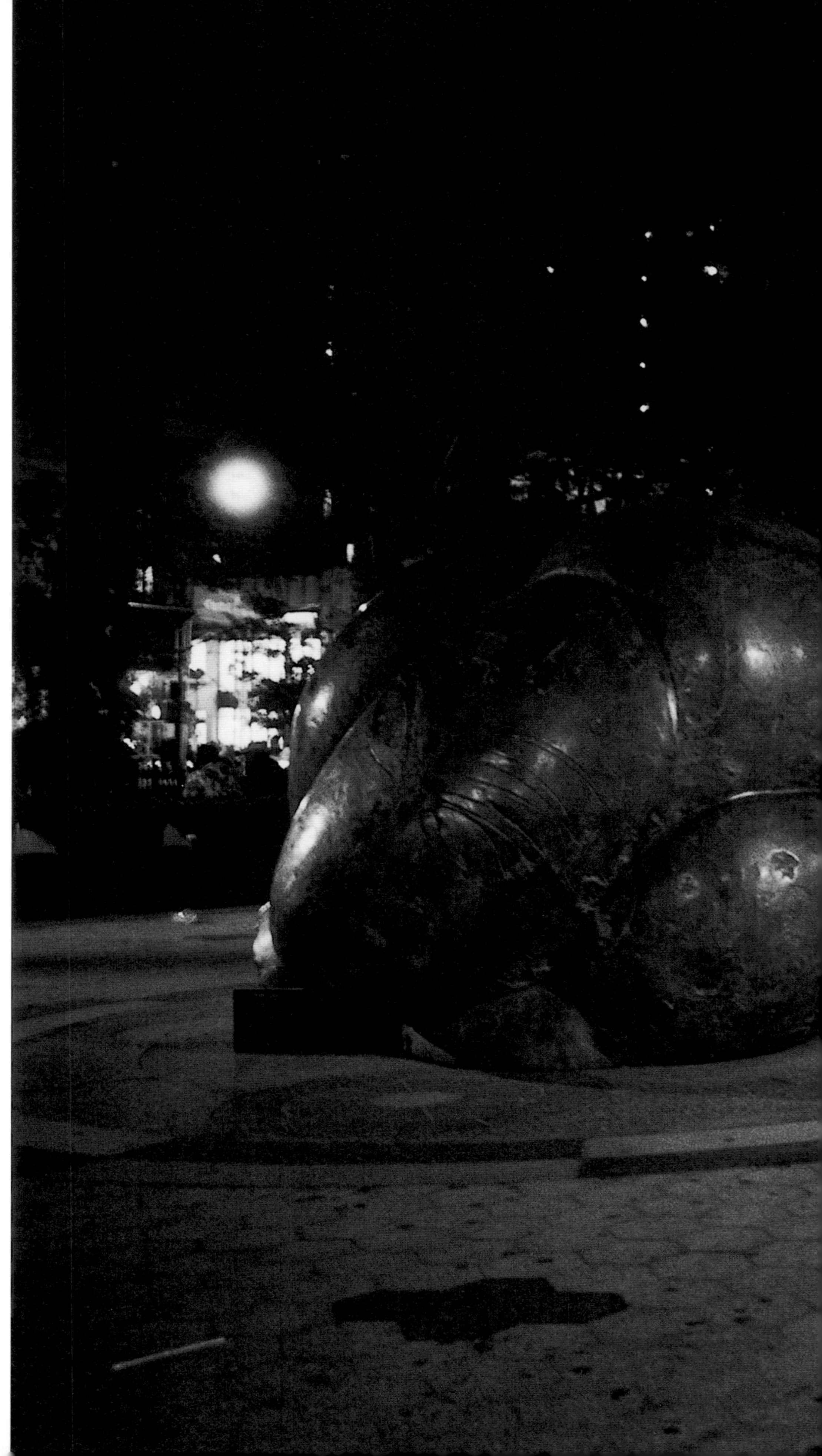

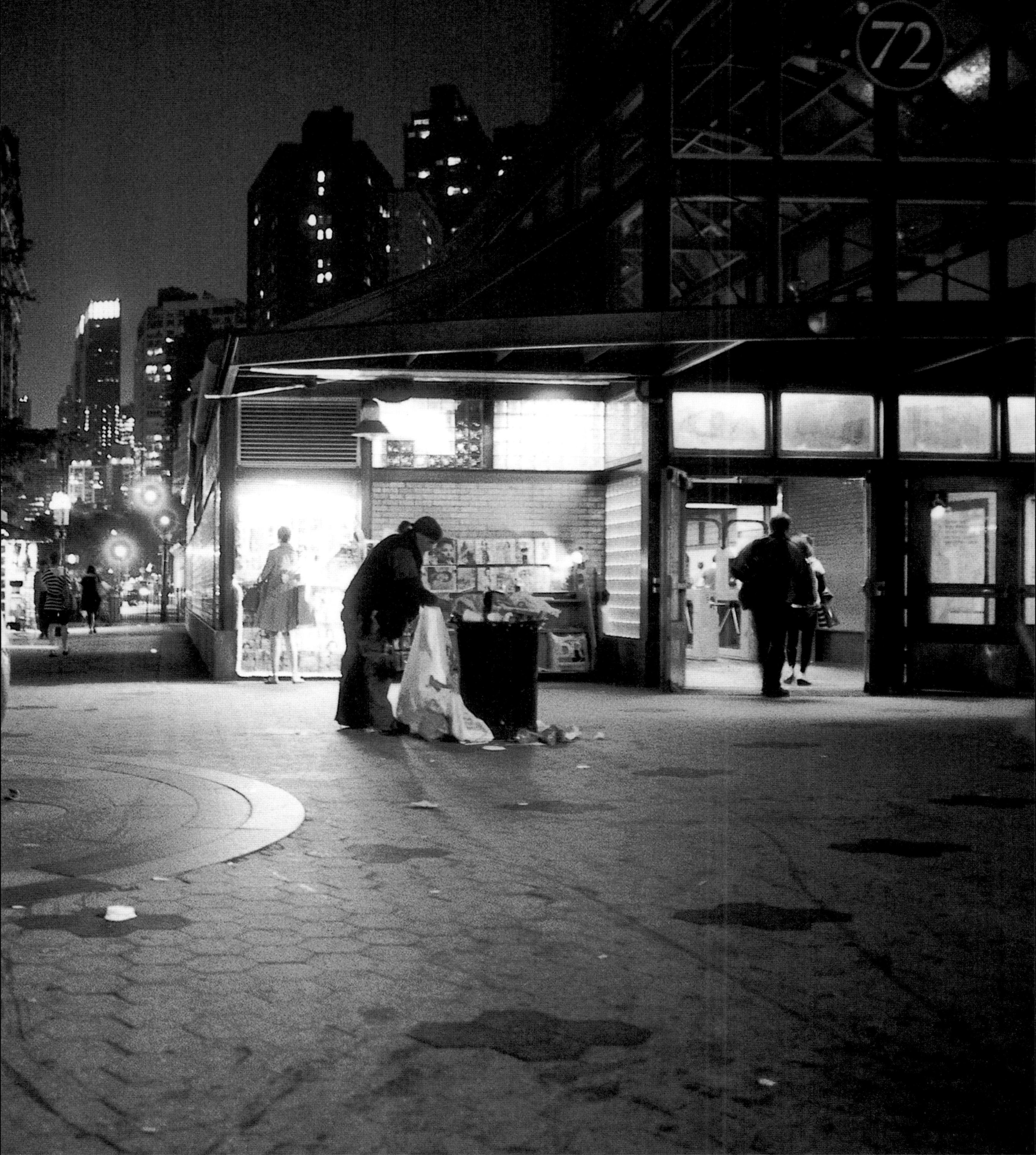

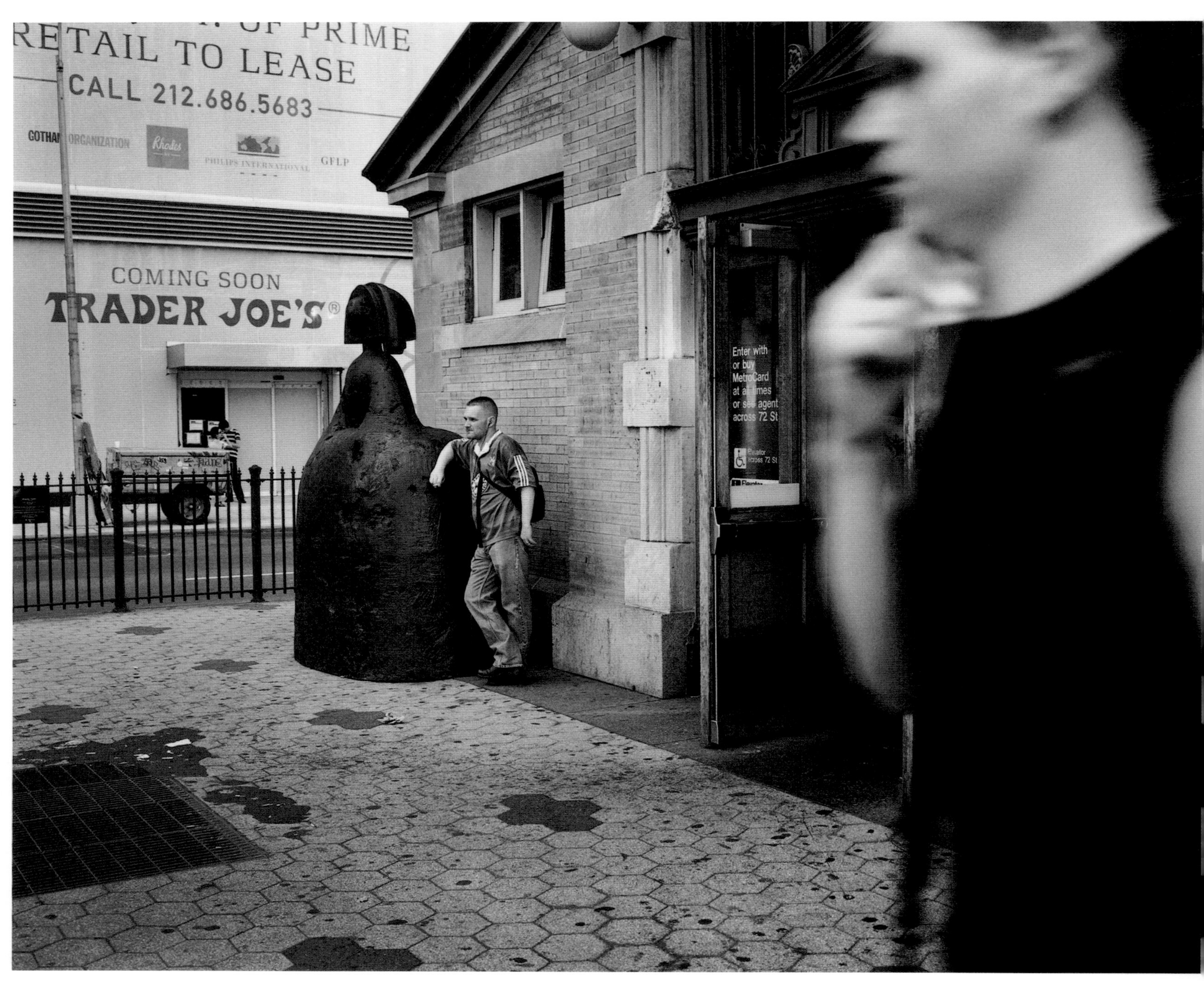
OF PRIME
RETAIL TO LEASE
CALL 212.686.5683
GOTHAM ORGANIZATION
Rhodes
PHILIPS INTERNATIONAL
GFLP
COMING SOON
TRADER JOE'S®
Enter with
or buy
MetroCard
at all times
or see agent
across 72 St.
Escalator
across 72 St.

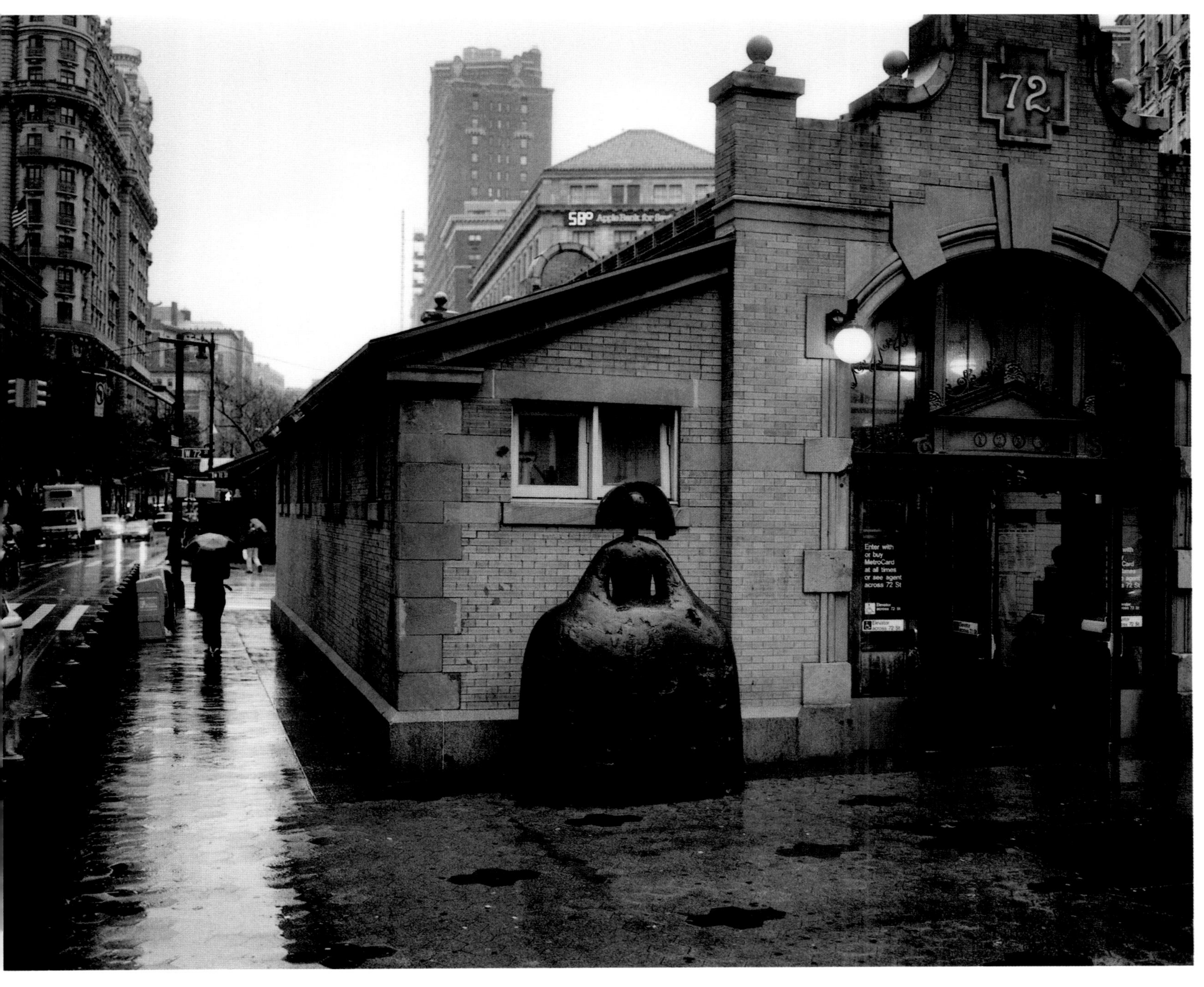
72
58° Apple Bank for Savings
Enter with
or buy
MetroCard
at all times
or see agent
across 72 St

that concentrates the absolute redemption of time.
Here the sculptures are more street, more immobile
artefacts among the acceleration that is overtaking
Manhattan. This is Midtown. The human landscape
changes again: it is no longer the group, the community,
the rite of several-party conversation, with its mad
chorus of voices, but rather the absorbtion of the man
who is waiting, who is strolling with a newspaper, who
is consulting his portable computer about a presumably
crucial question.

The *Marianas* are above all look-out points waiting for
the right moment. The moment for what? It doesn't
matter which moment. Stationed at the subway entrance,
with the attention and affection that New York deserves,
they see men and women go by with their destination
decided. And they rise delicately or vigorously as fickle
instruments of the day, as a necessary presence for the
start of the day in 72nd Street.

Don't they seem very much alone? "Don't you believe it.
They are greatly accompanied. They relentlessly welcome
the passers-by who enter and exit the subway. They are
two figures with a strange aura of perseverance. Look
at how people lean against their crinolines. There is a
constant commotion around them (if it is not raining or
snowing), which makes them permanently topical. They
provoke enraptured astonishment in those who look

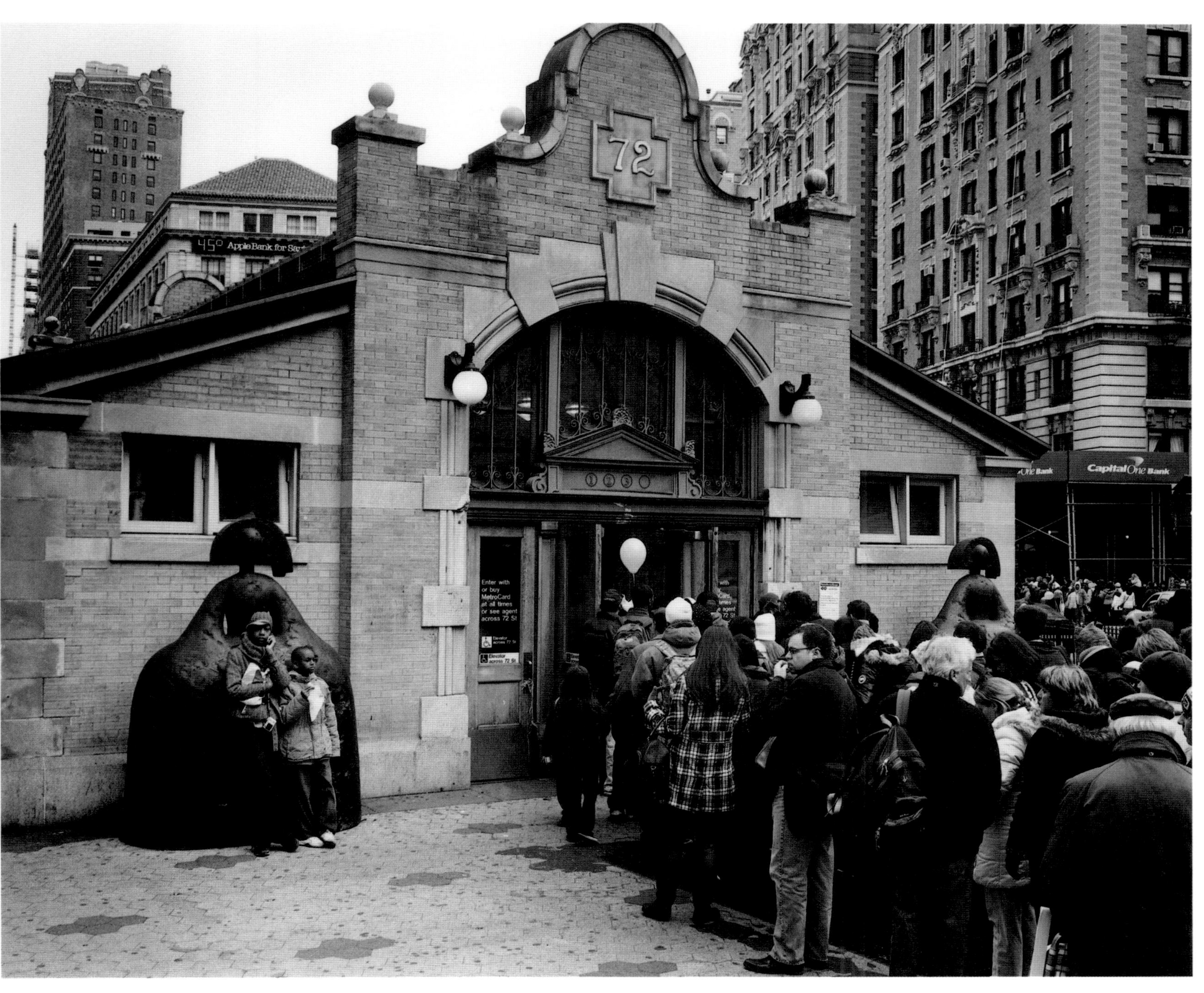
72
45° Apple Bank for Sav
Capital One Bank
Enter with
or buy
MetroCard
at all times
or see agent
across 72 St
Elevator
across 72 St
Elevator
across 72 St

at them. They hold us spellbound because they possess
something of self-portrait of each one of us."
Two ballet dancers from the Lincoln Center twirl around
them for a few minutes. Andrea is watching the birth of
her photograph. Through the sculptures she perceives
the day changing its skin, its evanescent mutation, its
insistence, its acceleration, the city's restless drifting,
which has already completely evolved, which at each step
shows its convulsive agreement with the unexpected. And
thus, little by little, everything takes shape or magnificent
pretences are created.

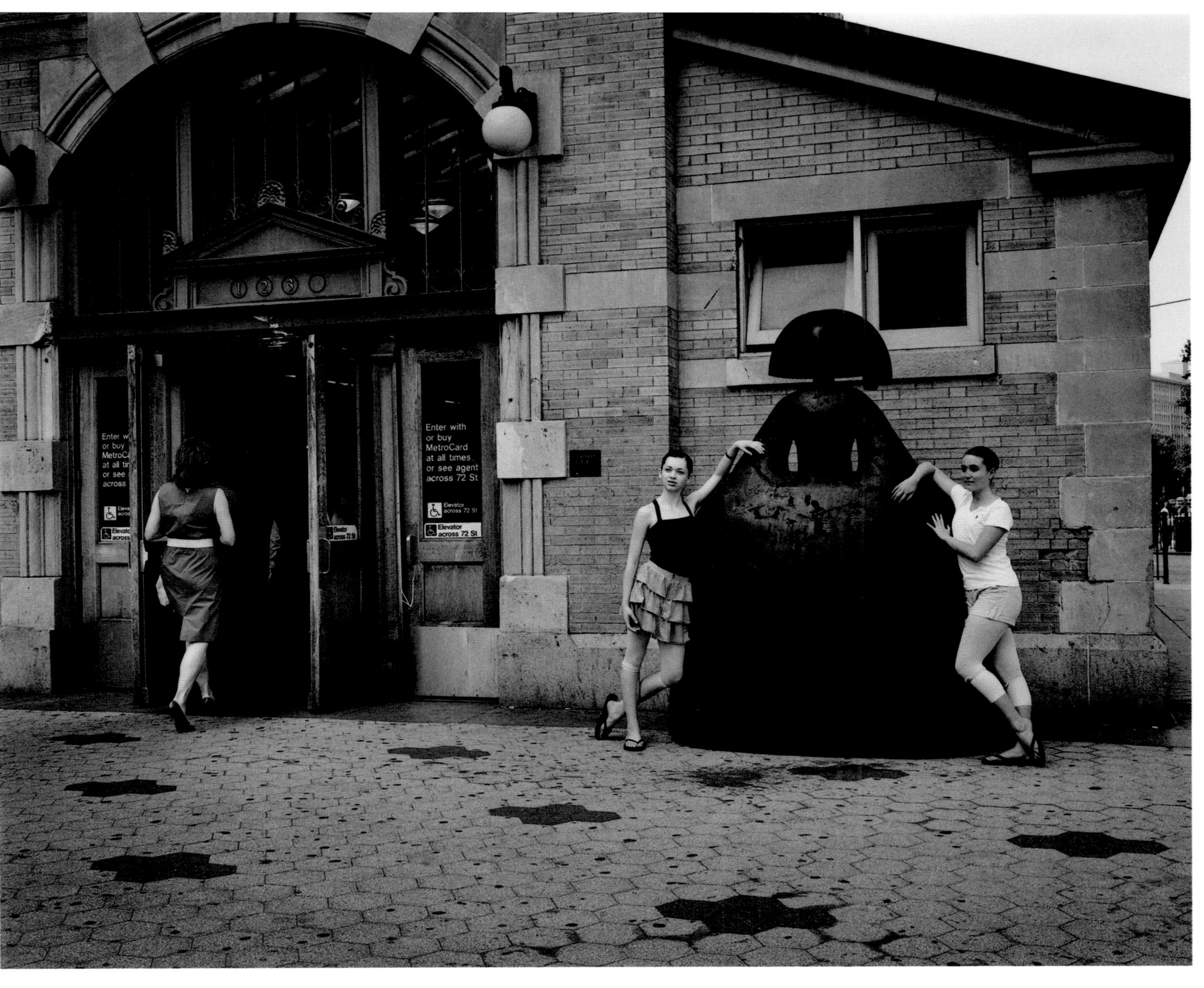
Enter with
or buy
MetroCard
at all times
or see agent
across 72 St
Elevator
across 72 St

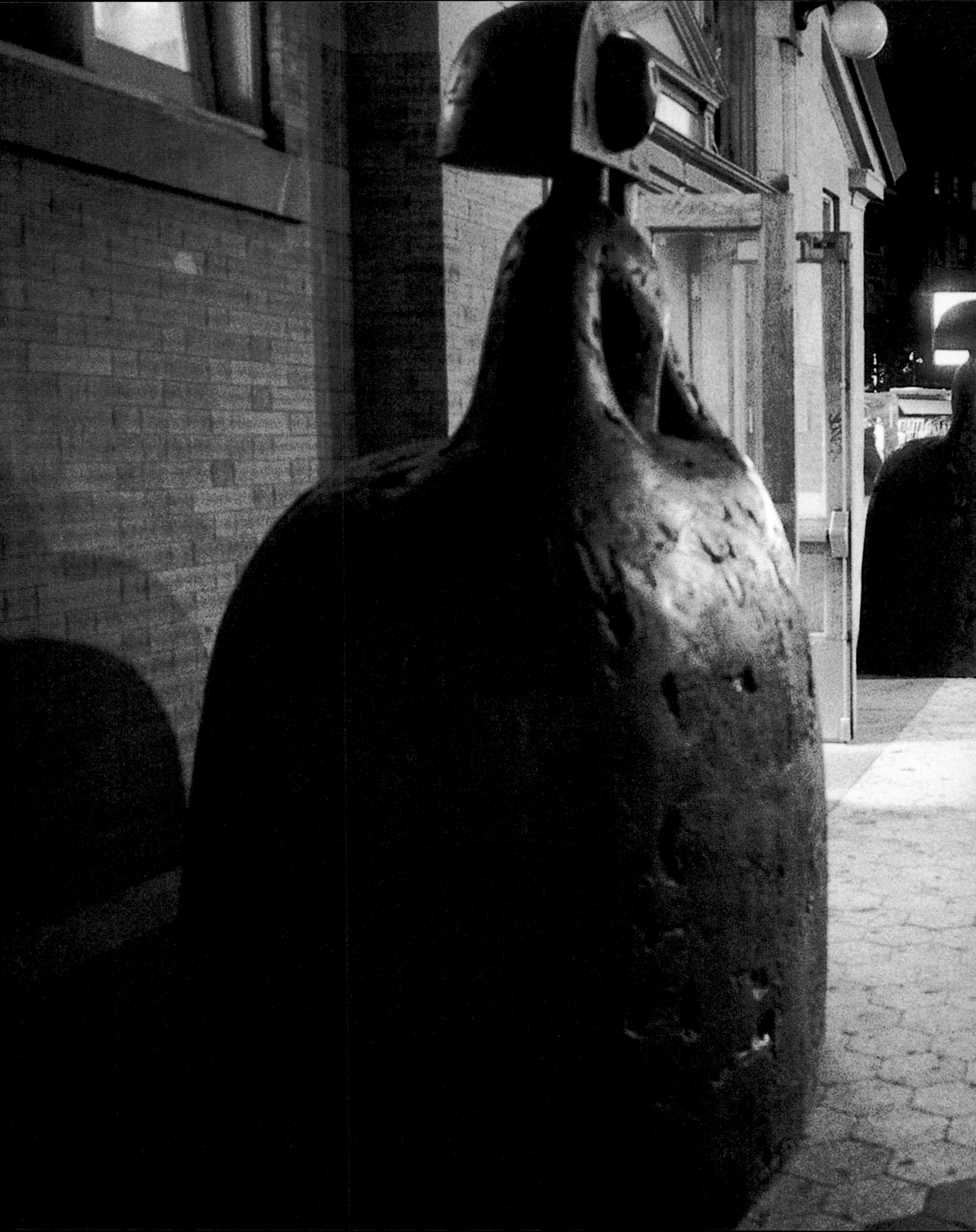

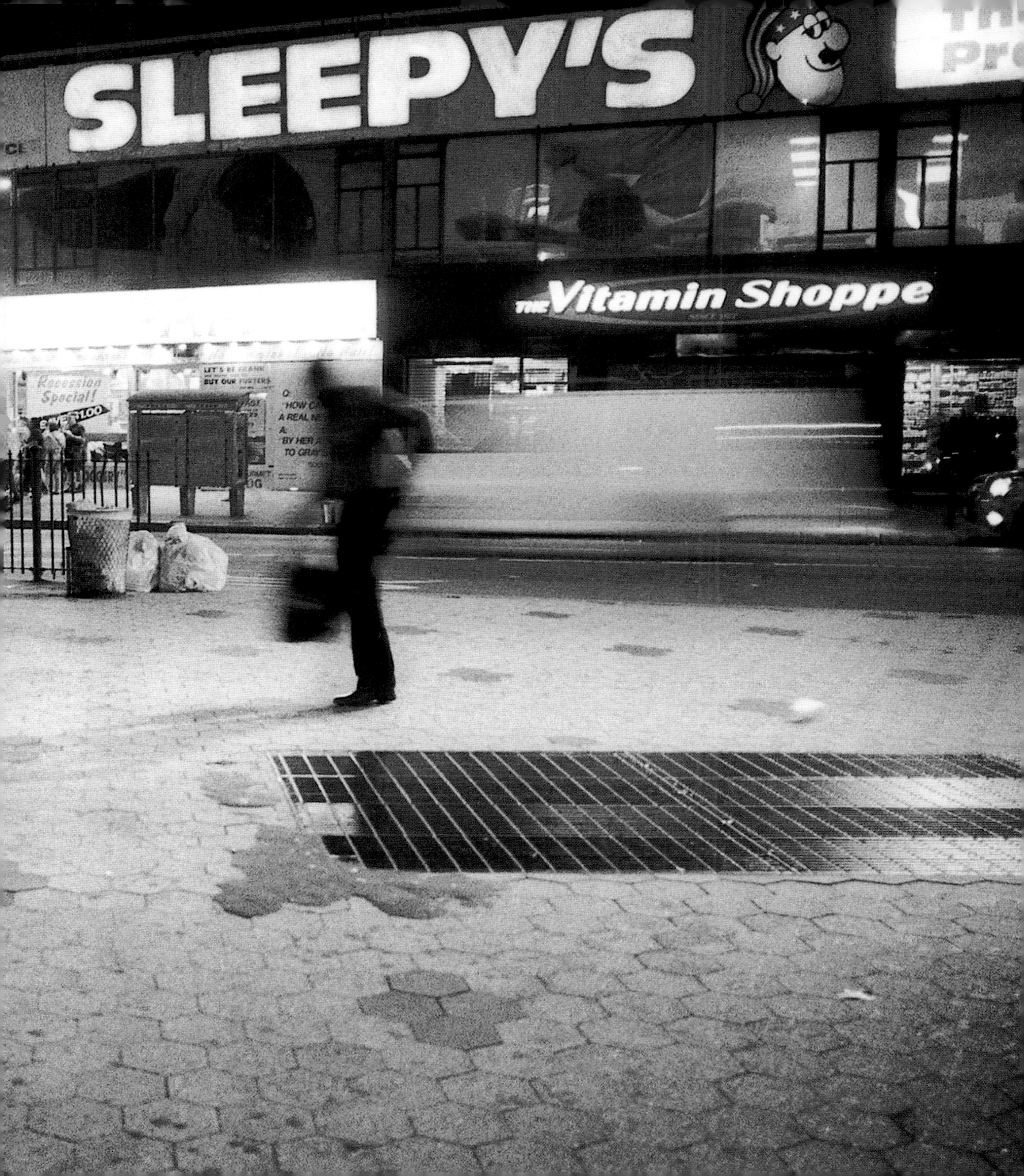

SLEEPY'S
THE Vitamin Shoppe
Recession Special!
SAVE $100

DANTE PARK

[DAMA II]

We go down to 63rd Street in search of *Dama II*. This long route from Domican Harlem is a pleasurable pilgrimage, almost a declaration. It is a summary of the metropolis and its informal borders.

Dama II has a long neck and a hairstyle of superimposed right angles. She is in a park. Nearby is the Lincoln Center. She occupies a small piece of ground in Columbus Avenue and is camouflaged under a leafy covering of trees, at the corner of a crossroads where everything is in transit. *Dama II* gives this urban junction the warmth of a totem pole, of a bronze amulet, of a feminine obelisk where we went to make secret filigree offerings. Her head is a mad type of architecture that competes with the branches of the plane trees. Haste does not dazzle her slender serenity, nor spoil the firmness of a face of Brancusian sparkles. She seems like a figure from the Cyclades, from the 3rd millennium B.C. And in unison with the figures who go by, she conceives an intrigue. Andrea searches for all the angles of the scuñpture. She prowls around it like a cat. She is familiar with the folds, the texture, the intimacy and the simplest movements

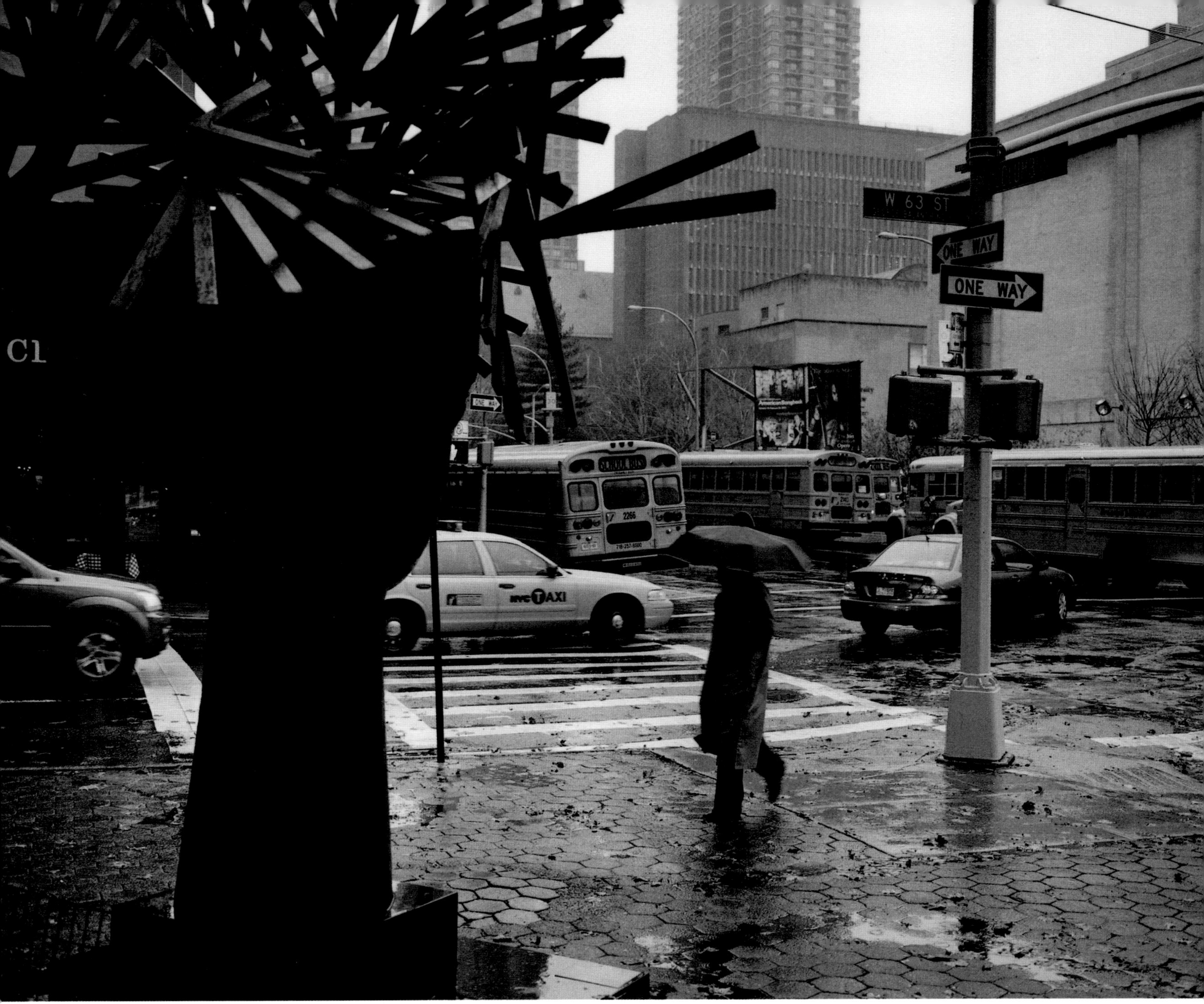
C1
W 63 ST
ONE WAY
ONE WAY
ONE WAY
NYC TAXI
2266
718-257-8500

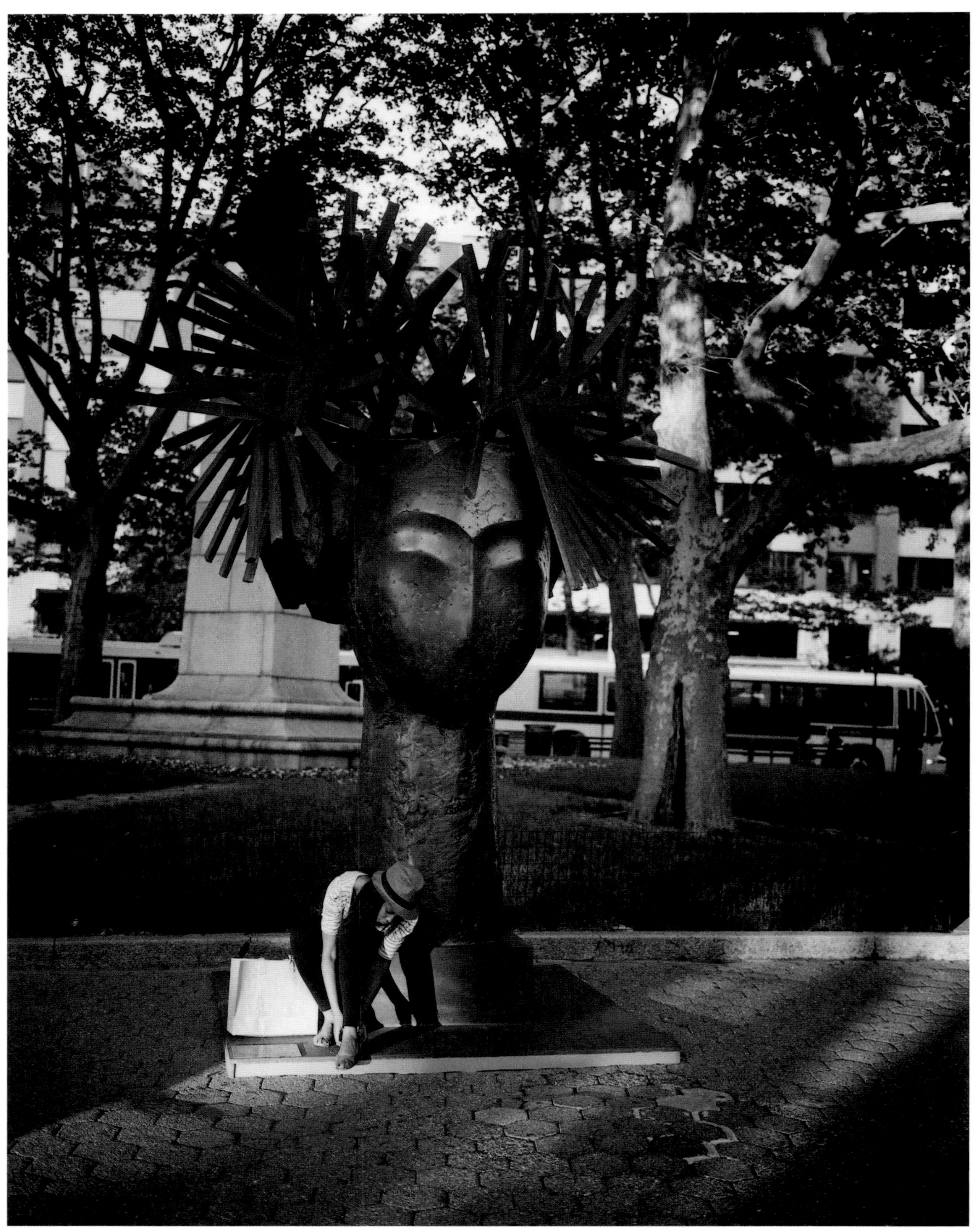

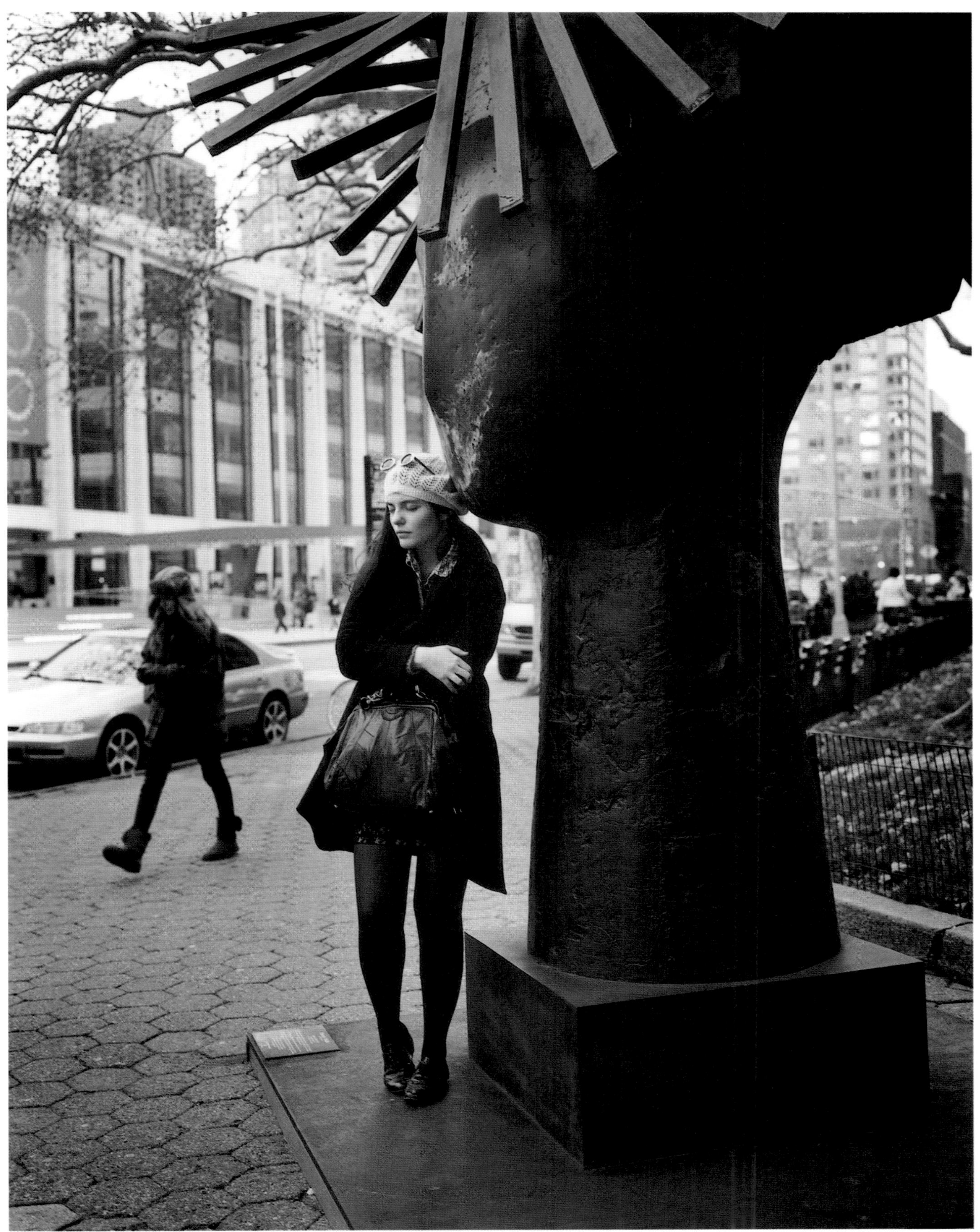

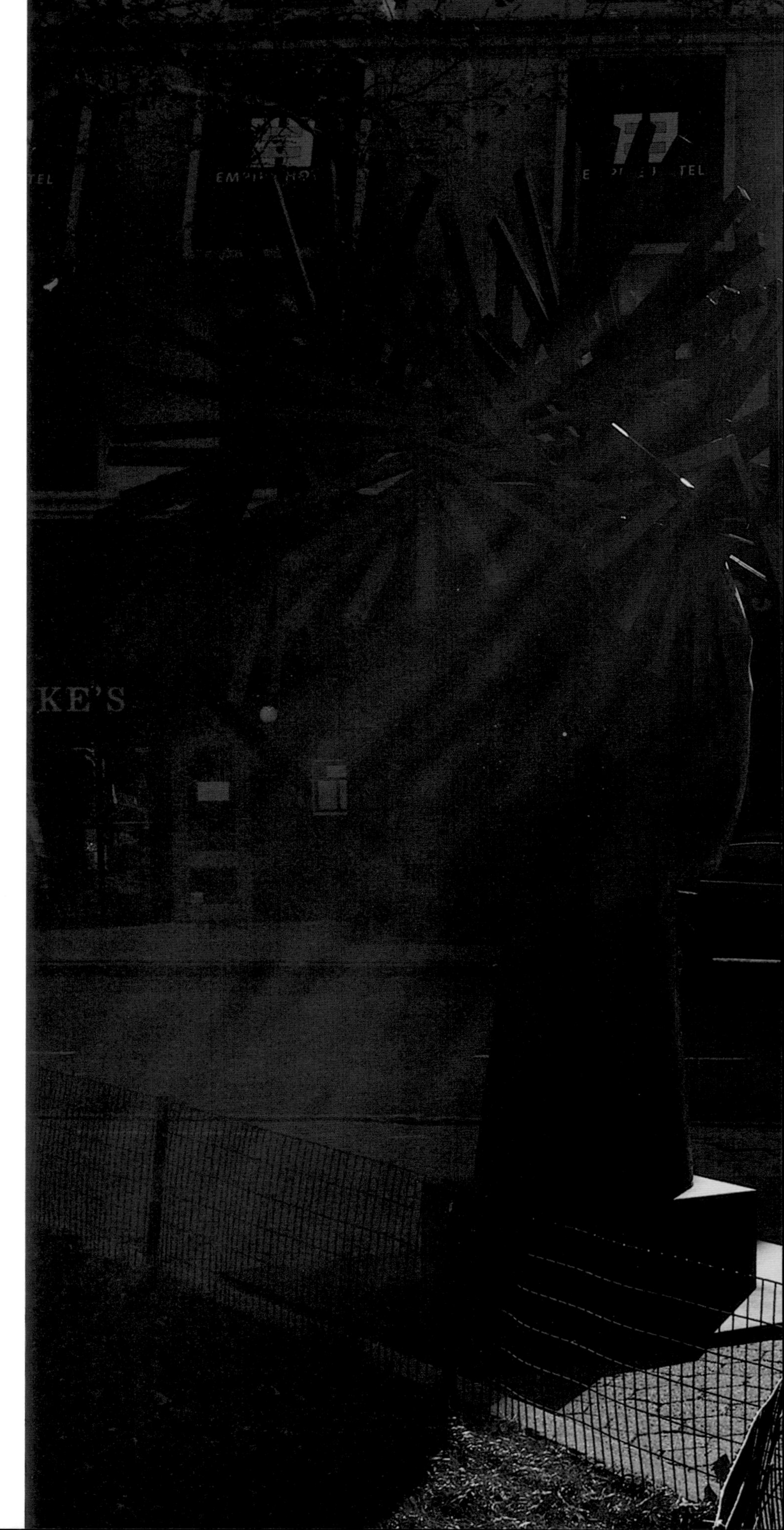

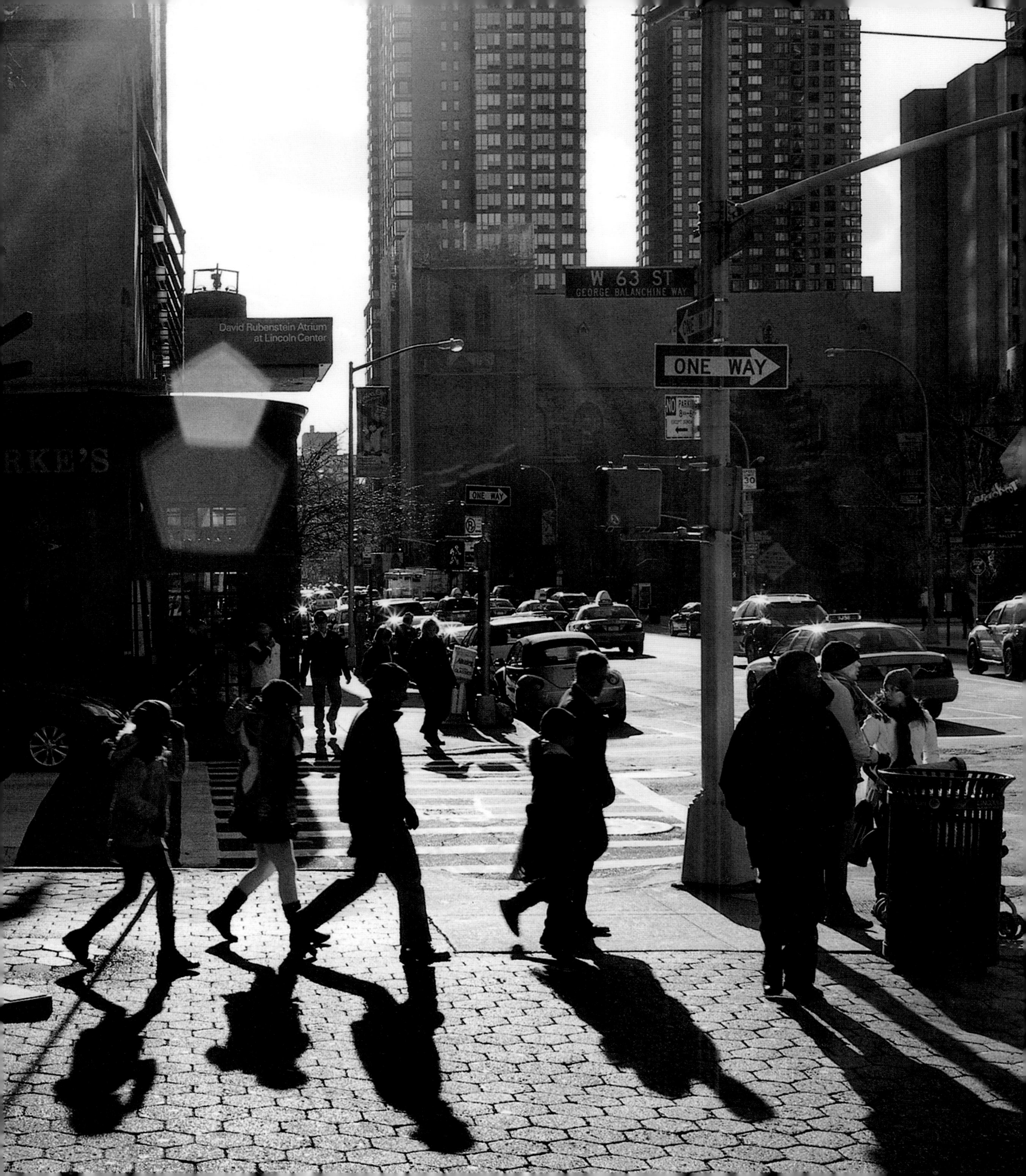

David Rubenstein Atrium
at Lincoln Center
RKE'S
W 63 ST
GEORGE BALANCHINE WAY
ONE WAY
ONE WAY
NO PARK
30

of the cast bronze. But she continues to be surprised
at each flicker of light, at each onset of night that falls
upon them. She undertook her safari with no other
strategy than that of a map, in order not to get lost.
And as of then the story of this procession wrote itself,
accepting the long-delayed phrasing of those who, at the
beginning of the route, stop in front of the sculptures,
camp and make of them another point of reference in that
precise instant.

As the tourist advances, the landscape becomes colder.
The conjuring becomes a distant observation, a fleeting
encounter. To such an extent that at the last halt on
the tour, the codes of relationship with the works have
changed radically. This is felt in the excitement of
Andrea's photographs, which respond to a fascination of
seeing the plot of the people and the plot of the sculptures
as if it were complicity or surprise. The architecture is
not outside her field of observation. Nor is the successive
activity that takes place in each of the streets in which
the works are displayed. There is no disfigurement of the
spaces or of the scales, but rather a compensation that
detects with the camera trigger in her hand. Braiding
the details lovingly, as Nabokov demanded.

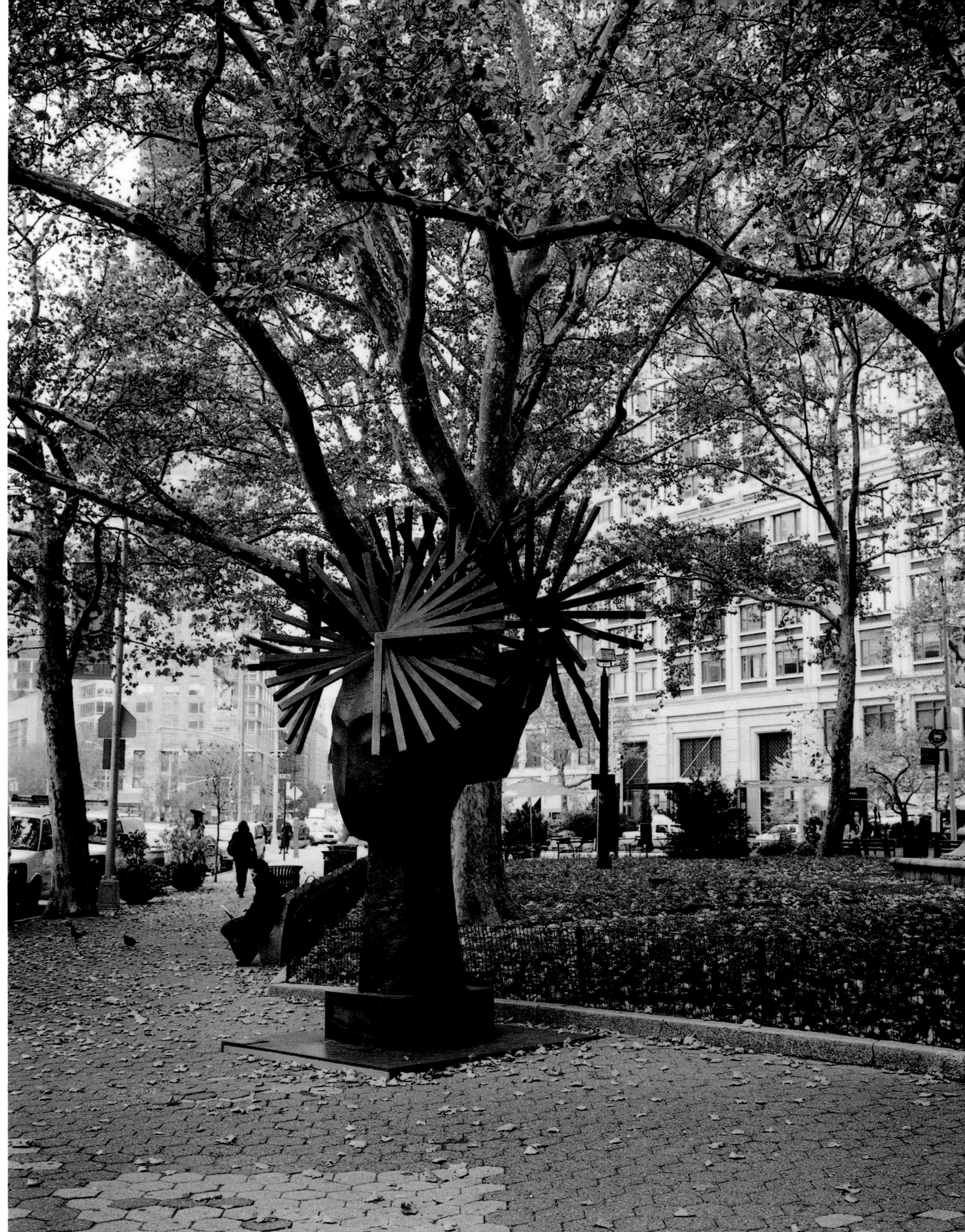

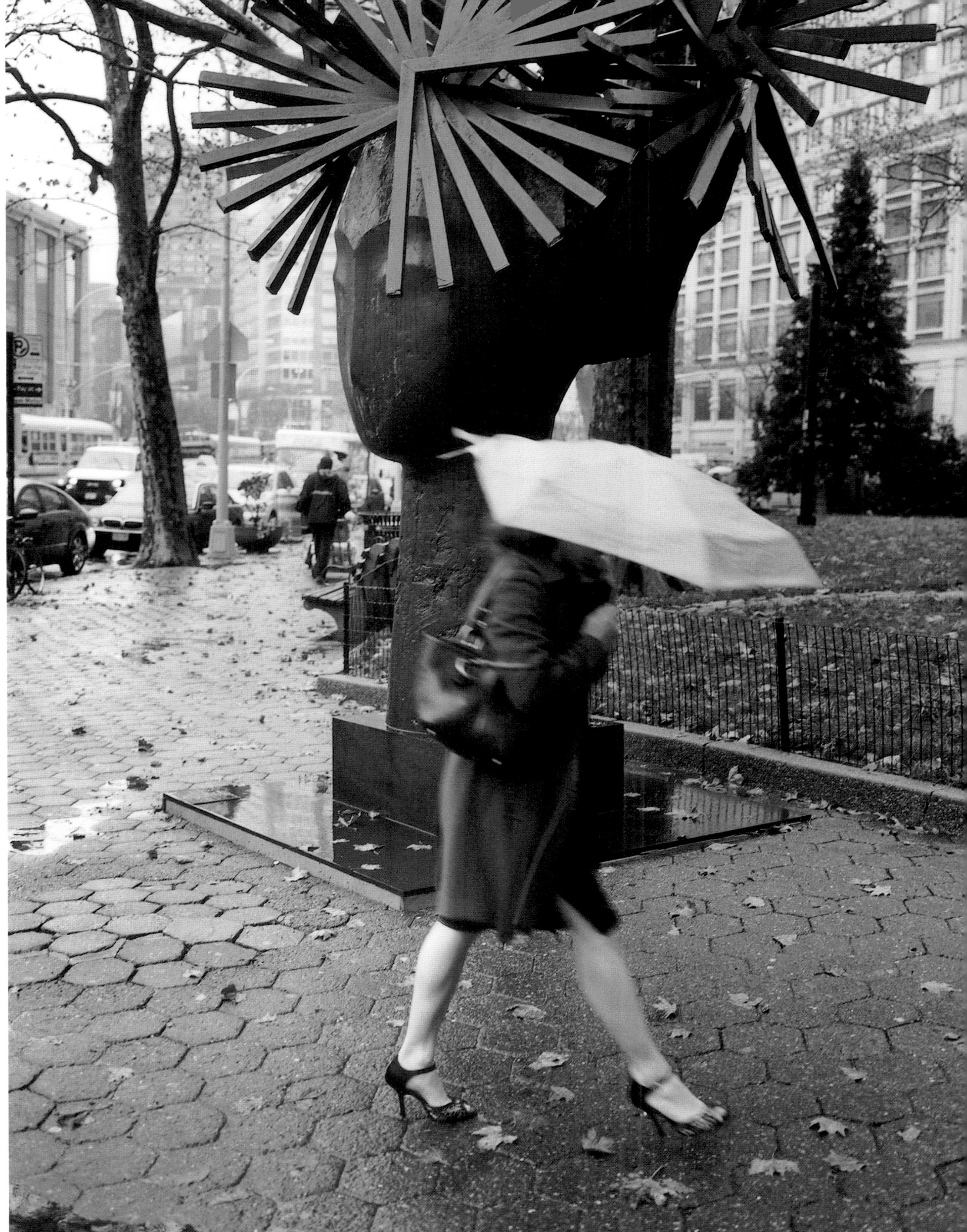

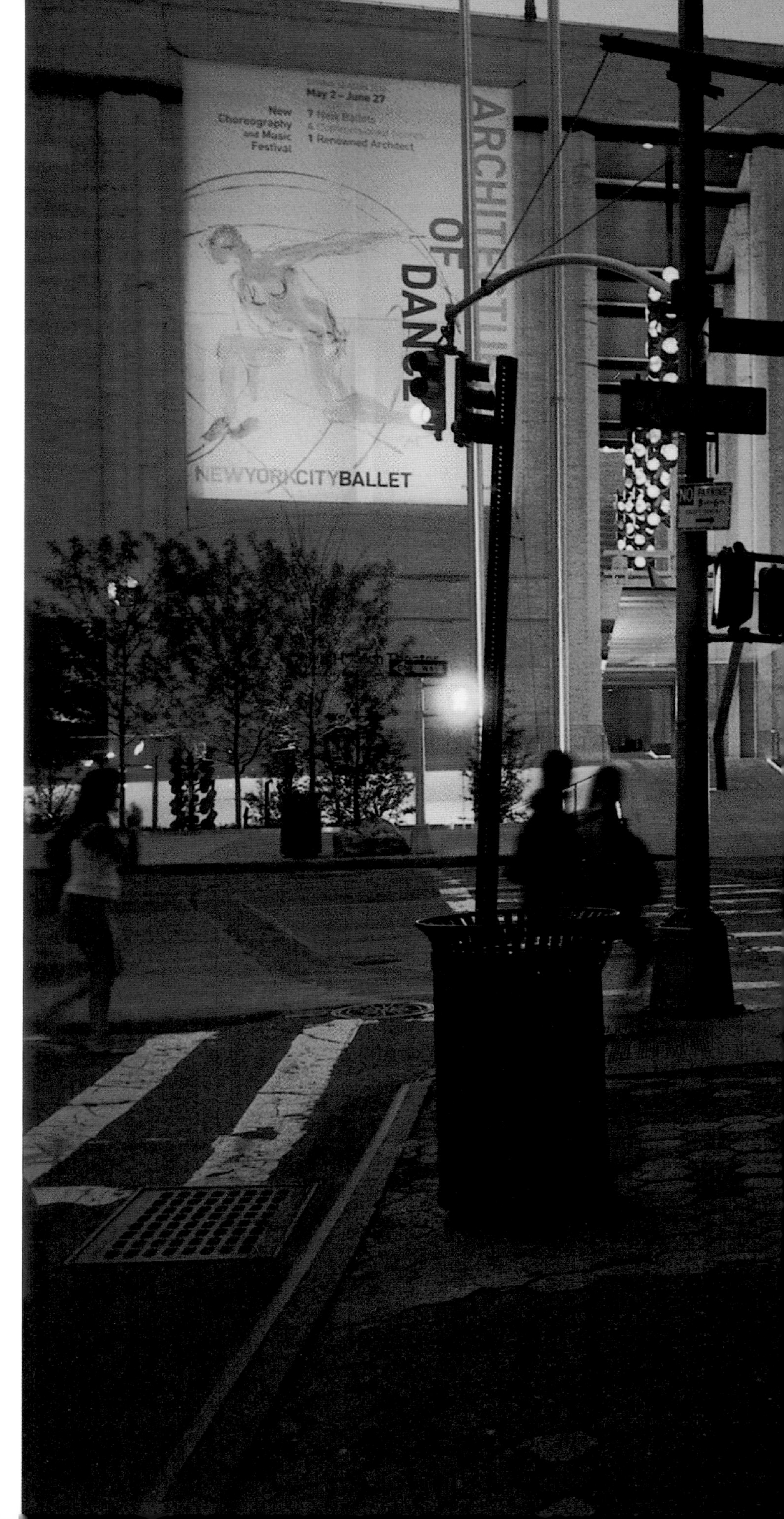

May 2 – June 27
New
Choreography
and Music
Festival
7 New Ballets
1 Renowned Architect
ARCHITECTURE
OF
DANCE
NEWYORKCITYBALLET

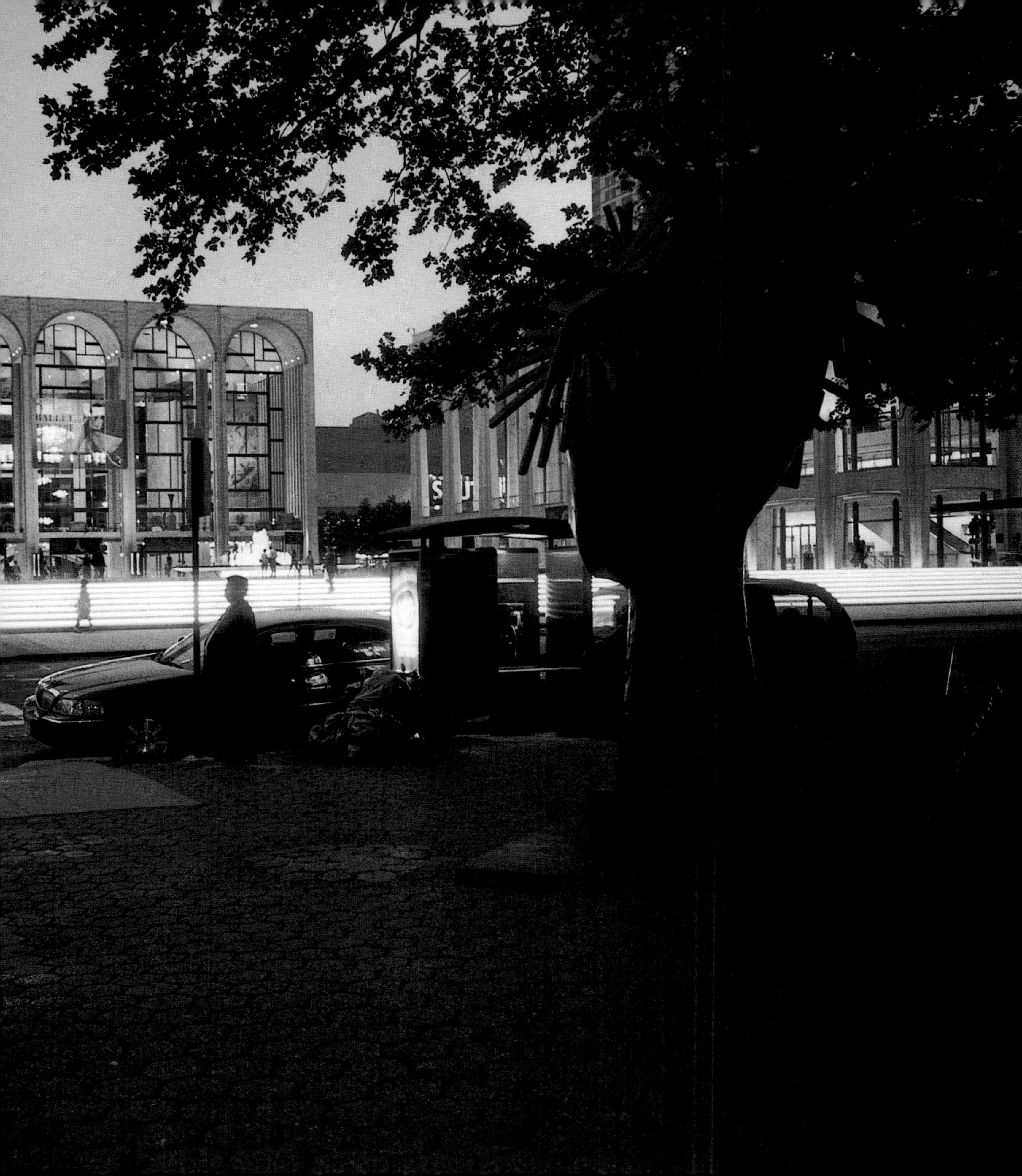

BROADWAY
COLUMBUS CIRCLE [MARIANA]

– We have already reached the end, Andrea.

– But the end is also a beginning: the mirror of an infinite journey; a journey that neither has nor requires a specific order. It is a return trip. The last stage is something of an apotheosis. There are four figures in the *Reina Mariana* and the *Dama a caballo*. They surround the statue of Christopher Columbus. And surrounding them are murmuring lovers, executives from the office buildings and people crossing to Lincoln Jazz. This square, Columbus Circle, has something of a moving self-portrait of New York executed in real time. In autumn, in spring, in summer and in winter, I have taken photographss during every season of the year. And I have never seen a moment when one of the sculptures became detached from its surroundings.

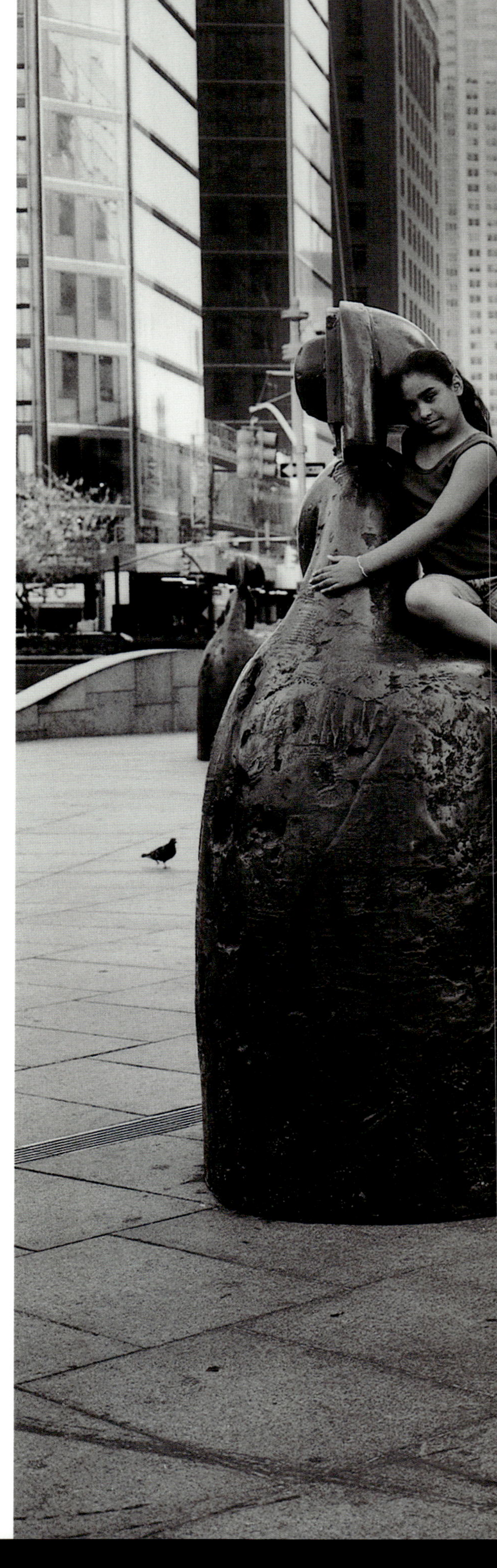

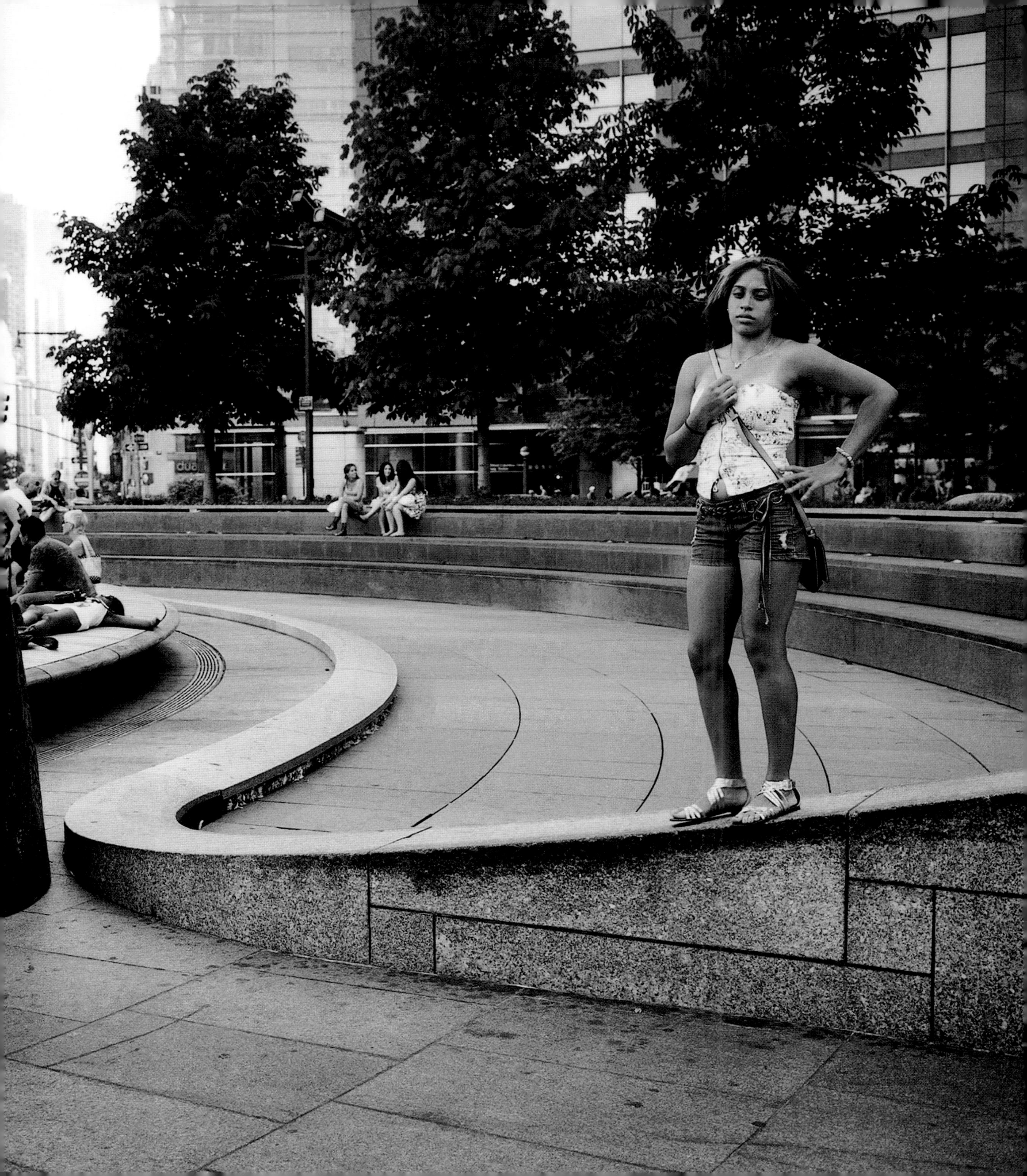

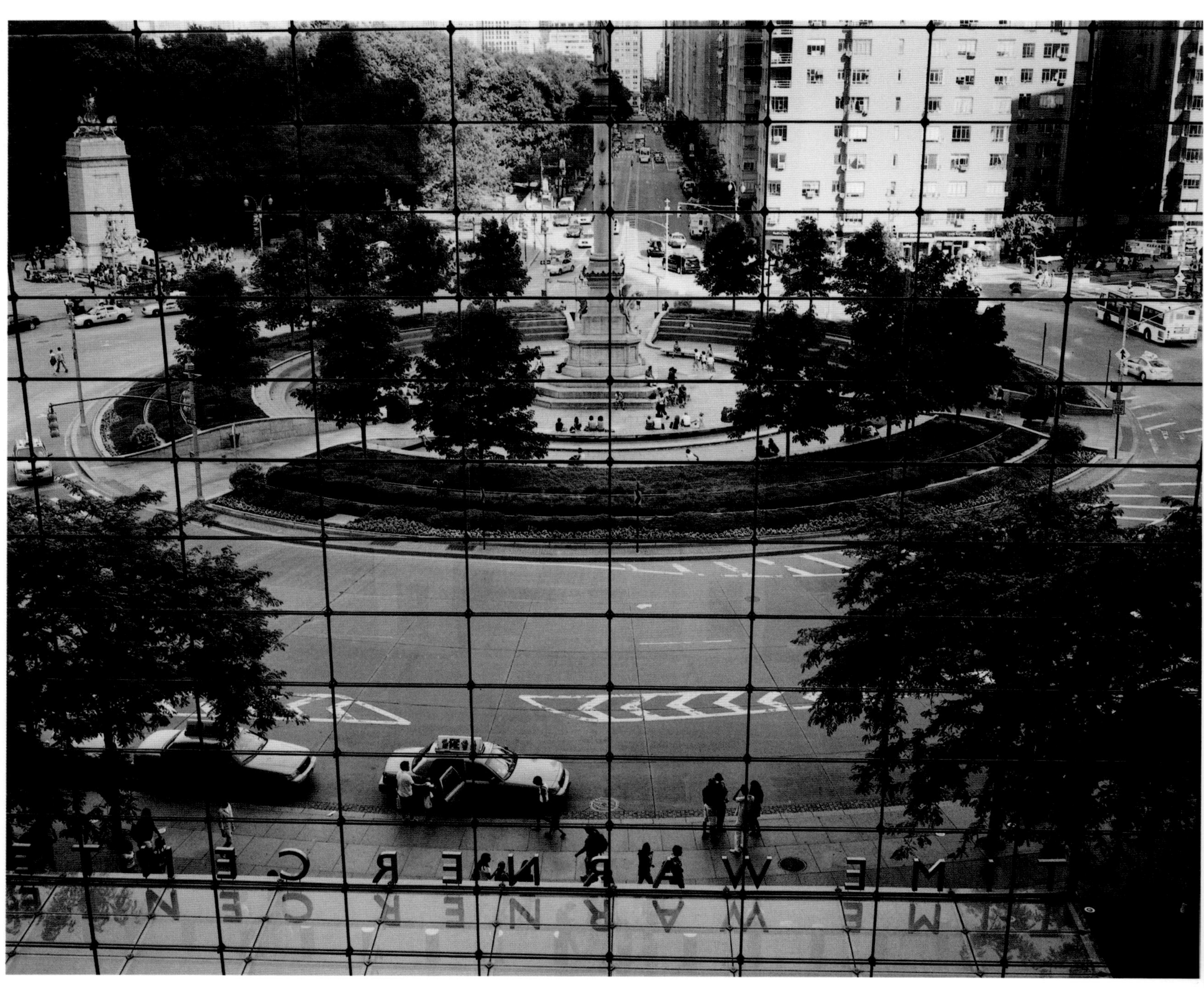

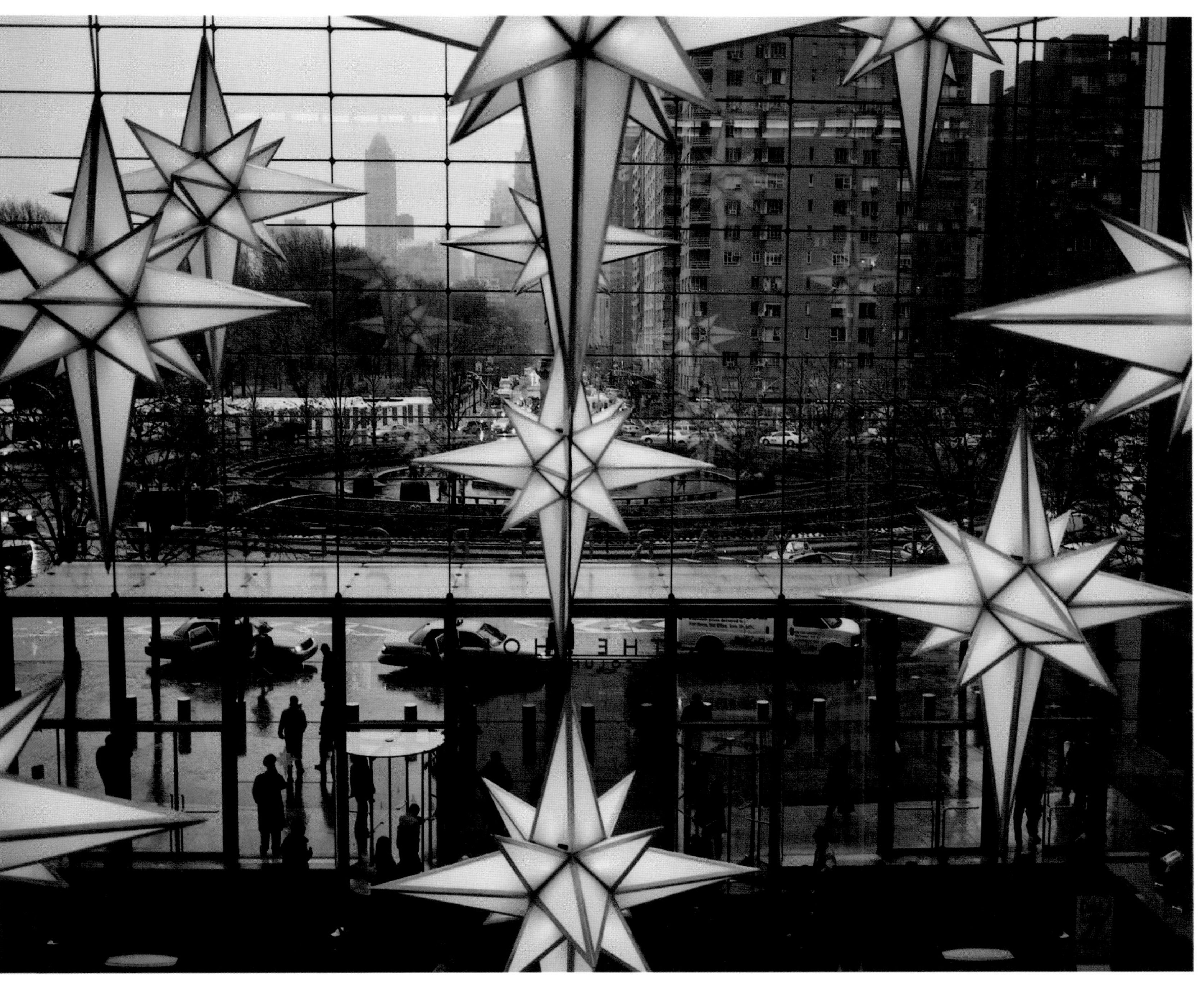

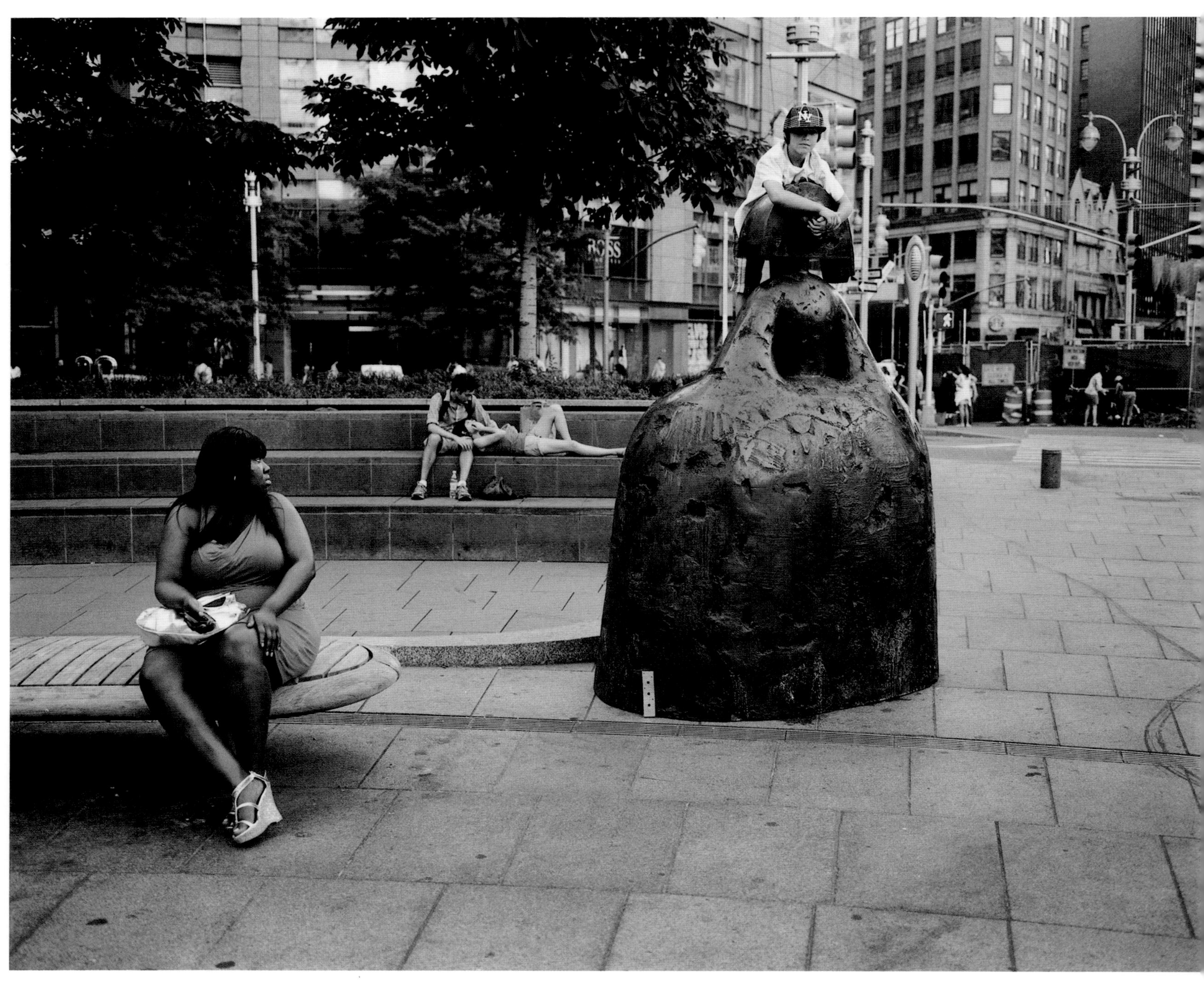

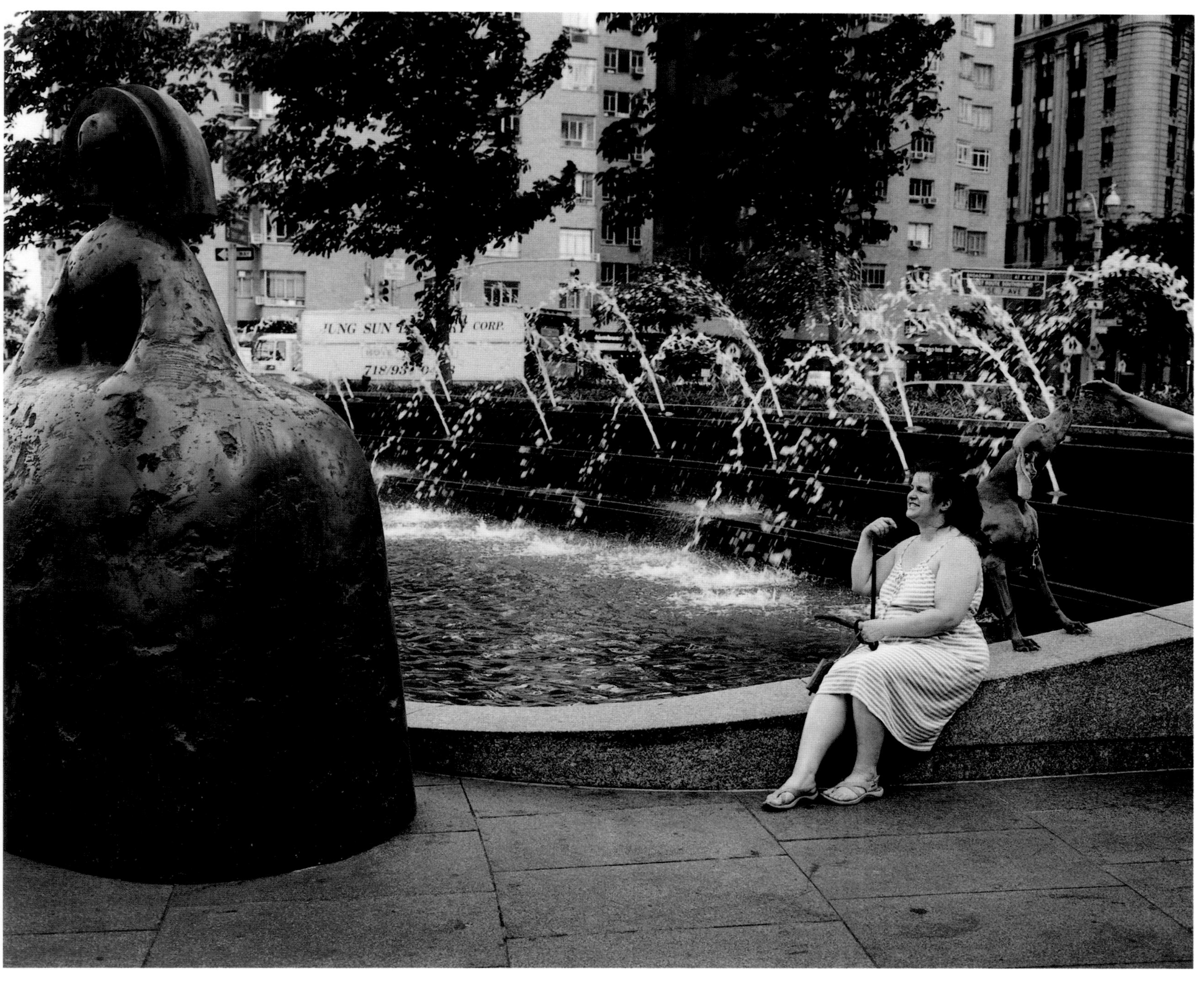
JUNG SUN ... RY CORP.
718/93...

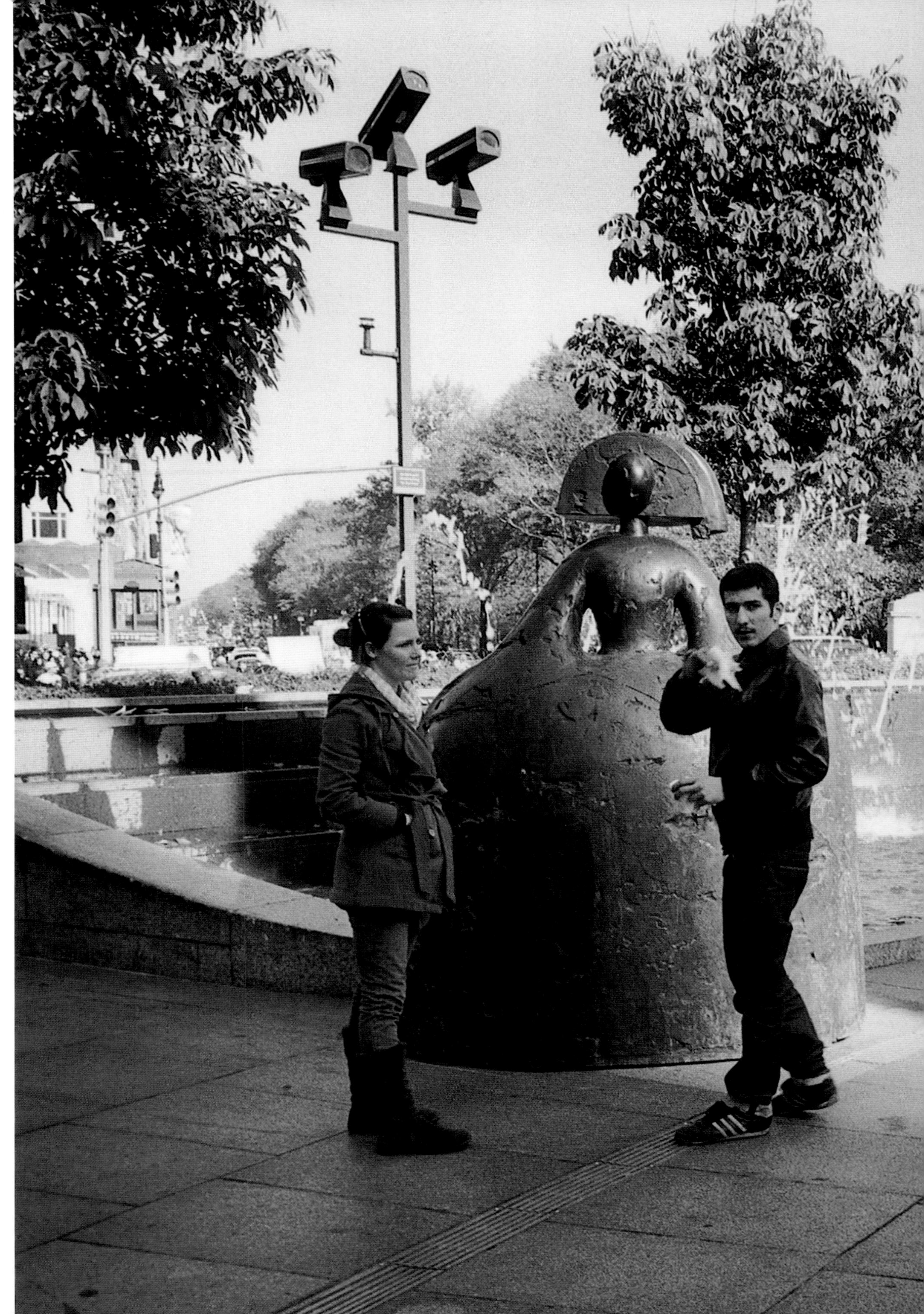

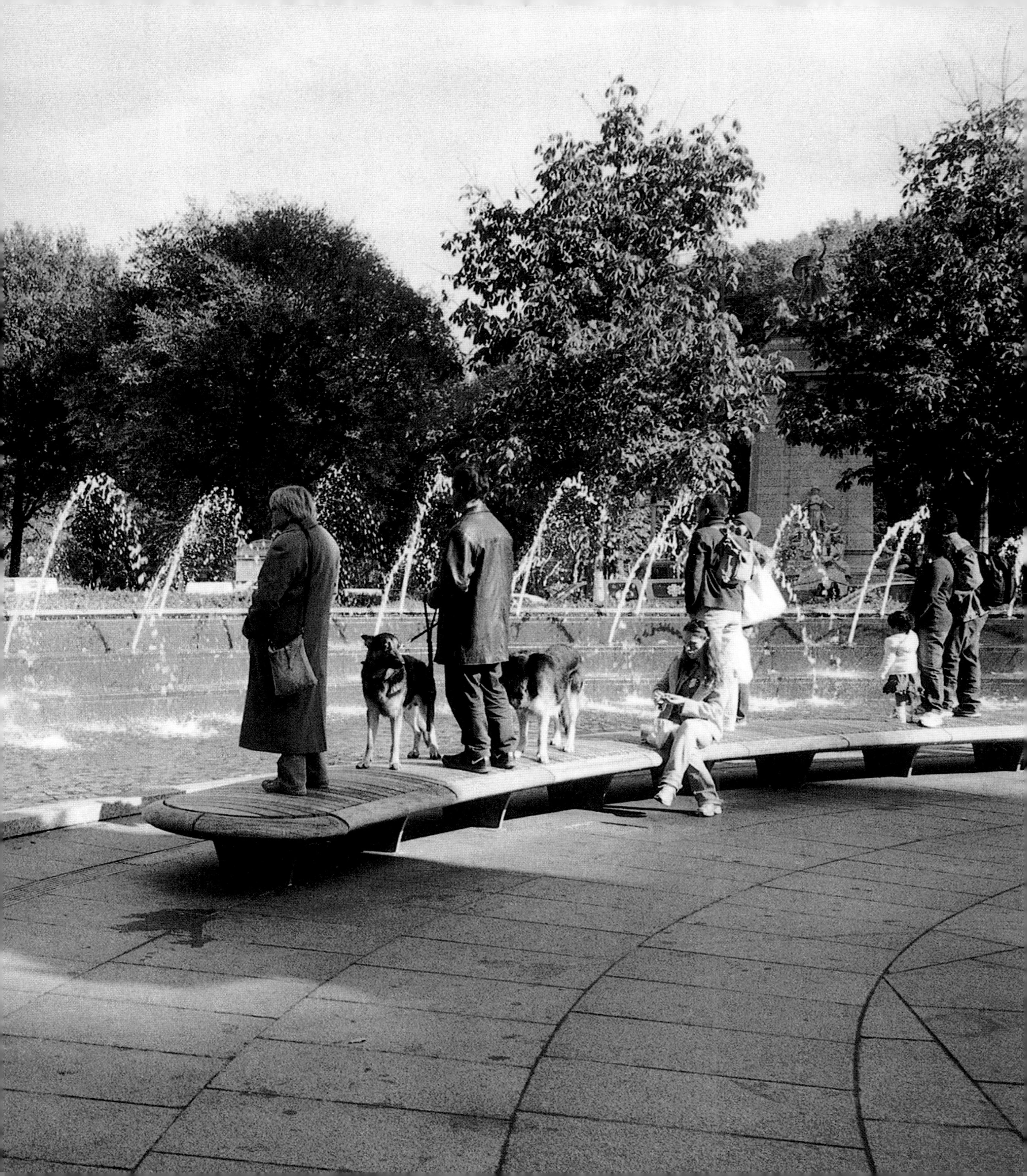

They all maintain that attitude of company, of a chest full
of accumulations, of human experiences that have pierced
the hard metal plating and have settled inside, giving them
lust, sensuality, density, lechery and perhaps a slight fever.
It seems that they have been here since the beginning,
with the slopes and the hills and the natives and the seeds.

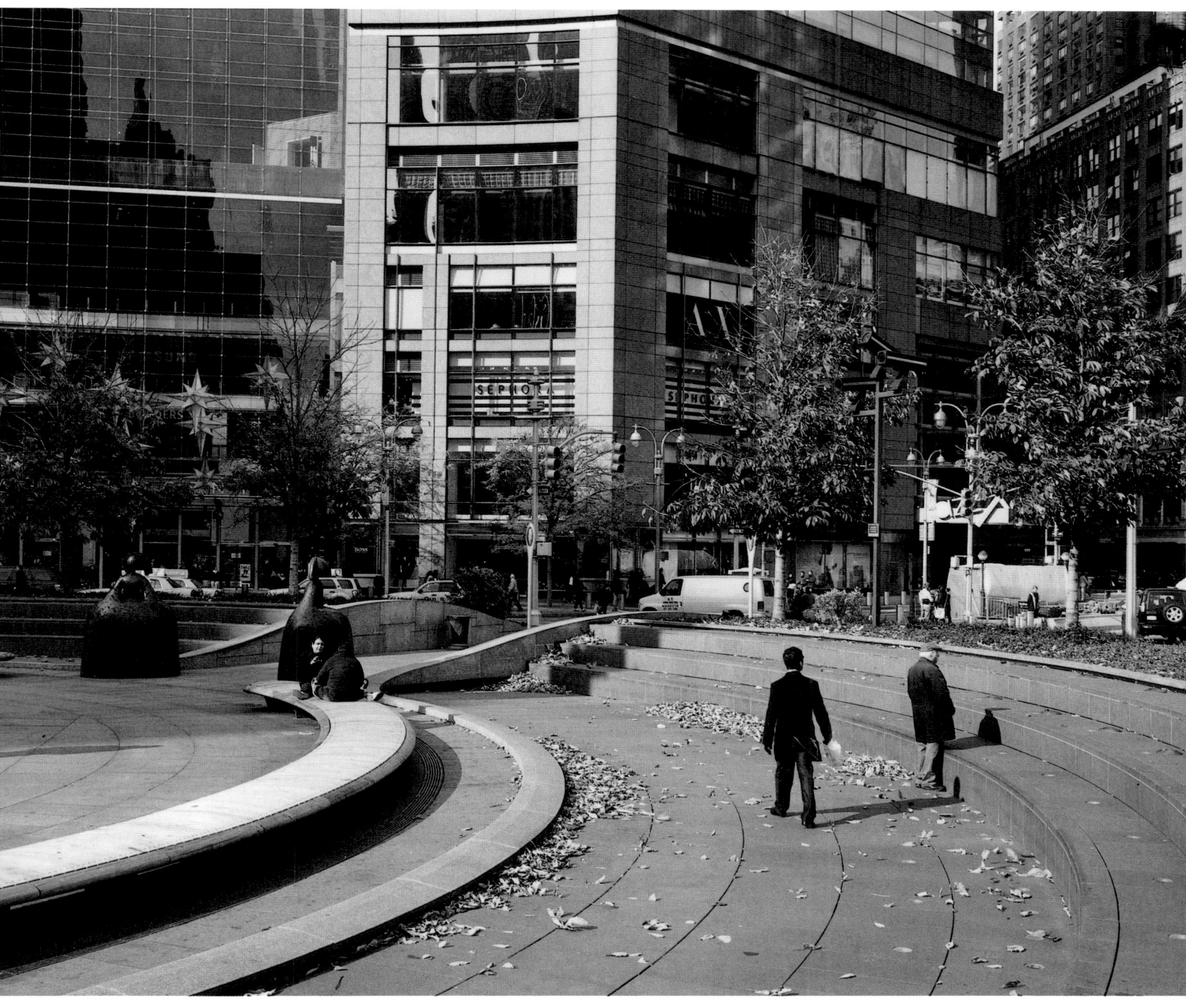

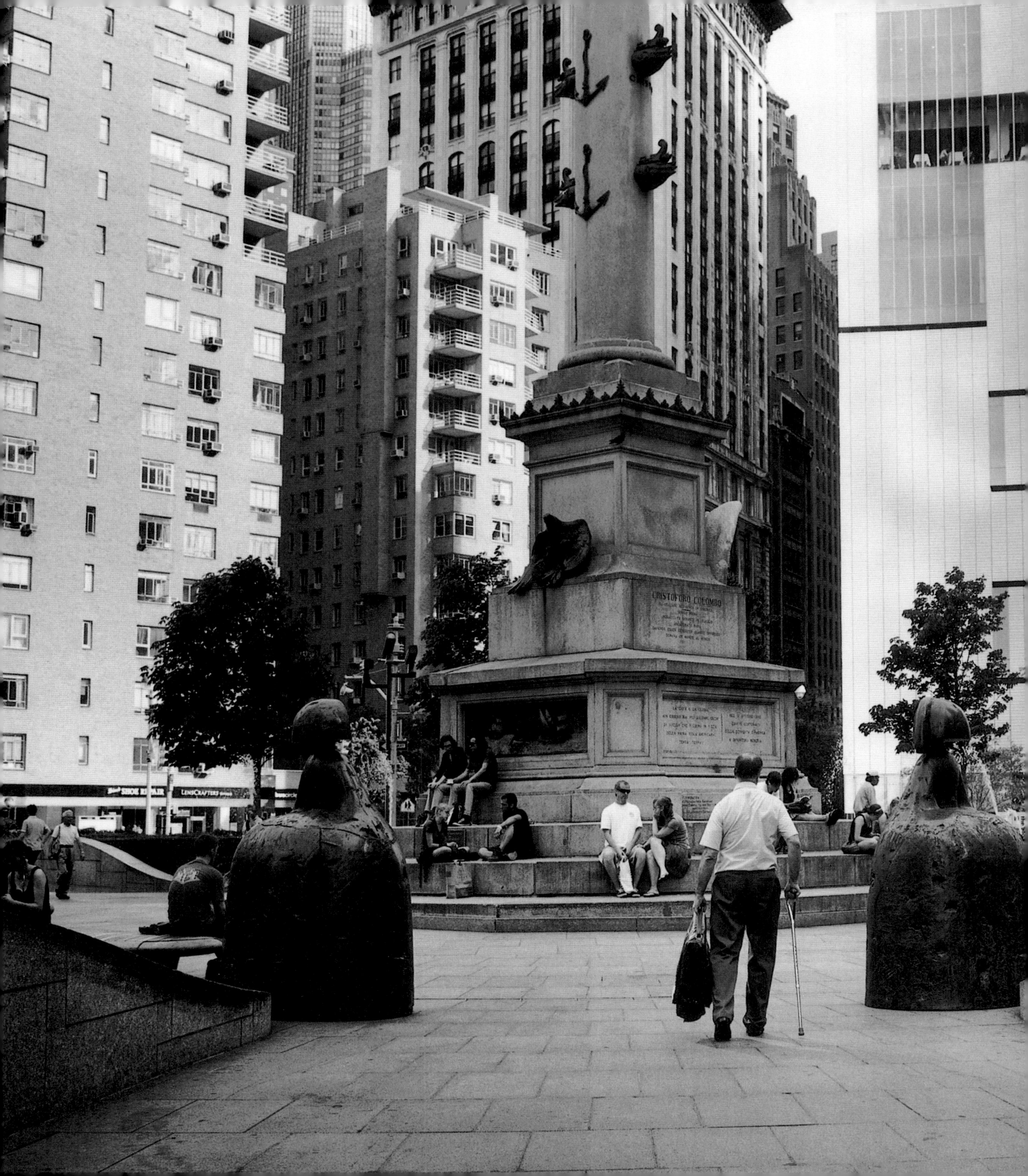

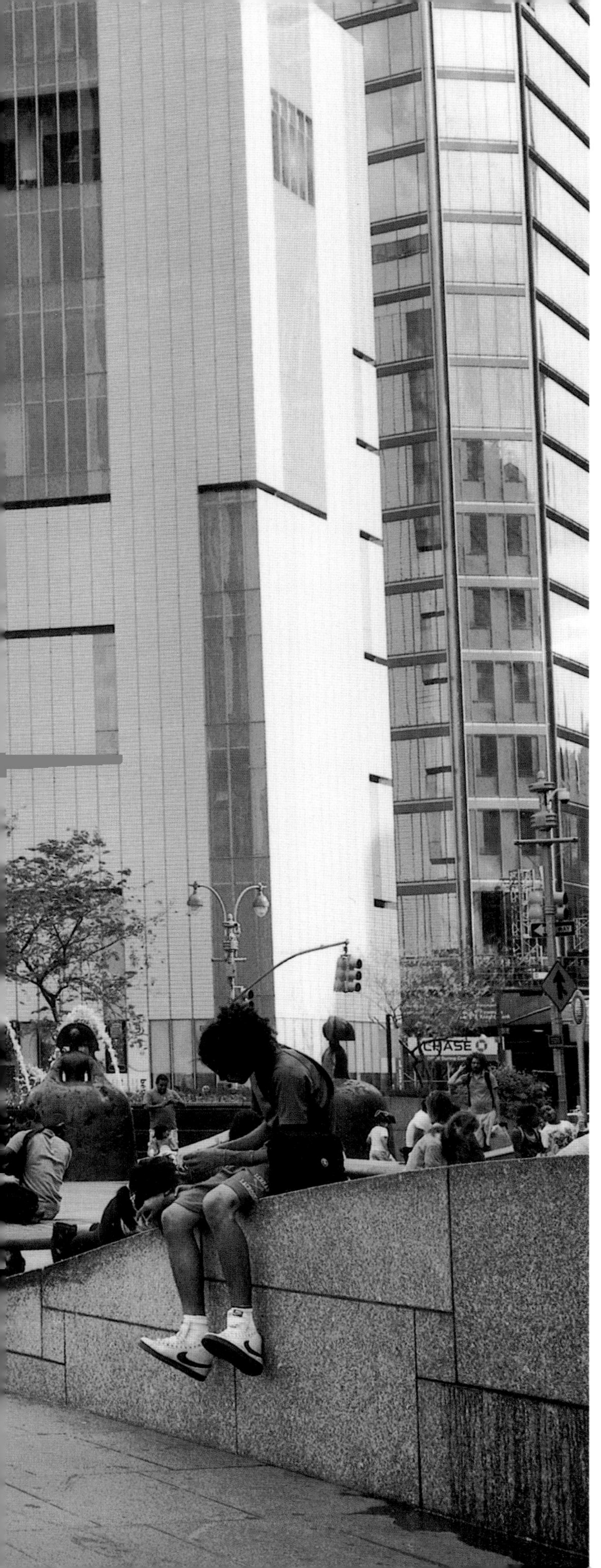

BROADWAY
COLUMBUS CIRCLE [DAMA A CABALLO]

The sculptures are arranged in a long corridor.
A pedestrian realizes this when he has covered the
kilometers of sidewalk, one by one, following their trail.
They establish a kind of remote hallucination if one
thinks of them from a distance. One's gaze hovers slowly,
tranquilly and gradually.
The gaze that Andrea guides with her mosaic of images
experienced, like that of the dancer with slow-moving feet
who composes the choreography around the last *Dama
a caballo*.
The sculptures are fragments of what has been seen
and experienced, shrapnel from memory that has
been dispersed by time. But the images remain, as the
reconstruction of a stirring sketch in which everything
is entr'acte. The memory that the photographs bring is
like that, with the intensity of nostalgia. Not only are we
nostalgic about things that we have experienced, but also
about what we have not known at first hand and someone
has described to us. For example, a sequence of scenes
that enabled us to construct a mental picture that cannot
be displaced.

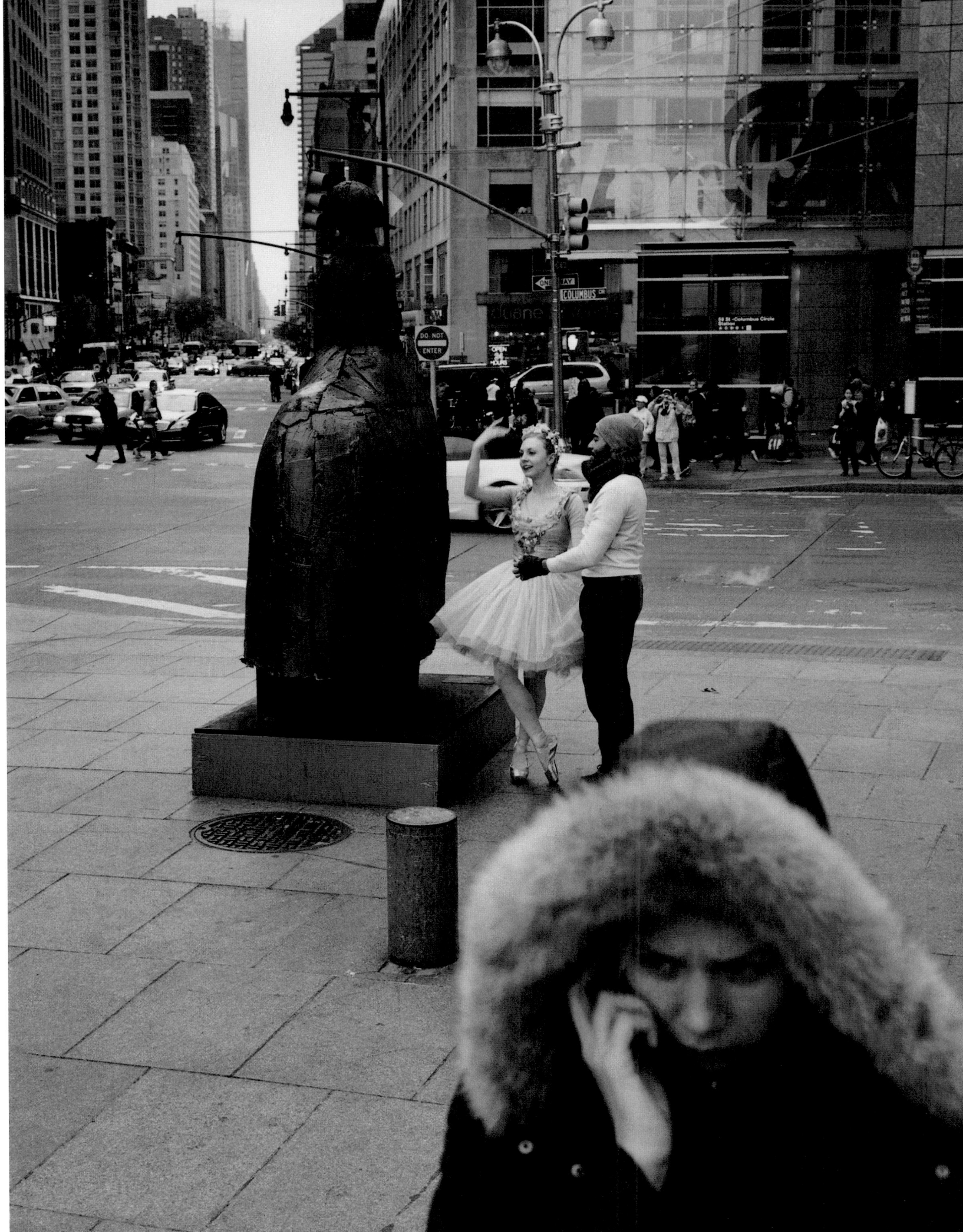

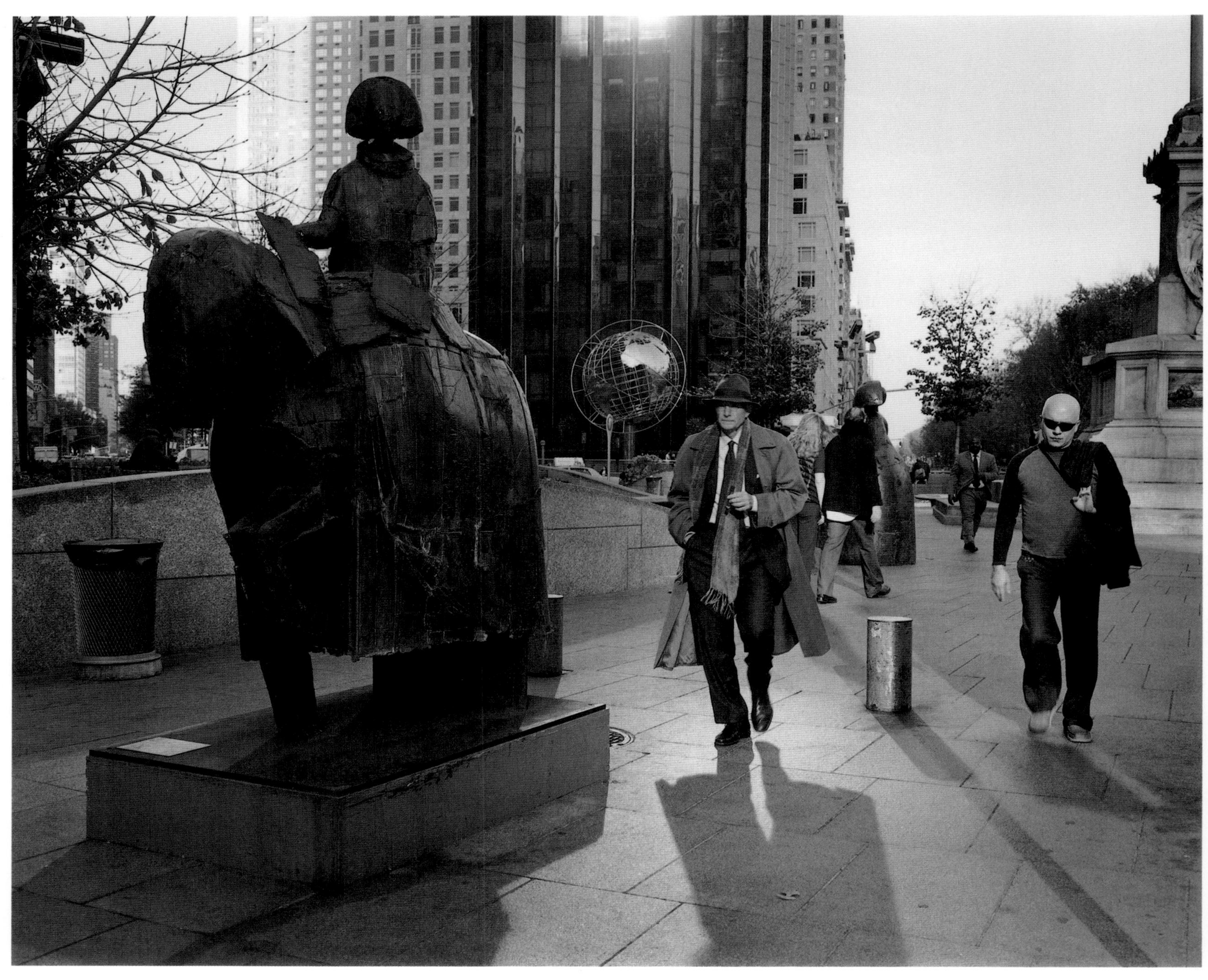

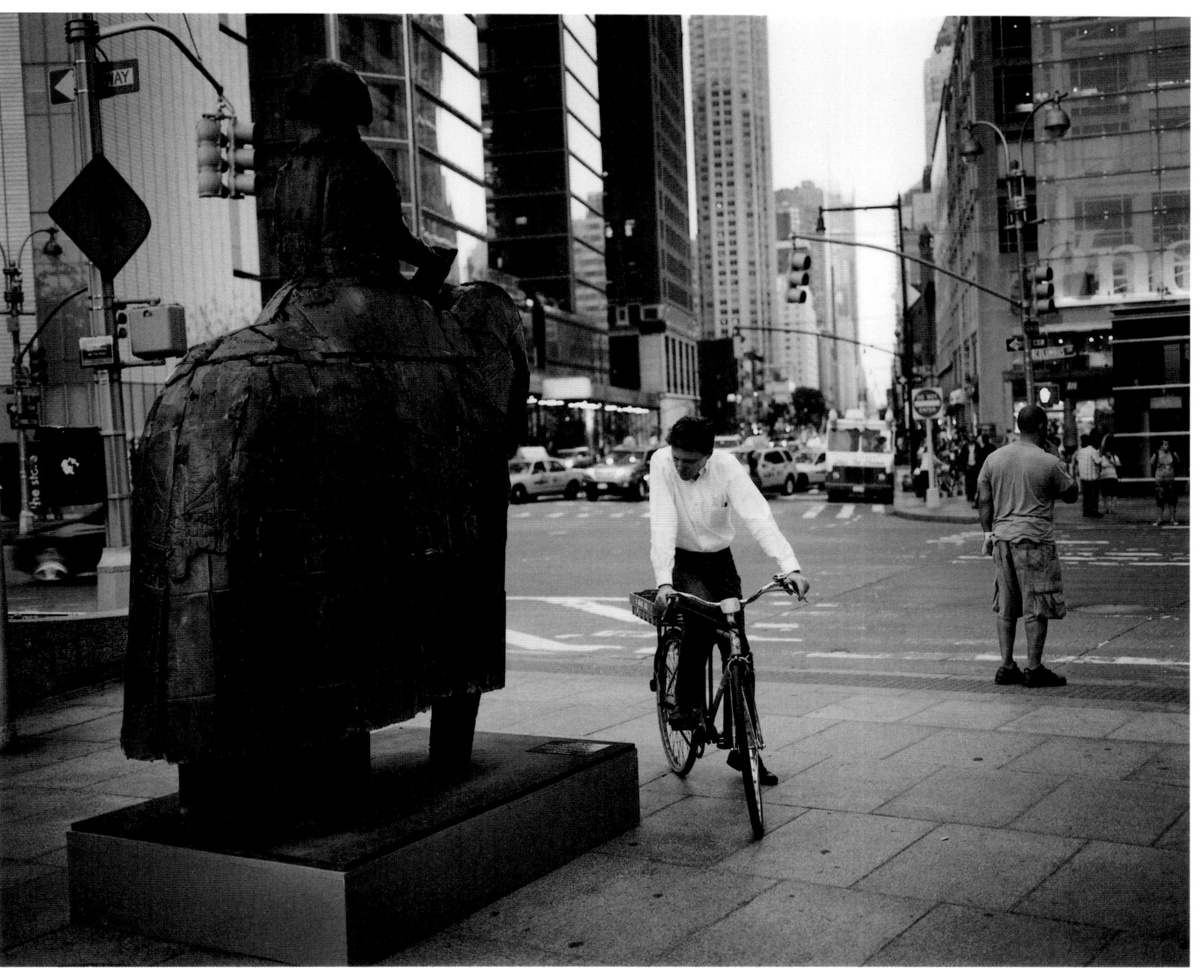

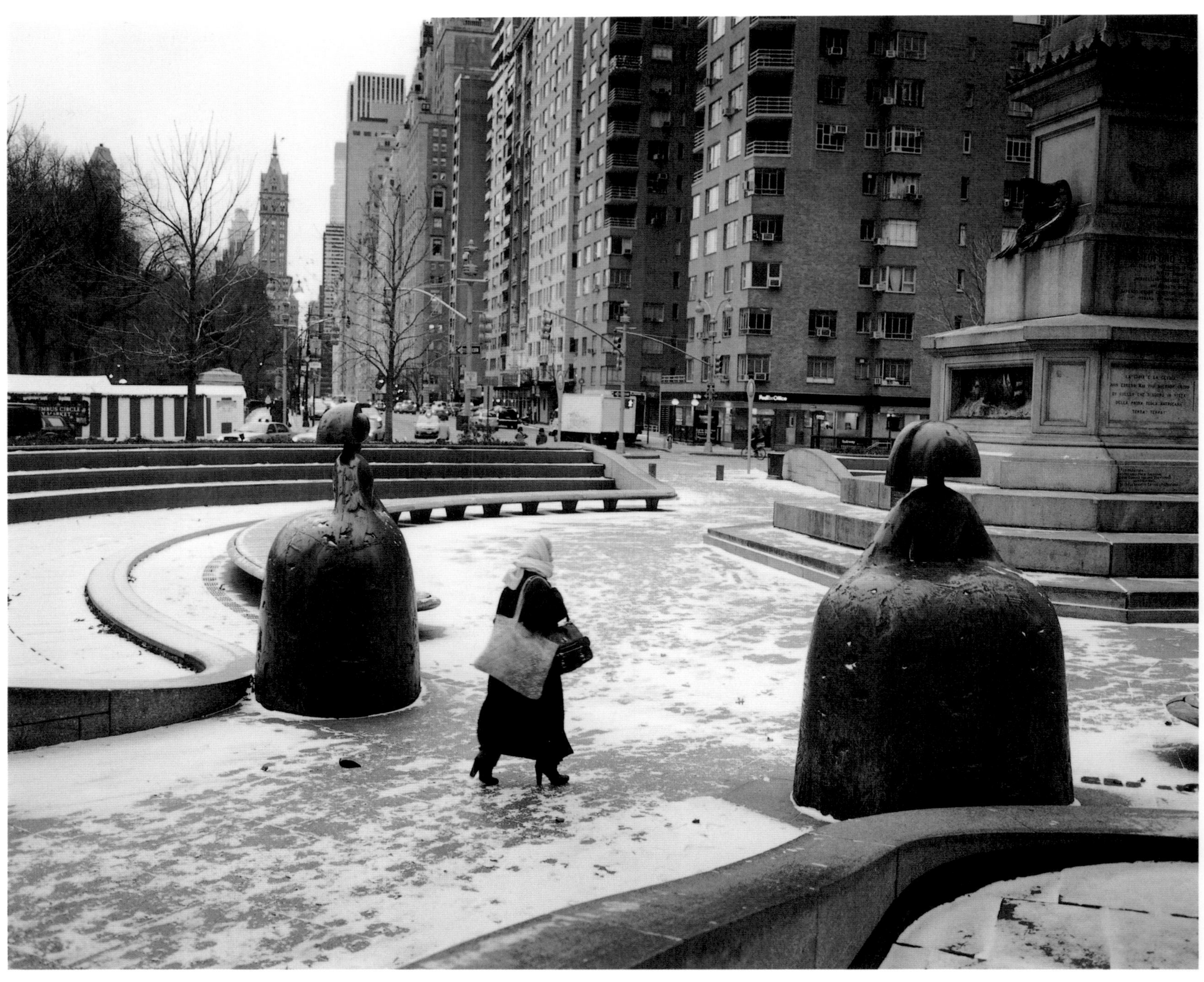

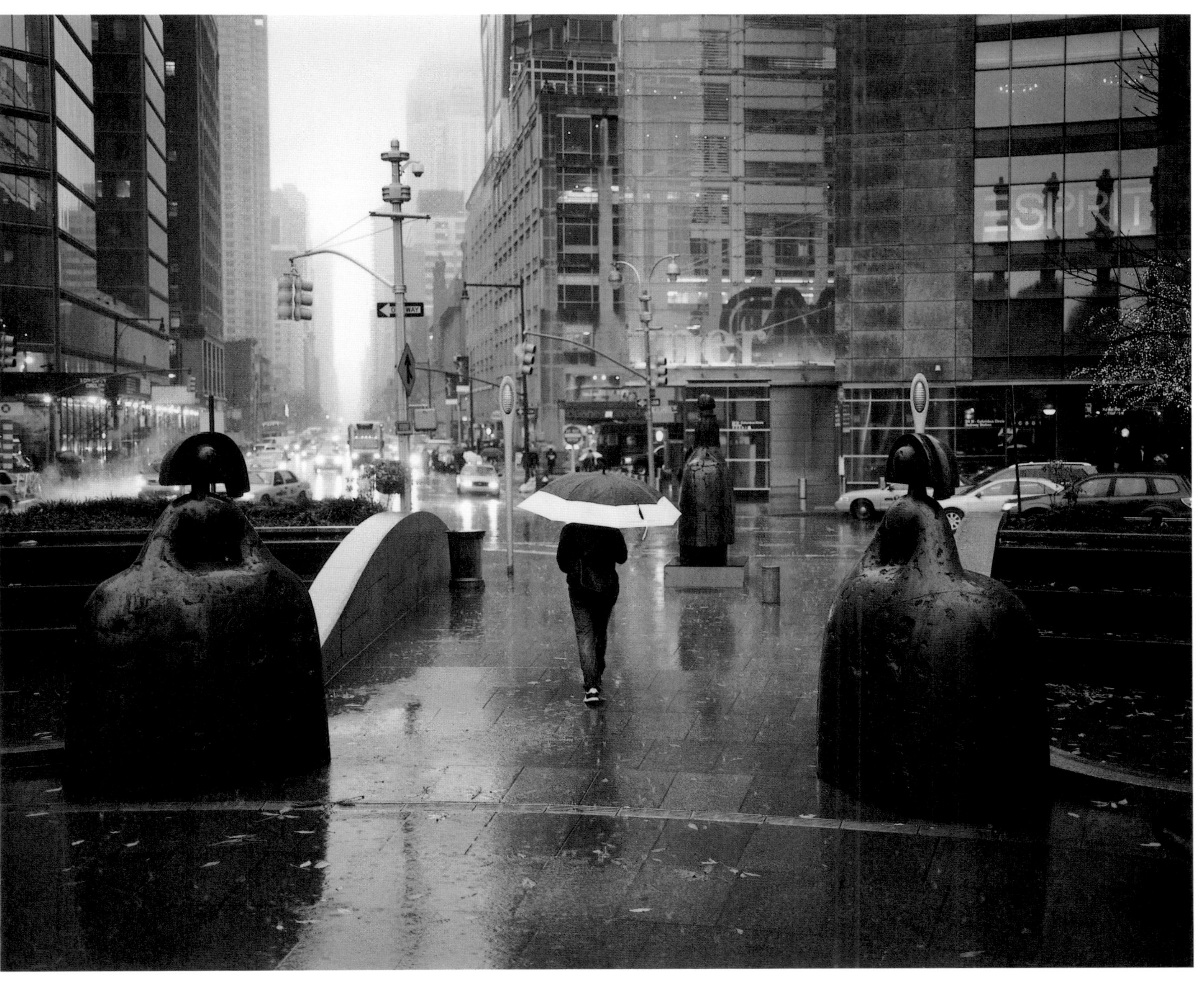

ESPRIT
ONE WAY

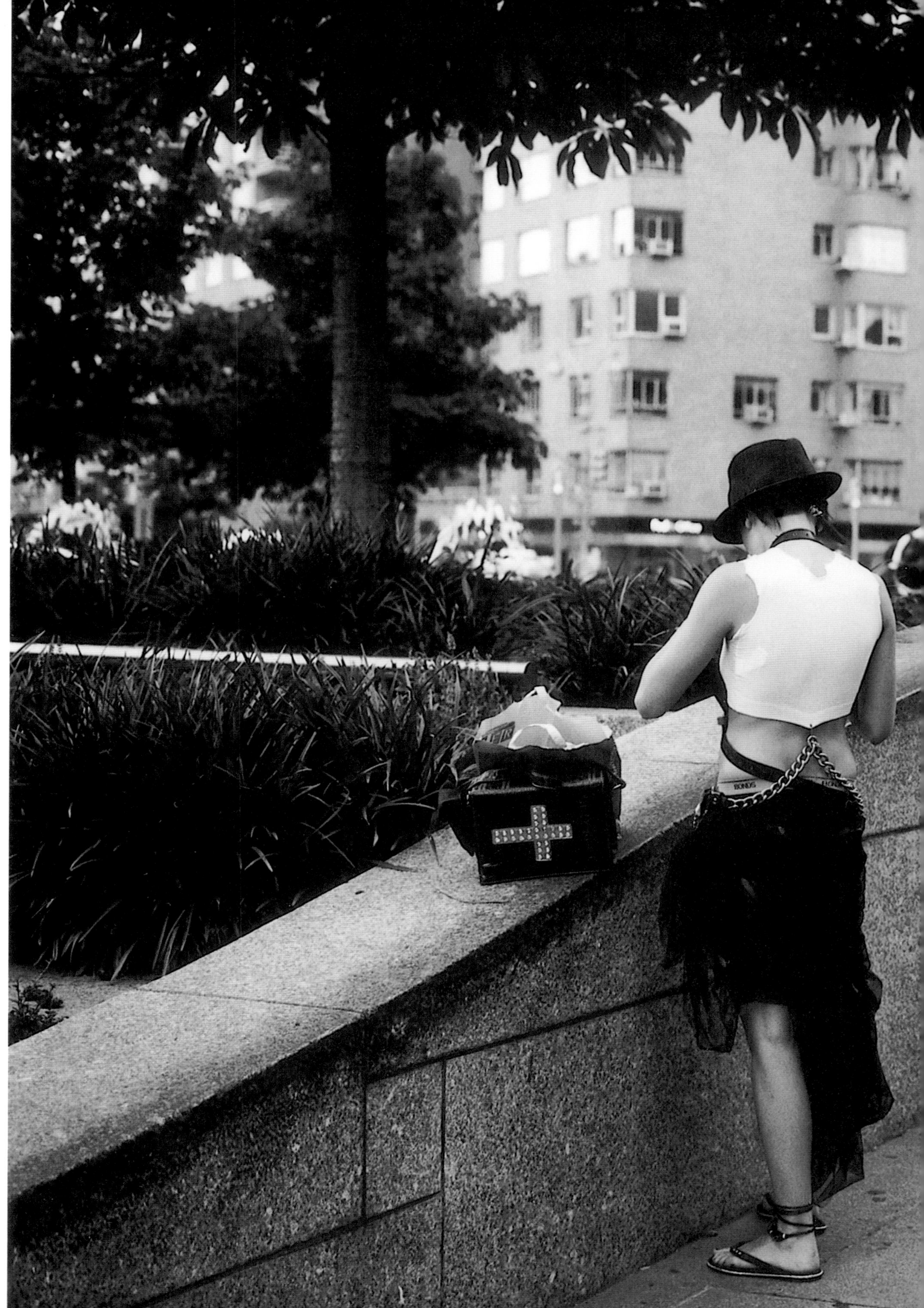

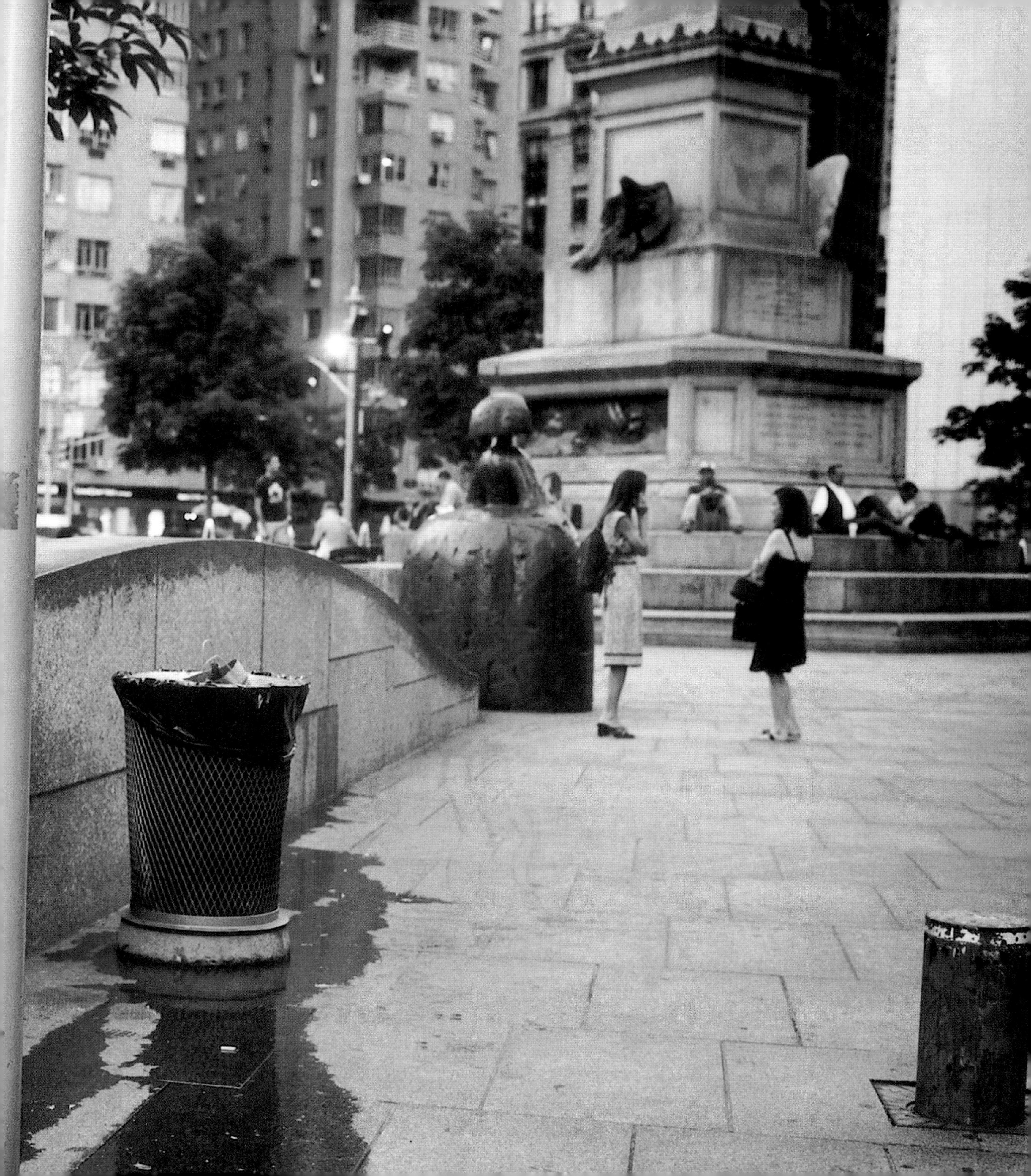

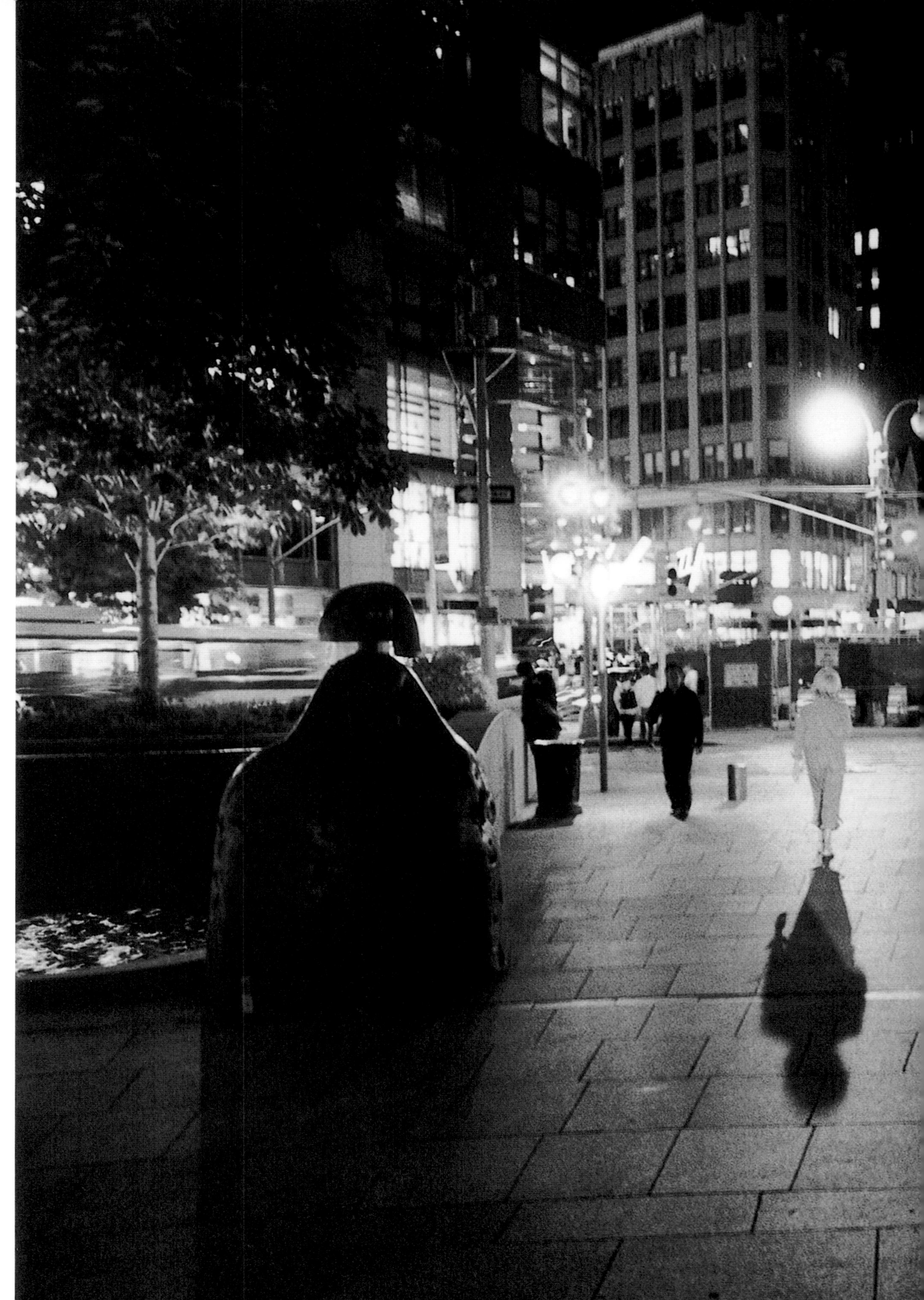

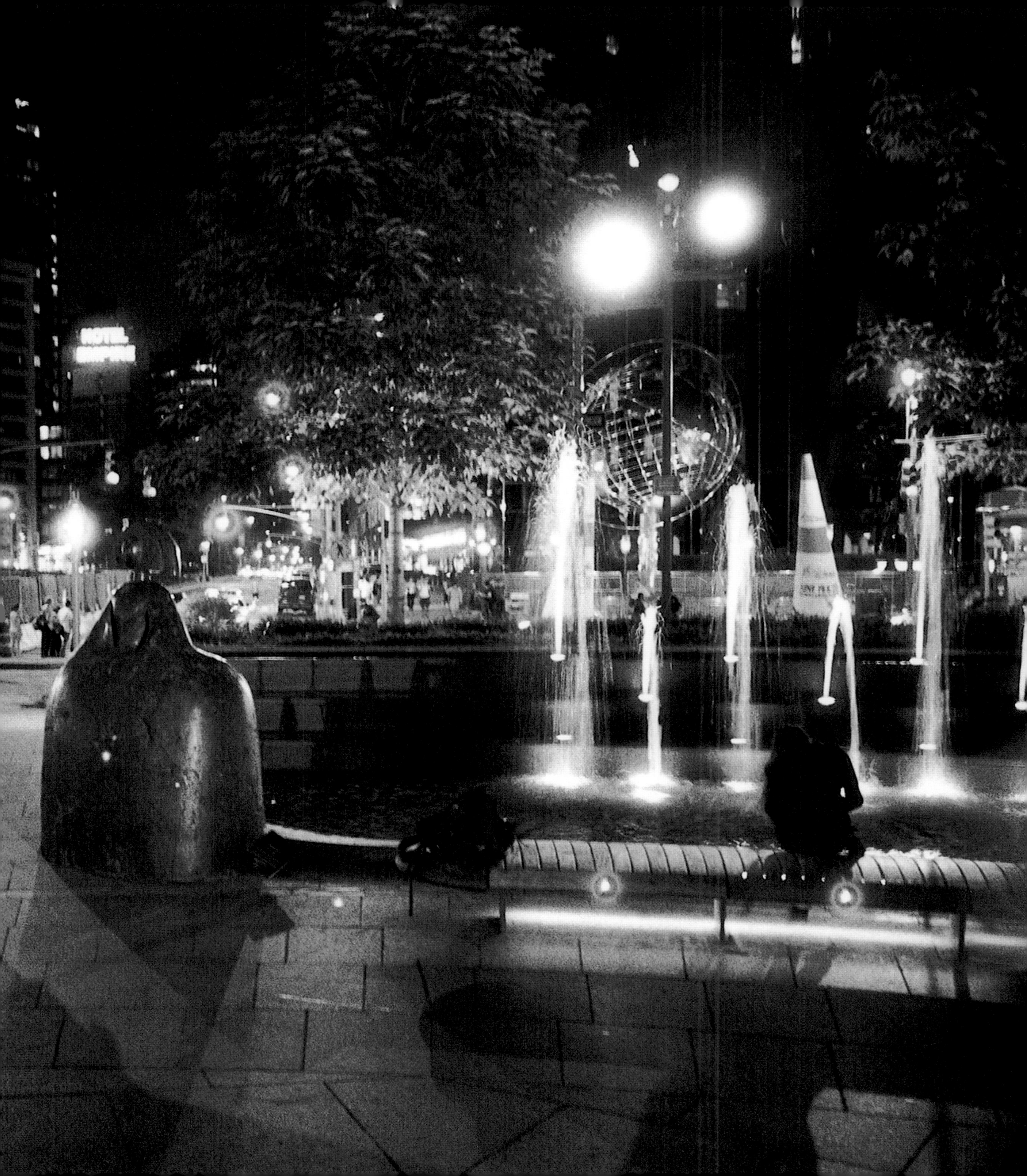

Andrea has prepared this landscape for us. And seeing her snapshots we feel as if we were really enjoying a story. Like that of walking among the inaccurate realities of Manolo Valdés's sculptures, in the same way that this man walks alone through the park, with his dog, and both of them tread on the fallen leaves of autumn, following the footsteps of something that has yet to be told.

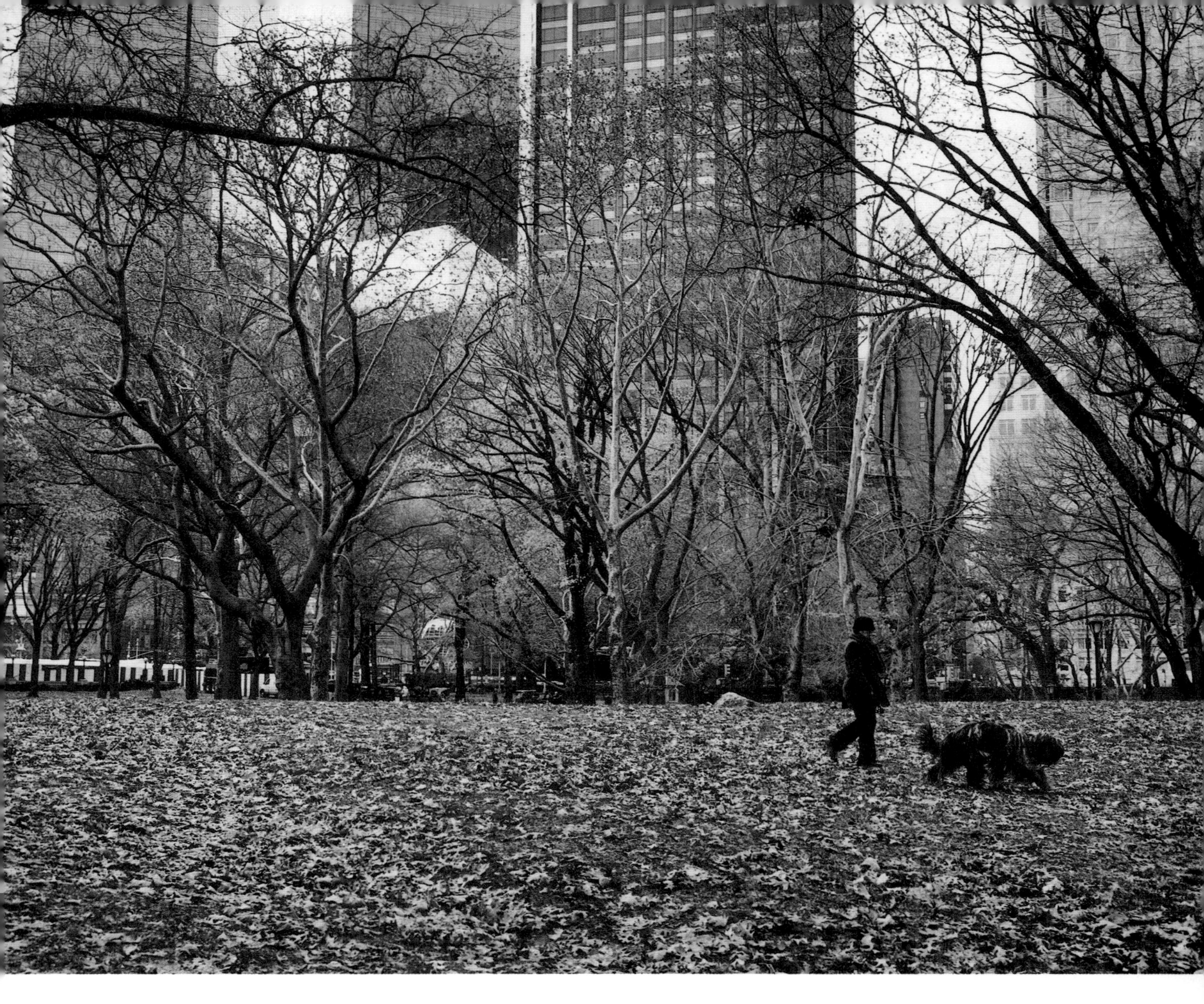

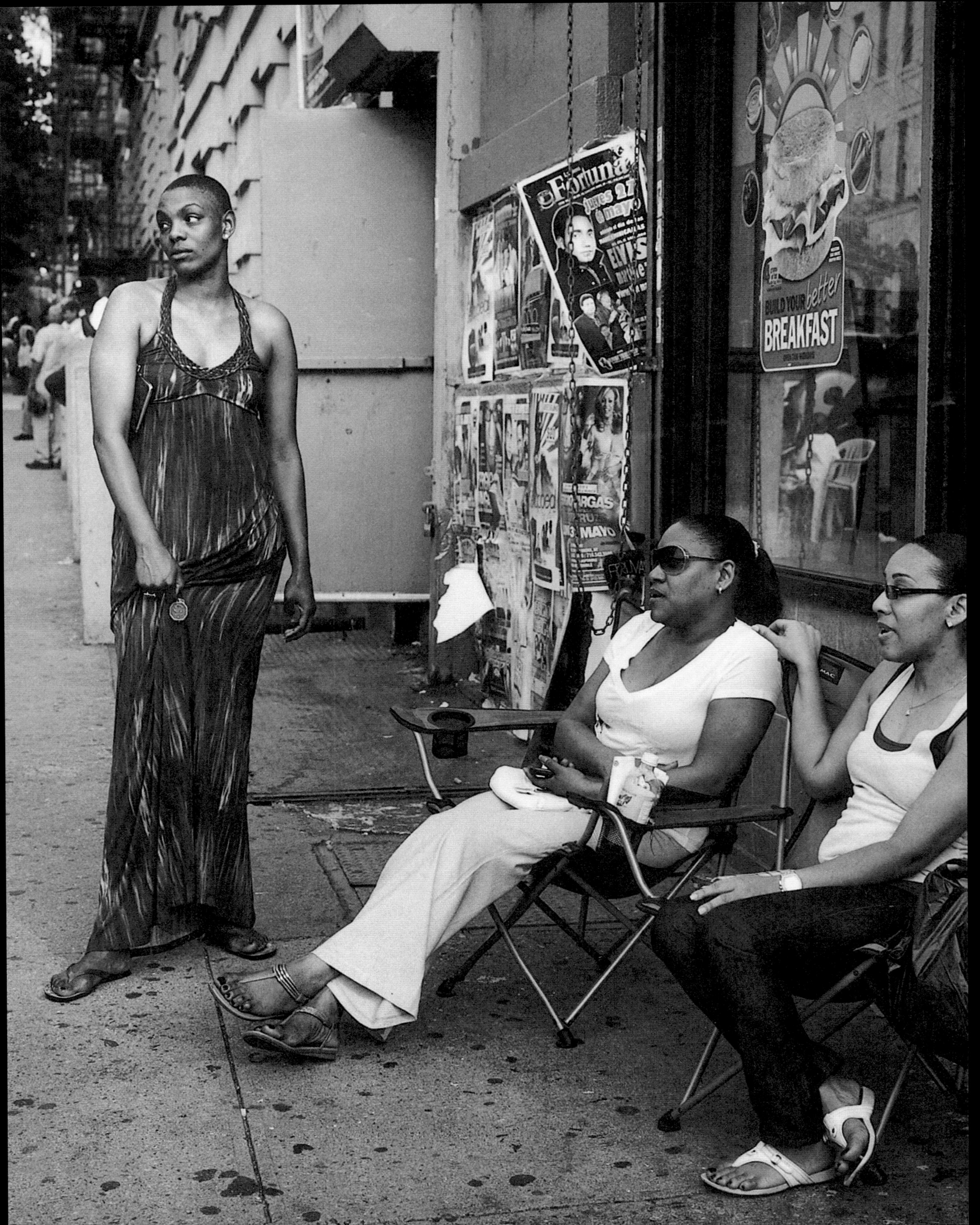

Fortuna
BUILD YOUR better
BREAKFAST
VARGAS
MAYO

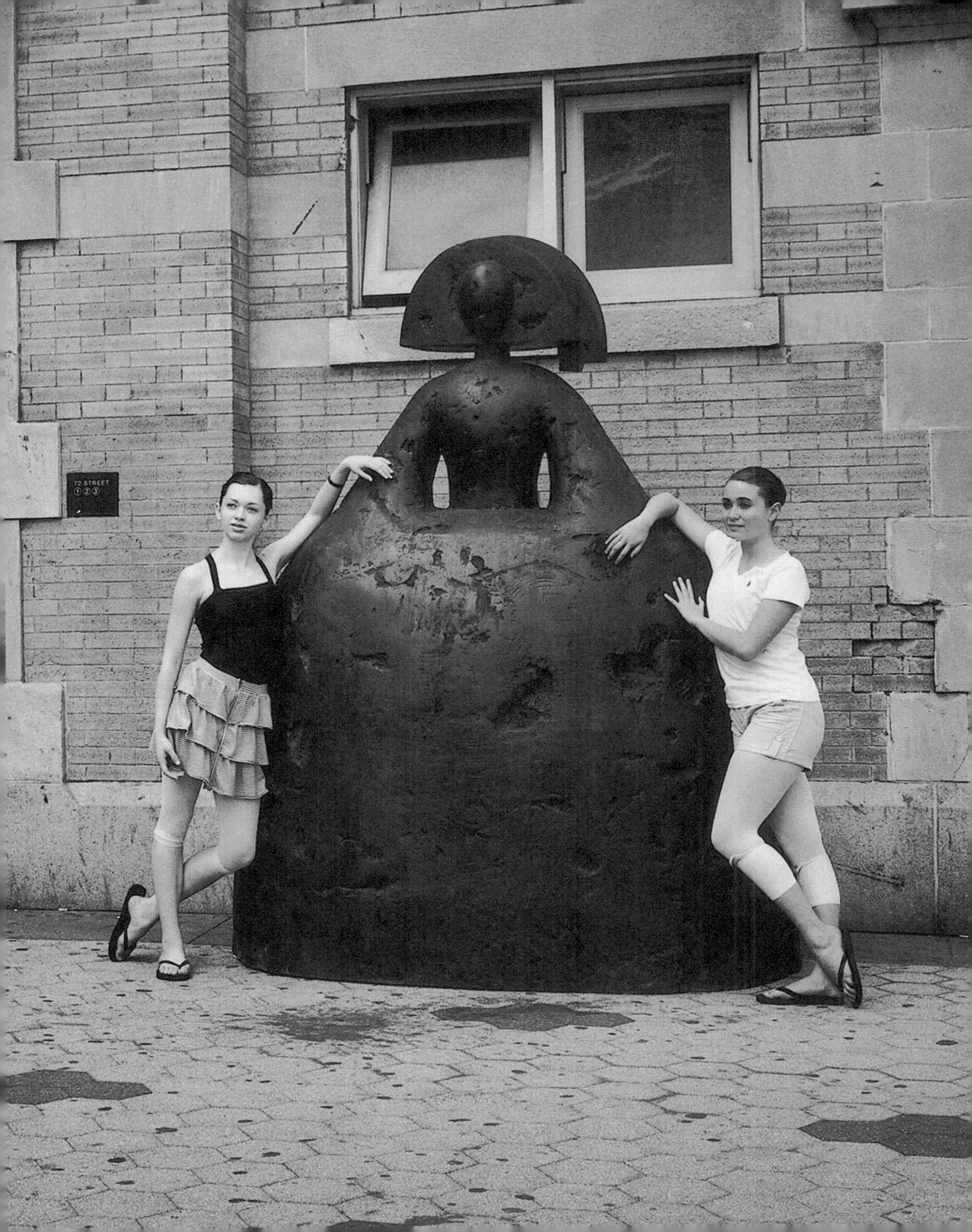
72 STREET
1 2 3

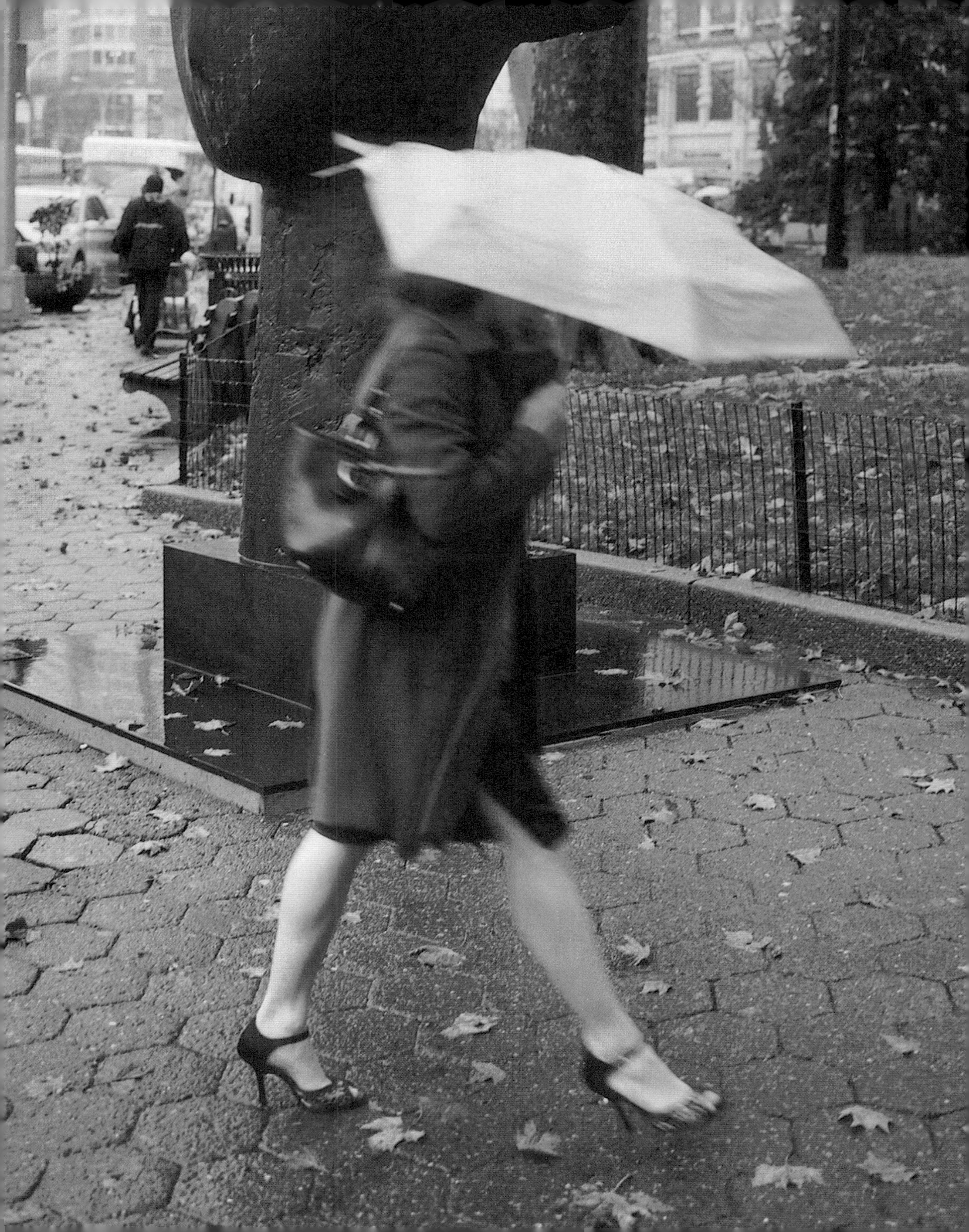

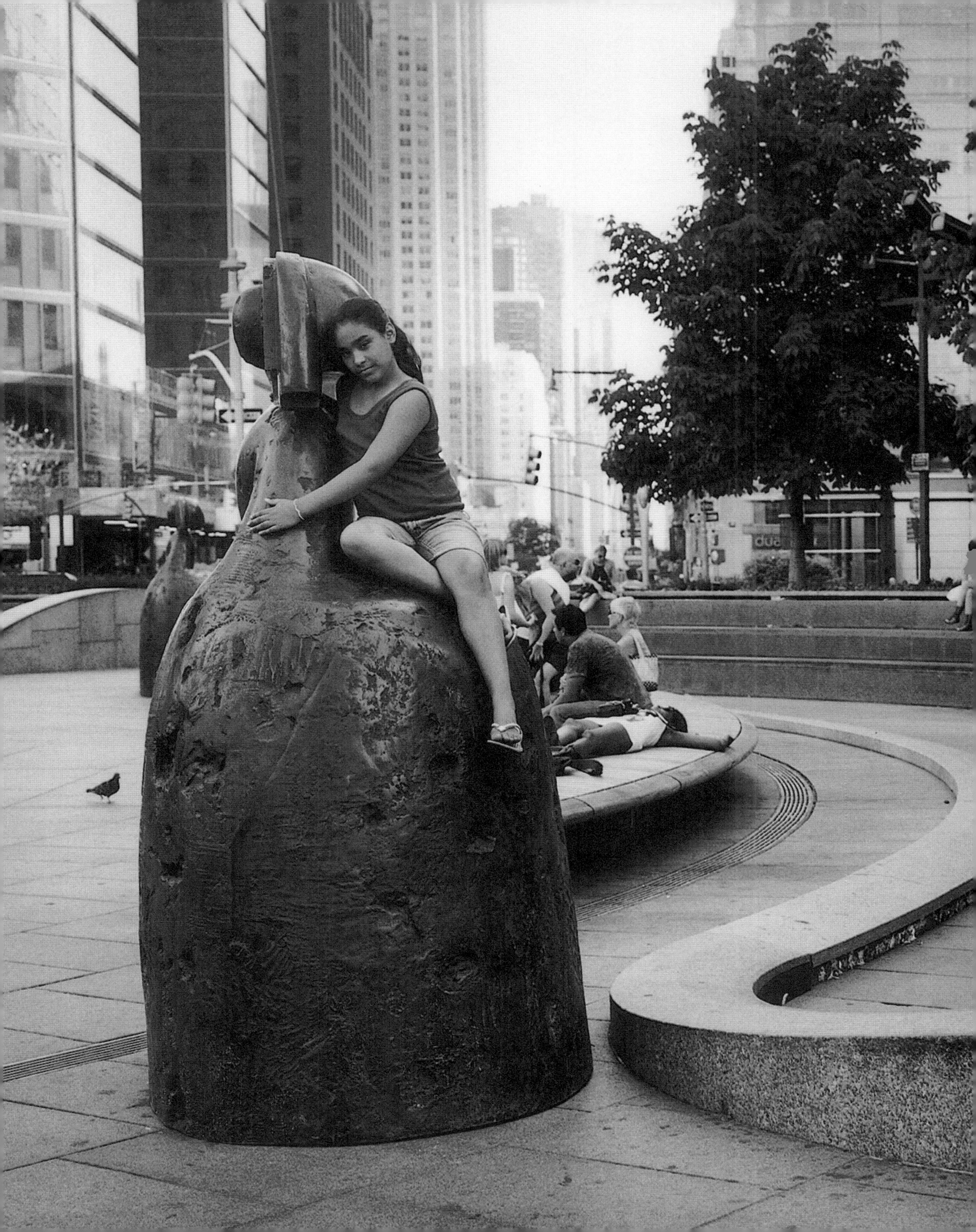

All the photographs were printed by John Cyr
using gelatin-silver bromide
The copies measure 11 x 14"

© Publication: TF Editores 2011
© Manolo Valdés 2011
© Photographs: Andrea Santolaya 2011
© Text: Antonio Lucas 2011

Graphic design
Juan Antonio Moreno. TF Media

Publishing co-ordination
TF Editores

Translation into English
Ann Canosa

Pre-printing
Cromotex

Printing
TF Artes Gráficas

ISBN: 978-84-15253-00-6
Legal Deposit: M-19346-2011